PRAISE FOR

The Lisu

"A real triumph. The Lisu should be proud to have Michele Zack, a keen observer with an unfailing eye for the revelatory image or event, to chronicle their amazing history and culture. The Lisu reputation for independence, equality, adaptability, 'repute,' and cultural cohesion despite steep odds comes across in her vibrant prose."

—JAMES C. SCOTT, YALE UNIVERSITY

"You don't need to be fascinated already by the Lisu to be fascinated by Michele Zack's spectacular new book about the Lisu. You just need to start on page one, travel with Zack into the Lisu world, and succumb to her remarkable evocation of this little-known but endlessly interesting people. If you cannot live years of your life with the Lisu, this is the book to read, at once a rigorous ethnography, a lively travelogue, and a beautifully written memoir. The best books are the products of love: this book is the product of a passion enduring decades."

—MISCHA BERLINSKI, AUTHOR OF *Fieldwork*
and Peacekeeping: A Novel

"This is a loving, inviting, and accessible portrait of the Lisu people. . . . The book is richly illustrated, well organized, and packed full of fascinating observations and insights. It is bound to reach and inspire many readers, both students of culturally diverse Asia and the general reader fascinated with the richness of our shared world."

—MAGNUS FISKESJÖ, CORNELL UNIVERSITY

"Journalist-historian Michele Zack provides rich images of Lisu across the entire region. Her keen observations and lucid writing unify what until now have been isolated bits and pieces of a much larger picture and for the first time show us the range and variability of these remarkable highland people."

—E. PAUL DURRENBERGER, AUTHOR OF *Uncertain Times, Gambling Debt,* AND *The Anthropological Study of Class and Consciousness*

"Michele Zack's book is packed full of insights and information. . . . Together with intimate portraits of individuals and communities, it asks important questions about opportunities and constraints facing indigenous people in a fast-changing world and concludes with interesting thoughts on possible futures for the Lisu."

—DR. ASHLEY SOUTH, AUTHOR OF *The Politics of Peace in Myanmar*

The Lisu

The Lisu

Far from the Ruler

MICHELE ZACK

UNIVERSITY PRESS OF COLORADO
Boulder

© 2017 by University Press of Colorado

Published by University Press of Colorado
5589 Arapahoe Avenue, Suite 206C
Boulder, Colorado 80303

 The University Press of Colorado is a proud member of
Association of American University Presses.

The University Press of Colorado is a cooperative publishing enterprise supported, in part,
by Adams State University, Colorado State University, Fort Lewis College, Metropolitan State
University of Denver, Regis University, University of Colorado, University of Northern Colorado,
Utah State University, and Western State Colorado University.

∞ This paper meets the requirements of the ANSI/NISO Z39.48–1992 (Permanence of Paper).

ISBN: 978-1-60732-603-8 (pbk)
ISBN: 978-1-60732-606-9 (ebook)
DOI: 10.5876/9781607326069

Library of Congress Cataloging-in-Publication Data

Names: Zack, Michele, author.
Title: The Lisu : far from the ruler / by Michele Zack.
Description: Boulder : University Press of Colorado, [2017] | Includes bibliographical references
    and index.
Identifiers: LCCN 2017021816 | ISBN 9781607326038 (pbk.) | ISBN 9781607326069 (ebook)
Subjects: LCSH: Lisu (Southeast Asian people) | Lisu (Southeast Asian people)—History. | Lisu
    (Southeast Asian people)—Social life and customs.
Classification: LCC DS731.L57 Z33 2017 | DDC 305.895/4—dc23
LC record available at https://lccn.loc.gov/2017021816

All photographs by author except where otherwise indicated.

Contents

Prologue

Yunnan, China, late October 1997

As darkness falls, very cold slips into freezing. The chill slices easily through jeans, thick jersey, and wool. Our quest to contact an isolated group of Lisu is stymied by the slippery mud of a mountain divide between Irrawaddy and Salween watersheds. The map shows a highway, but what we've been traveling along is more of an unpaved, and deeply rutted passage through the mountains. It would not rise to the definition of *road* in most places, never mind highway, and it runs between Tengchong and Guyong before carrying on into Burma.

Ahead of us a semi-truck loaded with four mammoth teak logs is wallowing at a disturbing angle, up to its axles in red mud. Traffic is blocked in both directions, and lengthening lines of mucky, government-issue baby blue trucks wait—those heading toward Burma are hauling consumer goods and weapons, those returning are laden with the teak giants. A few private vehicles, mainly small jeeps like our basic Japanese model, are also stranded. This is the third such obstacle of the past two hours in which we've advanced maybe 40 kilometers; our high spirits evaporate into shivers as a group of truck drivers argue without conviction, thigh-deep in the wet, cold clay.

Just as the sun dips out of sight, a thin backlit figure crests the hill and maneuvers carefully down the slippery alley toward us. His huge basket, brimful of kindling, knee-length blue trousers over embroidered gaiters, and crossbow identify him as Lisu. *"Seushae dja"* (go slowly), my companion, sixty-seven-year-old anthropologist Otome Klein Hutheesing, advises as he passes. The all-occasion greeting among the Lisu in northern Thailand seems apt.

He stops and smiles, taking in the situation as he shifts his burden. If he's surprised to be hailed in his native tongue by this grandmother clad in unfamiliar, Thai-style Lisu clothes and her companion of indeterminate age and tribe, he doesn't show it.

"Why don't you come back to my village?" Then he adds, stating the obvious: "This is no place to spend the night."

Preface

The Lisu—with their direct, sharp looks, bemused, intelligent faces, and quips from smoky, long-ago conversations—have haunted me for thirty years. A mix of bravado, *"Shu ma da"* (We can never die), and self-deprecating, dark humor reveals a sensibility forged by hard lives and survival against the odds. In myths, Lisu blame themselves for their misfortunes.

They are united in China, Myanmar (formerly Burma), and Thailand by the conviction that they are important and that their story should be told. This knowing they are as good as anyone else intrigued me from the start. My promise to help share their egalitarian-minded culture's worldview remained with me even after the first publisher of this book went out of business in 1999.

Where to begin in updating a manuscript about the Lisu written in the 1990s? On one hand, the changes in their lives are *just* a microcosm of vast change everywhere in the world. But because in thirty years the Lisu have undergone change that transpired across generations for most westerners, looking at them then and now is like viewing an ethnographic peepshow of humanity's journey from border-free tribal groupings to nation-states and the global market economy.

We live the results of this journey every day, but most of us don't remember it because ancestors, not we, made the trip. The Lisu remind us of this and perhaps that few of us long to return to our ancestral huts. Dwellers of nation-states have usually forgotten, internalized, or mythologized how they became citizens of this or that country. The inevitability of nationalism as the winning system is not in dispute, and perhaps those giving it thought might simply conclude that wins have outweighed losses.

Globalization, corporatism, and the rise of a shared popular culture have coincided with measurable increases in state authoritarianism in both democratic societies and undemocratic around the world. Whether or how this relates to Claude Lévi-Strauss's mid–twentieth-century assertion that "mankind has opted for monoculture" is an intriguing question.

Could one answer be that during 99 percent of human history most people, such as the Lisu, lived out of state reach on the peripheries of national control? As one of the final "holdout" people, the Lisu have important lessons to teach us about the political choices and tradeoffs "modern" people have made, and continue to make, in becoming subject to the state and adapting to global culture.

Dramatic change has occurred *everywhere* in the past thirty years, nowhere more than in China, Myanmar, and Thailand where the majority of Lisu live (tiny populations are also in Laos and India). The act of focusing on the culture and experiences of one group in this most diverse and rapidly changing region in the world creates a sharp lens through which to view the bigger story. History compressed makes pattern and difference discernible. Because of their independent and egalitarian values, witnessing adaptation from pre-literate to literate, pre-state to state, largely subsistence to largely market economy, and inaudible to louder political voices reveals a shared human history with which people living in societies that value democracy can identify. Their experience sheds light on how *we* got to where we are in our attempt to balance the values of independence and egalitarianism with the benefits and drawbacks of living in nation-states. Wikileaks, Edward Snowden, and Apple versus the FBI have highlighted our own evolution on such issues.

Timing has been critical. I began thinking about the Lisu and other nonstate minorities in booming Thailand in the mid-1980s, and I returned in 1990 as a journalist and economic migrant from recession-plagued California. Living as an illegal immigrant the first four of eight years there was relevant to writing about the Lisu. The 1990s was the last possible time to see them in remote corners and hilltops where they lived in circumstances affected by national and market economies but still retaining strong traditional elements and memories. In 1985, my first trek to a Lisu village in Thailand had been through un-electrified territory, far from roads. Things hadn't changed much ten years later when I began this project. Anthropologist Otome Klein Hutheesing and I visited Lisu enclaves in China in the mid-1990s before rope bridges across the raging Nujiang gorge had given way to suspension ones, before roads impassable in the rainy season had been improved, and before electricity and cell phone service had reached every village.

In Myanmar in the 1980s and 1990s, the Lisu (and indeed most Burmese) were in dire straights: Lisu women were bearing a dozen or more children, of whom half often died. Lack of medicine and disastrous government policies threatened Lisu and other minorities caught in the crossfire of fifty ongoing civil wars, including in the Kachin, Shan, and Wa States where the Lisu live.

By 2015, conditions in all three countries had altered almost beyond recognition—each differently. Thailand is no longer the booming "Land of the Free" but is overseen by a military junta called the National Council for Peace and Order. China is today the second largest economy in the world, globally integrated, with a power grid and other infrastructure reaching its every corner, without the government giving up central control. Myanmar has opened up surprisingly, is more peaceful, and has made dramatic reforms, including Aung San Suu Kyi's National League for Democracy's landslide victory in November 2015.

Without dwelling on my personal circumstances, I do pop up in the pages of this work, especially in book II. I want readers to understand why this project has compelled me over the years: the Lisu connect us to our own journeys to the present and help us interrogate the process, its losses and gains. I am a journalist, not a social scientist. I commit to telling the truth, with understanding that all attempts to tell true stories are shot through with omissions, imperfections, and outright blunders.

Acknowledgments

Going back more than twenty years and two publishers and now in an updated and completely new form, this book offers its author great scope for failing to credit key individuals who helped along the way. I apologize upfront and issue a blanket but heartfelt thank you to the scores of people who assisted me in creating this first-ever book-length work on the Lisu. My utmost gratitude is reserved for the Lisu themselves, who never failed to offer warm hospitality. From bamboo residences perched above terraces of sesame seeds growing in China, to churches in Myanmar, to mud-floor homes in Thailand, even the poorest Lisu eagerly shared their stories. The Lisu know they are important.

Important to this book is Michael Loftus, who represented my original publisher and arranged funding for the first round of my research, fieldwork, and writing. When that venture folded, he went out of his way to ensure that copyright reverted to me despite my work-for-hire contract.

I can never repay American anthropologist E. Paul Durrenberger for his support from this project's inception in the mid-1990s up until the present.

His knowledge of the Lisu in Thailand, photographs from the 1960s and 1970s, and professional guidance have been invaluable. He helped revive this book by introducing me to the University Press of Colorado and advising me on its update.

Another Lisu expert, the Dutch anthropologist Otome Klein Hutheesing, was essential in sharing her work and network in Thailand. She hosted me in both Chiang Mai and Doi Laan, her study village and home of many years, and accompanied me to China in 1997 where her assistance went far beyond that of language interpreter. Mimi Saeju, a daughter in Otome's extended Lisu clan, carried on her legacy (along with other family members) when I returned to Southeast Asia in 2014 to update the work; she served as a translator, interview subject, and provider of essential international and Thai Lisu contacts, including to the ever-helpful Chome Orn-anong.

Insights from the Morse family, Christian missionaries resident in Thailand who lived with the Lisu for three generations in three countries, enriched both the original and final versions of this book. I especially acknowledge Eugene and Helen, who invited me into their Chiang Mai home and provided numerous introductions, including to their grown children and extended family members. One nephew, Bobby Morse, was my guide and translator in Myanmar in 1997. By 2014, both of the elder Morses had died; their son David, also a native Lisu speaker, was equally helpful, particularly in helping me confront and digest the dramatic gap of twenty years that updating this work required and in providing key introductions in Myanmar.

Julian Gearing, my excellent friend and colleague from *AsiaWeek* in the 1990s, was a perceptive sounding board, helping to refresh me on Thailand and the evolving political situation for Lisu and other minorities there since I left Southeast Asia in 1998. He and his wife, Khemjira Thianthong, drove me to Lisu villages near Chiang Mai, serving as translators. Victoria Vorreiter, also of Chiang Mai and an authority on traditional music in the Golden Triangle, helped enhance that aspect of the work, neglected in the original.

Senator J Yawu, the first Lisu to serve in the Upper House of Myanmar's Parliament, representing Kachin State, was instrumental in bringing the Lisu story into the present. He helped me grasp the complexity of minority/majority politics in his country and provided entrée to Chinese Lisu circles I could not have accessed otherwise. In helping me set up my Chinese Lisu crew and itinerary, he nimbly demonstrated the internationalization of the present Lisu world. The writer and scholar Ashley South, with superb on-the-ground knowledge of ethnic conflict, the peace process, and internally displaced people in Myanmar, met with me in that country as I endeavored to tackle these issues, provided useful introductions, and answered queries from afar as I reworked the material.

I owe thanks to the Putao Lisu Cultural Committee, chaired by Ngwa Pi-too, for arranging my walkabout in rural Putao, and to Ah-hin, guide and translator. In and around Myitkyina, Pastor Ah Dee-che, Joseph Gwa, and Selina ensured that I met as broad a spectrum of Lisu as possible and answered endless questions about Lisu/Jingpo cultural dynamics, civil wars in Kachin State, and religious divides among Christian Lisu.

Hill tribe writer Jim Goodman provided excellent, detailed advice on my Salween Valley itinerary. "Akha Jim" as I knew him in the 1990s has since greatly expanded his geographical reach and knowledge of minorities, and he shared freely with me. Lisu expert Reinhart Hohler arranged travel to China in 1997 and to Myanmar in 2014.

In preparing this work, I'm indebted to Alyssa Ribeiro for creating polished chapter notes and a bibliography from a disorganized pile of old and new notes, print material, and source lists and for taking on this partially complete project after the tragic death of my talented research assistant Carlee Merward.

Also gone now but his help never forgotten is my father-in-law, Walter Goldschmidt, who advised me on what I might achieve in a broad work for a popular audience. Many of his ideas inform this work, though I can't blame him for its shortcomings (he died in 2010).

My husband, Mark Goldschmidt, read and commented helpfully on every stage of this work for over twenty years and accompanied me back to Southeast Asia in 2014, where we climbed mountains and crossed rivers on the flimsiest bridges imaginable to reach Lisu living as far from the ruler as possible. His love and support have sustained me throughout.

Note on Use of "Burma" and "Myanmar"

In 1989, Burma's military regime crushed pro-democracy demonstrations and without notice or consultation with its citizens changed the country's name to the Union of Myanmar. Because no democratic process was involved, objections to the sudden change came from many quarters, including Aung San Suu Kyi, whose National League for Democracy had recently won at the polls but was barred from taking its seats in Parliament. English-speaking countries, including Britain, the United States, and Canada, continued to refer to the country as Burma. I was squarely in this camp when I wrote the first version of this book.

In updating it in 2014 and 2015, I adopted a different approach: I refer to the country as *Burma* historically and *Myanmar* from 1989 onward. The most important reason for the change is that when I returned in 2014, I asked perhaps a hundred Burmese, Lisu and otherwise, this question: by what name do you want your country to be known? Everyone said Myanmar, concurring with government reasoning that Burma was the name bestowed by the British, the country's former colonial ruler. They feel Myanmar is more "inclusive" because 40 percent of the population is non-Burman. But since both words have the same root, Myanmar might not *actually* be more inclusive. It is understood to be, however, and they prefer it.

My other reasons are practical. I want to avoid the awkwardness of the double-barreled Burma/Myanmar unless I'm referring to a long time period. The use of Burma when the reference is to events before 1989 and Myanmar after provides readers with an easy way to keep track of time context.

The Lisu

Introduction

It's good to live close to the water,
but it is better to live far from the ruler.
   —*Lisu proverb*

In known time, Lisu have roamed east and south from villages clinging to sheer slopes in or around the Nujiang, or Upper Salween River Valley, of Yunnan, China, and across mountain ranges in Southeast Asia. Theories diverge on where they came from, but they've since wandered from China into Burma, fingertips of India and Laos, and to Thailand's northern provinces. If vertiginous passes meandered on indefinitely instead of smoothing down into plains and deltas, Lisu would probably have kept on moving in search of the perfect, east-facing mountain with good soil and water and as far away from police, soldiers, or other authorities as possible. Today, while most Lisu still live in remote areas, many have settled at lower elevations and closer to rulers than their ancestors would have deemed wise.

Widely dispersed, numbering around a million and a half people, the lives and customs of Lisu vary from country to country and even from mountaintop to mountaintop. Yet they are bound by a language and political worldview that ignores distance and defies pigeonholing. Whether they wear long flowing skirts and black velvet tunics, as in the upper Nujiang gorge in Yunnan, or blue, orange, and red mini-skirts with rattan knee bracelets and embroidered gaiters, as in Tengchong 200 miles south, they are Lisu. Their cultural glue transcends the modern clothes many wear today as well as religion: whether they commune with nature spirits, their own ancestors, Buddha, Christ, a combination, or none of the above, they identify as Lisu. The variables of dialects in China, Myanmar, and Thailand are sufficiently minor as to allow Lisu everywhere to communicate with each other.

In 2014 I returned to Southeast Asia to update the research and fieldwork conducted in the 1990s that this work is based upon. Changes brought by modernization were so dramatic that my first impression was that differences between then and now were too great to span in one book. But I soon realized that while easy-to-spot markers such as traditional dress are far less prevalent than a generation ago, other continuities, more subtle and more basic, link yesterday and today. Outer values have become internalized, but cultural self-awareness, accompanied by unity movements in China and Myanmar, indicate that Lisu culture is not about to disappear. It is changing, though, and loss of language and integration into majority populations pose existential threats. Even in laissez-faire Thailand, where Lisu enjoy individual freedoms but have weaker citizenship and land-owning rights, I witnessed intent to preserve and bring a version of their ethos into the future. In 2015, Chiang Mai University in Thailand hosted one of the first meetings of Lisu from all over Southeast Asia, including Laos and India.

I witnessed a muscular will to cultural survival among Lisu in every national setting. In China, perhaps the most religiously and philosophically diverse of the countries, Lisu atheists, animists, and Christians equally value some construct of "traditional culture" as their world modernizes at convulsive speed.

One Lisu, out of more than a hundred I interviewed in 2014, responded negatively when asked about the importance of cultural identity—and he was most likely joking. A sixty-year-old atheist with a crew cut from Liuku, capital of Nujiang Lisu Autonomous Prefecture in China, he lives in one of the few places where Lisu make up the majority. In fact, one third of the world's Lisu population lives here. His denial was delivered with deadpan irony: "who has time to think about culture? Today all we care about is making money and doing business." He is married a second time to a second Lisu wife, speaks Lisu most of the time (even to conduct business), and went out of his way to show me old Lisu cable bridges still in operation across the Nu Gorge. Being an atheist did not inhibit him from having strong opinions on Lisu culture and religion. He was visibly disappointed when I was unable to visit his father who, until converting to Christianity ten years ago, had been a practicing shaman.

The Lisu are among the most egalitarian of all Southeast Asia's hill tribes, and their political style rejects hierarchical organization that could link them across villages or countries. Since until the past hundred years no standard Lisu writing system existed, the cohesiveness of their culture has always been mysterious—and never more so than today. They continue to adapt and change while identifying as Lisu.

Missionaries introduced Fraser's Romanized script of the Lisu language a century ago to translate the Bible, but this, as well as less-used and now defunct alphabets developed by the Chinese (in the late 1950s) and the Burmese (1970s), have yet to gain broad usage. Lisu children began attending school and learning to read and write Chinese, Burmese, and Thai scripts a few generations ago; but through most of the twentieth century it was oral tradition—songs, myths, proverbs, and grandiloquent speechifying—that informed Lisu existence. Lisu men in particular are renowned linguists able to converse in several languages.

Unlike other preliterate, less anarchic people including the Hmong and Karen in Southeast Asia, the Lisu did not take to expressing themselves in writing until recently. Because Fraser's script, the most universal Lisu writing system, was first developed to communicate Christian content, there was push-back from animists and atheists against its broad adoption. If the Lisu language itself remains viable, however, this could change. The Lisu version of Christianity is growing and today is practiced by close to, if not an outright majority. Led by China, Fraser's has become the Lisu writing system accepted by nations, and the Lisu Fraser keyboard is now available via Unicode, the computing industry standard built into today's operating systems including Microsoft and Java. Within more modernized Lisu enclaves in all three countries, a modified version called Advanced Lisu Script (ALS, a script without backward and upside-down Roman letters) has gained ground, as it is convenient for texting.

I traveled extensively, mostly in tribal areas of Thailand, Burma, and China, in researching this book. It was a marvel to see Lisu living so variously and

Yunnan's Dansha Valley near Tengchong, where Lisu have settled at lower elevations. Author photo.

yet cut from the same cloth. Whether worrying about their *myi-do* (repute), preparing a smoky meal around the fire, or arguing about new political realities, the Lisu in all three countries—in the 1990s and today—face life with a blend of practicality, fatalism, and distinct humor riddled with what they call "talk play." Most still live in relatively remote areas and practice agriculture even as roads, electricity, and the Internet connect them to majority cultures and the world beyond. A growing proportion has moved to cities and towns. Lisu everywhere are empowered by mobile and smart phones to communicate and to maximize whatever economic advantages life hands them. While for most these remain modest, new emphases on prosperity and education have taken off, growing exponentially with the rise of a new class of "untraditional" Lisu leaders in culture, politics, religion, and business.

Lisu with undergraduate and advanced degrees number perhaps 1,000. I met the Lisu foreign minister of Nujiang's Autonomous Prefecture in Yunnan (a Communist Party cadre), the animist/Buddhist daughter of an illiterate Lisu woman who runs a US-based tech company from Chiang Mai, Thailand, and the first Lisu senator in Myanmar, a defrocked Roman Catholic priest—among others.

Such variety makes defining the essential quality of "Lisuness" or teasing out its distinctness from other highland peoples in Southeast Asia, such as the Lahu, Akha, Shan, Hmong, Karen, and other minorities, tricky. Yet the Lisu *are* distinct, even in perpetual flux. Descriptions ranging from the Chinese label of the "Merry Nationality," to "anarchists of the highlands," or Paul and Elaine Lewis's "desire for primacy" and "the Lisu want to be first"—all capture long-observed aspects of Lisu pith. Lisu was translated as "the loud custom people" by Eugene Morse, a Christian missionary who spent his life among them. The "wraparound people" is another frequent translation. Rice, repute, getting one's daughters well married, and avoiding authorities are all ingredients—yet the recipe remains offhand. Newer research provides a useful non-state perspective on their stateless culture by locating Lisu within "Zomia," a Europe-sized but heretofore unidentified "idea-realm" in highland Southeast Asia. (But that doesn't help much in distinguishing finer grains.) My approach, as much as possible, is to let the Lisu define themselves in their own words, songs, stories, and proverbs.

Whether it is an old Christian woman in Burma running out to her muddy fields to dig up roots to feed unexpected guests, a Lisu man in Southwest China inviting strangers to stay the night, or a family in Thailand gamely entertaining tourists—images of hospitality, directness, and a nutty zest for life against great odds come to mind when I think of the Lisu.

This work is neither definitive nor academic but one that introduces a people and their environments—in China, Myanmar, and Thailand. I refer to those living in India and Laos, whom I did not meet. Country-specific material is integrated throughout, but most contemporary material is in Book II.

Book I includes mythic, historical, and ethnographic sections on village, childhood, economy, and religion—and is a fairly un-restored 1990s ethnographic period piece describing traditional Lisu lifestyles before national setting had as much impact as today. Some newer material is woven in to offer a taste of the dramatic change occurring in the single generation since. While the past refuses to be contained in a separate box, I wish to preserve a version of the original work I did because it was undertaken in the last moments when it was possible to glimpse Lisu living more or less as they had for centuries.

In the past thirty years, many isolating effects of physical remoteness have decreased or vanished—and national governments have tightened their grips on frontier areas via improved infrastructure, technological reach, and political integration.

Book II includes country-specific views of the Lisu, based on some research from the 1990s but far more on fieldwork and on sources I've encountered since 2014. Sketches, stories, and interviews provide contemporary snapshots of life in Thailand, Myanmar, and China. Descriptions of Lisu in all three countries inform this section and bring the book up to date, so readers may follow the Lisu journey across space and time and capture a sense of the varied political landscapes they inhabit today.

I aim to make Lisu reality present by exposing the universality of their journey and by interrogating some of the choices they've made as they evolve from stateless outsiders into something more compatible with citizenship in modern nations. My father-in-law, the cultural anthropologist Walter R. Goldschmidt, was of invaluable assistance in Book I, first in framing what would be useful in a nonacademic short work on such a broad subject. Well into his eighties, he accompanied me to Otome Klein Hutheesing's study village of Doi Laan in northern Thailand in 1997 for his last fieldwork. He died before I revived this project and so has not been here to advise me on the update. He had strong ideas and opinions, however; I've relied on my understanding of them to help frame Book II and my conclusions.

There has been excellent scholarship on the Lisu, mostly in Thailand, and I am indebted to the works of both academics and missionary-ethnographers. But only *5 percent* of the Lisu live in Thailand, and they remain relatively unstudied elsewhere. They were even less so in the 1990s when I began this project.

Since the British Colonial Period, little new material has been written about the Lisu in Burma-Myanmar. In 2014 I interviewed the chair of the National Lisu Culture and Literature Preservation Committee, who shared parts of a draft of a new volume on Lisu history and custom about to be submitted to the National Archives. It is part of a larger national project on Myanmar's minorities and *after government approval* will be published simultaneously in Lisu, Burmese, and English.

Chinese scholarship also exists but is politically influenced and controlled. Outside a small body of unreliable translated material, most of what has been written about the Lisu is inaccessible to non-Chinese speakers. Because Chinese government websites are so wildly off on basics (in one, Lisu population was wrong by a factor of 10), I chose not to rely on this source. Although several Chinese scholars have focused on Lisu gender roles, such as Yang Guangmin's *Women Not to Be Blocked by Canyon*, such material is not considered reliable in its particulars. Chapters titled "Farewell to Slash and Burn Agriculture" and "Throwing off the Shackles of Primitive Culture" do highlight Lisu women's equality and leadership.

Taking the broad view and compared to larger groups such as the Hmong (or Miao), Karen, or Mien, however, far less is known about the Lisu outside of their own world.

Perhaps because of this dearth of material—especially in Myanmar and China, where 95 percent of Lisu in the world live today—and the specialized nature of scholarly work, no professional anthropologist has written a general overview of this group whose independence and all-over-the-map quality leave so many loose ends to ponder. The impossibility of substantive analysis—and reticence over sinking into generalizations on one hand or interminable relativizing on the other—make such a study frankly unanswerable to standard academic scholarship. While understandable, it is a shame because as the world changes rapidly and the Lisu with it, it was too late to *begin* this task in 2014.

There is diversity among the ways of Lisu in China, Burma, and Thailand; and country setting influences culture and fate. Policies toward minorities on issues of citizenship, land tenure, and religious freedom vary widely. But this is one book, not three, which emphasizes cultural patterns and place over time, remarking on national variations.

The Lisu tapestry is complex and doesn't fit neat progress narratives woven by nation-states. Still, comparing and contrasting the lives of Lisu in flux in three very different countries offers a unique lens through which to examine culture and adaptation and is the broad perspective this book offers. Its appearance makes good a long-deferred, much worried-over promise I made to share the Lisu story with a broader audience.

May the myi-do (repute) of all Lisu who helped me tell their story increase with this publication!

1

Who Are the Lisu?

When you've lost your *myi-do* (repute) it's already too late,
You can't pick up spilt water.
—*Lisu proverb*

The Nujiang gorge of Yunnan Province (*nu* means "angry" and *jiang*, "river" in Chinese) is also known as the Salween River. It is the heart of Lisu country. Thirty percent of the world's Lisu live in this dramatic environment, where mountains—increasingly treeless in areas given over to agriculture, still forested in others—spring vertically from a narrow gorge carved by the torrential river. The Biluo mountains (13,000 feet, or 4,000 meters) bank it on the east and the Gaoligong mountains (16,500 feet, or 5,000 meters) on the west. Vertical drop to the river below is 3,000 to 4,000 meters (10,000 feet to 13,000 feet). Un-tethered boats in its powerful current are rare, and it gives up few fish. The steepest part of the gorge extends 310 kilometers, with a valley floor ranging from a few hundred meters wide in most areas to a couple of kilometers in a few places. The Nujiang wasn't convention- ally bridged until the 1980s and remains un-dammed—one of the longest free-flowing rivers in the world. Lisu settlements perch in wooded valleys above and behind the big gorge, and trails and a single narrow road paral- leling it are the main highways.

Although today there are modern bridges, until the late 1980s Lisu still often found it more convenient to cross the torrent at a height of a few hundred feet on a cable slung across the gorge at narrow points. Most cable bridges have been replaced with pedestrian suspension bridges only in the last few years. Some still exist; in 2014 remaining old cables were well-known enough that people stopped along the road at these spots in hopes of capturing an image or video of a human crossing on their Galaxies and iPhones. As recently as 2010, on market days it was not unusual to see Lisu men, women, and youth use the old cables as the regular mode of transportation across the river, carrying children, produce, and other possessions. Suspended aloft in a rope sling with a wood or metal slider, they get a big push to start and then pull themselves the rest of the way when momentum ceases. Showing fear is not Lisu custom.

Lisu are distinct from the Akha, Lahu, Haw, Hmong, and other minorities with whom they have intermingled, married, and shared villages and outsider status, as well as from Han Chinese, Burmese, and Thai majority populations. Lisu men are known as highland farmers and crossbow-wielding hunters with a flair for languages and storytelling. Lisu women in traditional dress are impossible to confuse with others. They are also distinguished by a reputation for being entrepreneurial, as hardworking equals of their men, and as family purse-string holders. Those who marry Lisu are very likely to "become Lisu" themselves. Early explorers and geographers used terms such as "fine race," "superior people," and "fair complexioned" to describe them. In 1933 Major C. M. Enriquez of the Burma Rifles noted that Lisu are "armed and independent, and ready to migrate if interfered with in the smallest degree."

However, anything more than superficial study reveals fluidity and a culture impacted by a dizzying number of influences. A relatively small and widely dispersed group, even among minority populations, Lisu today live mainly in China's Yunnan Province (700,000), Myanmar's north, east, and central areas (400,000), and Thailand's north (50,000). Numbers are only slightly more reliable today than in the past. National bureaucracies have made progress in counting Lisu and other minorities in the twenty-first century but do not always make data public. Perhaps a thousand live in Arunachal Pradesh in northeast India, at the northwestern limit of the Lisu, and small Lisu settlements exist in Laos and Tibet.

Nujiang gorge. Author photo.

Numbers and even names applied to minority groups by nations are not consistent and shouldn't be assumed to be accurate, particularly in areas of conflict. This is most true in Myanmar, where the government counts people but doesn't release ethnic identity data. Census data may be intentionally inaccurate and identities ambiguous—groups exaggerate their population to appear "bigger" as they vie for political power. Questions of what constitutes or how to define an ethnic group (or its political activities) are becoming more, not less, contested today than in the past.

In Myanmar, for example, most Lisu live in Kachin State. Lisu there are classed as Kachin by the government, along with the largest ethnic minority, the Jingpaw, and three other minorities. However, they are not particularly close linguistically or culturally to the Jingpaw, who dominate Kachin State and whose insurgent army has battled the central government for fifty years. The convenience of the state or reasons unconnected to identity often end up defining groups.

It is not my purpose or within my expertise to sort out these hugely significant issues; however, they must be acknowledged. *Self-identification as Lisu* is the single criterion I used to define who is a Lisu in this work.

There is much to be learned from the Lisu—a strong people with a culture that defies space and has deflected annihilation throughout its long unwritten history. In spite of being so few and scattered, they have continued to adapt their unusually egalitarian culture without losing identity. The hardships of living in the crossfire of many countries' national conflicts, politics, and wars, their land pillaged by international logging interests, the drug trade, and environmental disaster, hasn't defeated them.

What is their essential strength, and how does it renew itself? What can the Lisu teach us?

Language is the most obvious characteristic shared by Lisu across differing habitats and national settings. Despite a 25–30 percent difference in vocabularies among the dialects spoken in Thailand, Myanmar, and areas of China, all Lisu understand each other after brief contact. Beyond this, defining traits that never fail to be noted—whether by anthropologists, missionaries, development workers, or government officials—are pride, individualism, and intolerance of authority.

These traits support each Lisu's desire to accumulate and increase his or her *myi-do*, or repute. *Myi* means name but also connotes fate and productive capacity, and *do* means power in the sense of accomplishment, according to anthropologist Otome Klein Hutheesing who works among Thai Lisu. Missionary David Morse, who now lives in Thailand but who was born and grew up in Burma as a native Lisu speaker, translates *do* as news, in the sense of transmission. They agree on repute as the closest English translation and that myi-do is the most highly ranked of Lisu values. The quest for myi-do is an individual one; the person—not the family, village, or lineage—obtains myi-do by working hard, taking care of obligations, speaking well, and following the dictates of Lisu custom.

Such outward, action- and results-oriented values encourage the behavior of a people who do not like to be bossed around and who historically chose statelessness over belonging to a larger group or nation.

All who have observed closely or lived among the Lisu note this attitude. The label "anarchists of the highlands" has stuck but probably misstates the case. The common association of anarchism with violence and "smashing the state" doesn't apply when looking at a pre-state minority culture, according to scholar James C. Scott. The author of *Two Cheers for Anarchism* and *The Art of Not Being Governed* suggests that "seeing like an anarchist" and appreciating the potential for voluntary cooperation *without* hierarchy resonates more closely with Lisu political sensibility—which is rational and practical and embeds mechanisms that encourage cooperation. It is true that Lisu do not rank harmony enforced by hierarchy as highly as other groups, such as the Karen or the Akha, and have been known to resort to killing in upholding group or personal justice—especially in dispatching Lisu headmen with authoritarian impulses. Their social code is embedded in *illi* Lisu (Lisu custom,) the constant reference used to judge human behavior. "It is custom" or "there is no custom" are the final words in many arguments. The fact that Lisu custom varies doesn't destroy its evocative force.

Throughout their history, the Lisu have migrated frequently and far—to seek new land, as an individual or group response to internal conflict, and to avoid war and domination. Their willingness, *eagerness* even, to pick up and move on is another defining characteristic. It was true of all Lisu in the past and, though constrained by land pressure and political realities today, is often still true among Lisu outside of China. While there are several groups of shifting highland agriculturists, the Lisu style of migration is distinct.

They are more likely to migrate in small groups and to establish independent hamlets in isolated places than are others, asserts Eugene Morse, father of David Morse, who lived with Lisu and other groups in China, Burma, and

Thailand his entire life (1921–2011). This explains how a relatively small group came to be so spread about. Eugene Morse also asserted that Lisu are not as clannish within their social organization or as inward-looking in their world-view as other migrating groups. They are risk takers. His view was seconded by an old Lisu Christian man I interviewed in Myanmar in 1997, Eligah Illia, who told me: "We're explorers and hunters and not afraid of going into the forest or to someone else's country."

Anthropologist E. Paul Durrenberger applied the model Sir Edmund Leach suggested in *Political Systems of Highland Burma* to take up the question, "who are the Lisu?" Leach's pioneering study made use of the Kachin terms *gumsa* (hierarchical) and *gumlao* (egalitarian) to identify contrasting political styles, as well as to note the dynamic between the two polarities. The Lisu are renowned for being on the egalitarian-most side of the scale because they essentially disclaim hereditary power, headmen, and ongoing councils of elders. Their social organization leaves room for great autonomy for the majority of individuals.

Durrenberger concluded that a chief difference between the Lisu and other mountain people is political style. Other sub-groups, such as pockets within the Karen community, could also be termed egalitarian, but not to the same degree—and the spirit of individual freedom and gender equality is common to Lisu groups scattered across thousands of miles and in every national milieu.

In 2014 I saw evidence of a pragmatic shift toward appointing leaders and officials, especially in China and Myanmar, where Lisu are developing political power within the state. That and cultural survival demand more organized social structures—which several generations of Christianity seem to have pre-pared them to build.

Lisu in Thailand, the smallest, least Christianized group, provide an exam-ple of adapting outwardly while maintaining egalitarian internal values. This country is extremely hierarchical, and Thais recruited headmen to create administrative links between each village and the government. While Lisu headmen use the position to make economic gains (they are paid by the Thai government) in the same way they would use any advantage, they do not develop patronage in the Thai way or extend power to their sons. In an elec-tion for village representatives to a council overseeing spending in Doi Chang in late 1997, the son of a popular Lisu headman of twenty-three years lost soundly. His son was not un-liked, Abeno Leeja explained to me, but it is individual repute, myi-do, that determines leadership. Leadership among the Lisu tends to be situation-specific; villagers judged that the son simply didn't have what it takes to be a good negotiator of village interests when dealing with Thai bureaucrats.

Few reliable historical references go back far, so it is possible the Lisu "live free or die" reputation has been over-weighted. However, the Lisu penchant for avoiding concentrations of power that dynastic setups encourage, especially compared to the Shan in Burma, has been well-observed since the end of the nineteenth century—allowing the gumlao label to stick. A possible exception is among Myanmar-Burma's Christian Lisu, who began developing leadership (not synonymous with hierarchy but perhaps related) to survive in that war-torn and impoverished regime, as well as to accommodate their adopted religion. The sons of ministers often become ministers themselves, and so spiritual authority has become vested in certain families. It was not that surprising in 2014, as that country's political economy was undergoing dramatic reform, to see a Lisu political class, as well as cultural leaders, emerging. Most Lisu in Myanmar are evangelical Protestants—however, in true Lisu fashion, the first Lisu senator in the country emerged from a tiny group of Lisu Roman Catholics.

The Lisu way is to make important decisions individually but in consultation with others. If a group is involved, consensus is reached by discussion. This works as a pressure valve, allowing venting of individual differences. In *Exodus to a Hidden Valley*, Eugene Morse says: "The Lisu do not hold with the common democratic concept of majority rule. They feel that the losing minority is bound to be unhappy . . . and so problems are discussed and discussed until an obvious answer emerges." To the Lisu, "It seems only logical that . . . each individual should be granted as much participation as possible in the decision-making process . . . There is no set prerogative, status, or authority among individuals." Minority views receive a degree of protection through this long-winded process.

While Lisu cosmological views may look hierarchical if all the spirits they propitiate are considered, in practice they aren't. Daily spiritual lives are most concerned with balancing dualistic opposites (man-woman, heaven-earth, east-west, top-bottom) and negotiating among the forces of ancestors, nature spirits, bad-talk spirits, and lost souls—not in ordering or beseeching them in

Ponies mean prestige. Author photo.

a particular way. Lisu recognize two interconnected worlds, the visible and the invisible. Ritualizing and other communication with the unseen world is necessary and constant because being on good terms with spirits is required to be successful both places. Even Christian Lisu, who ignore lesser spirits in favor of Wu-sa, the creator and sky god, in formal religious practice, keep track of their former system and use it as a common reference. They do not deny the reality of the spirit world; they have simply changed their interface with it. This has economic consequences, as Christians primarily raise pigs to sell instead of to feast the village. But practically speaking, Burmese Lisu are too poor to feast the village and instead host smaller gatherings.

The extreme, remote environments Lisu inhabit, such as the Nujiang gorge and hilltops in Burma and Thailand, shape their worldview and support values of pride and independence. Whether cultivating steep mountain swiddens in Burma or Thailand or valley floors in China, each individual's effort is central to group survival. Every person who is physically fit has an equal chance to use his or her labor to reach life goals. Among Lisu, goals beyond having enough to eat are having children, sufficient pigs, and luxury items such as horses or silver. Nowadays, a motorcycle or pickup truck substitutes for horses and cash for silver. But one isn't truly successful unless, in

Lisu New Year group. Author photo.

addition, one distributes wealth back to the community in the form of feasts. Since feasts are always connected to ceremonial activities, repute and prestige are associated with taking care of one's responsibilities. Christianity has disrupted economic aspects of raising pigs for ceremonies, but the Lisu style of Christian practice has substituted other communal obligations.

The distinctness of Lisu identity came into focus for me after spending time with individuals across the ideological/religious spectrum in several countries. A dynamic core resonates across their culture, allowing them to borrow easily from other cultures, other religions, and other languages without losing "Lisuness." They are also bound by a common sense of humor and word play filled with wish reversals: something they like stinks or is called ugly; a hunchback is described as well-built.

This core is evident despite a wide range of customs, depending on clan, location, and religion. Among the Lisu, no lineage is considered superior, and none are formally organized. The main lineages in Thailand—the Bee, Wild Cat, Fish, Bear, Wood, Buckwheat, and Hemp—(see Chapter 2, Mythic Origins) are not the same as those in Burma or China. There has been much intermarriage with Yunnanese and other minorities so that clans have been added or at least assigned Chinese names by administrators who don't speak

Lisu: Li, Yang, Wang, Tao, Wu, Ts'ao, Ho Cu, and Cang are some of the larger clan designations, and they exist side by side with a Lisu name. It is impossible to accurately tease out one discrete set of Lisu customs or religious practices, although most are informed by the cosmic habit of pairing opposites. Christians continue this, so one has to list a set of lineage names as well as the ethnic, country, and religious label to identify a Lisu with any specificity. However, according to virtually everyone I interviewed, those who marry Lisu are far more likely to take up Lisu habits than is the Lisu partner to surrender identity. The exception is when a Lisu physically moves away from his or her environment and joins majority populations.

In practical matters, personal allegiance is not to the larger group or even to village or clan but to the group of households with whom one links economically. This may or may not cross clan lines to include other kin. Usually, three to six families affiliate for economic reasons and socialize together. But the clique leaves room for fluidity and individuality; it is not unusual for a Lisu to drop affiliation with one and pick up with another. That is why it has been suggested that the ultimate political unit among the Lisu is the single household or in some cases the individual. This characteristic, more than any other, has supported Lisu in remaining one of the last stateless people.

In addition to other characteristics that bind them, a final one worth mentioning is their continual reference to non-Lisu such as Thai, Burmese, Indian, or Chinese in their own judicial and political actions. Like minorities everywhere, Lisu define themselves against majority populations. Better to be a Lisu with myi-do than to enter a majority culture at the bottom rung—the spot invariably reserved for them. This doesn't stop Lisu in Thailand from seeking or gaining national citizenship as a way to access benefits conferred to members of the larger society. In China and Burma the Lisu already are citizens. As practical people, in all three countries they are trying to figure out what these benefits, which have so far mostly eluded them in Myanmar and Thailand, might turn out to be.

2

Mythic Origins

A black dog builds a fence and walks back and forth behind it;
The clawless bird falls to the ground, and ants bite it.
  —*Lisu parable*

Before in the world there were no people. Wu-sa (sky god) made people,
one man and one woman. He made them of beeswax patties. They could
not marry because they were the same, brother and sister. Wu-sa told them:
If there is no love, if you do not want each other, you cannot stay here.
One, the woman, goes to the north, and one, the man, goes to the south.

Lisu origin myths vary, there is no written record, and memorized versions
differ. Lisu in China, Burma, and Thailand often disagree on how it all
started—the above was told by an old woman from Doi Laan, a Lisu-Akha
village in northern Thailand, and recorded by anthropologist Otome Klein
Hutheesing. The fact that the "first woman" went to the north in the story
and the man went to the south is odd because at home the Lisu divide
space as in the mythical Chinese Court, where male-female principles are
represented by an east-west, left-right duality. At the end of their migration
trail in Thailand, however, south could refer to centuries-long southward
migrations. In a flood myth variation the two survivors of a flood, a brother
and sister, survive by riding it out in a large gourd. Incest is the common
theme.

It is notable that in both cases, man and woman are "the same" or equal.
In the first, they are equal because they are made from the same material
(beeswax) rather than one being made from a part of the other, as in the
Adam's rib Old Testament account, and in both, siblinghood bespeaks

sameness or equality. This manifests in the equal status women and men share in Lisu culture.

In all Lisu origin stories involving siblings, brother and sister get together to save the human race, usually after a period of testing. If there is love after this trial, they are allowed to marry. In a story told in China, a pair of grinding stones is separated and then rolled down opposing mountaintops by *A-heng-pa*, the brother, and his sister *A-heng-ma*, to determine if heaven wants them to marry. In the valley, the two stones meet and fit together perfectly, one on top of the other.

A seventy-year-old dashipa (healer) of the Guapa (multiply) Clan living outside Liuku in Yunnan reinforced the sameness theme with a story he told of the original incestuous couple reproducing nine sets of twins, each a girl and a boy. Each set married and went out into the world to start up the world's races and nations.

These pairs commit divinely sanctioned incest to save humanity in Lisu myths, and their children and grandchildren go off to repopulate the world with Akha, Karen, Yao, Wa, Shan, Tai, and other people. The grinding stones are sometimes just two rocks, pieces of wood, or gourds, but the tale is found in all countries where Lisu live. In one, the first couple comes up a girl short, so the man destined to continue the Akha line goes into the forest and marries a monkey.

The Doi Laan grandmother in Thailand's origin tale continues, explaining the endless wandering of the Lisu:

> Eventually, a Lisu king marries his daughter to the Chinese king's son. No children are born, and so the husband takes a second, Chinese, wife. Still no children are born, and the man becomes restless: gambling, smoking opium, going out with girls. The Lisu wife, by now a queen, thinks to herself "Eh? I stay alone, stay like this? I will be hungry and then die." So she goes back to her Lisu father without telling her husband (a common Lisu survival strategy until today).
>
> War ensues over this family breach: "Lisu king, I have come to kill," the Chinese king says. The Lisu king was killed, and the Lisu people, without his protection, had no place to stay. Even though they fought and killed the Chinese it was not possible to stay, so they fled in all directions. "Since then, the Lisu have no country . . . that was long ago, maybe 4,000 years."

Another myth relates that long ago the Lisu were wealthy and powerful before the Chinese defeated them. Since then they wander but will serve no one because of their proud origins. This fits with the group's reputation for being dominant and unwilling to submit to authority, either from within their villages or outside them.

A creation myth that takes a different tack has it that Mupu-da, the creator, and Mupu-ma, the creator-female, had hammered the earth flat. But Mupu-da was talking so much that he accomplished only a fraction of what his wife had done. In a fit of pique he pulled up the world, thus forming the mountains and valleys.

The couple had one son. When he died, he was cut up into six pieces, with each piece buried separately. Each sprang up to become an original Lisu clan. The bit buried near a beehive became the *Bya-zo* (bee clan), the one interred underwater became the *Ngwa-zo* (fish clan), the piece planted near a tree became the *Se-zo* (wood clan), and so on to account for the Bear, Buckwheat, and hemp clans.

In the Upper Nu Gorge Lisu practiced a basic animistic religion free of Chinese influence with nineteen original totems named for animals, including bee, fish, bear, tiger, monkey, sheep, bird, mouse, snake, and others. They founded Lisu lineages when, magically disguised as men, they married Lisu women. Members of each clan are not allowed to kill the animal associated with it, which encourages cooperative hunting. Because tribe members trace origins to a human female ancestor, women receive great respect.

Women are revered as peacemakers: in one Chinese Lisu myth, two tribes go to war over a marriage, the men fighting with knives, crossbows, and lances. Terrible bloodshed occurs on both sides until an old woman climbs a cliff, takes off her long skirt, and waves it, shouting at the men to stop. The men cease immediately and return to their villages because custom at the time gave women a right to call for armistice. If the men didn't stop fighting, the woman would feel shame and jump off the cliff.

Myths explain why the Lisu have a hard life; in these the Lisu generally hold themselves responsible: Mupu-da and Mupu-ma gave the Lisu a language written on rice cakes. The Lisu get hungry, and thinking they would remember the script, they eat them. So they are forever at a disadvantage because they are not literate. In a variation, which could be the original "the dog

Wraparound fence to separate rice fields is held together with twisted grass. Author photo.

ate my homework" story, the Lisu language was written on an animal hide, which their trickster canine chewed up and made off with. Anthropologist scholar of anarchism James Scott argues that the rejection of writing systems by the Lisu and other preliterate people in Southeast Asia reflects agency: a tactic of less powerful people who practice "the art of not being governed."

One story recounts that when the world is being divided up, other people mark their territories with rocks or wood, but the Lisu are lazy and make boundaries from grass. The grass eventually rots away, and the Lisu are left without land and at the mercy of the Chinese, Thai, and Burmese nation-states. One actually sees twisted grass fences surrounding Lisu villages in Myanmar today—evoking the specter of a Lisu Three Little Pigs story in a country where the "wolf" of central government frequently blows down (or burns) their houses and confiscates their land.

The Lisu are pragmatic, and their myths reflect it. Klein Hutheesing argues that the psychological device they use to cope with homelessness is to forget and that they are a people who do not look back. Bad talk, offended ancestors, or just because Wu-sa has written it in a book—these are the causes of misfortune, and one needs the wit to accept what cannot be changed. James Scott notes that *not* having history can be a choice, that written history itself is responsible for creating winners and losers and hierarchies that undermine individual equality.

The best a human can do is to apply his or her individual energy to building up repute by following Lisu custom. In the end, what you *do* is more important that what you *believe*. Fate and life, *sya-mya*, are synonymous for the Lisu, who have no word for hope. In spite of this, in a favorite song they declare with typical Lisu bravado: *Shu ma da!* We cannot die!

3

History and Origin Theories

There's no land without running water;
there's no land the Lisu do not live.
—*Lisu proverb*

Myths about the origins and wanderings of the Lisu are more prevalent than historical evidence and could be as meaningful. Because the Lisu are a pre-literate society, not much studied, that receives scant mention in histories written by others such as the Chinese, solid documentation doesn't go back far. While Lisu in China and Burma used to memorize oral histories and genealogies, this custom has weakened through successive migrations.

Of older people who can still recite from memory, most recall fragments of stories, songs, prayers, or poetry in an archaic Lisu dialect they don't understand. More remember genealogies. These have practical use during bride price negotiations, when a common tactic is to claim incest to levy fines on the groom.

The Lisu and their forebears, like other hill tribes in South and Southeast Asia, may not have always lived in the hills or mountains or always been distinct groups. Many former tribal or pre-state valley dwellers were forced up into less accessible and fertile areas, often high in the mountains, by more powerful groups. Over the past few thousand years, even inhabitants of empires and nation-states have been squeezed up mountainsides and "back" into tribal existence. Segments of larger societies, such as armies or disowned peasant groups, have branched off to join others or headed for the hills to free themselves from taxes, slavery, or other domination.

An area of scholarship arising in the twenty-first century identifies a "non-state space" within this region that sprawls across highland areas of eight remote, mostly contiguous nation-states. About the size of Europe, it was first called the Southeast Asian Massif and, more recently, Zomia. Providing more than just a new name for lands the Lisu and other minorities escaping state control have traversed over the last few thousand years, Zomia creates an alternate way to *think* about the history and political choices made by millions of people as nation-states began rising and reaching what we tend to see as inevitable dominance.

One record from the nineteenth century places the Lisu in China before the Christian era. But there's no way to link this with the people who today call themselves Lisu. Mention of them appears in Fan Ch'o's *Man Shu*, written around AD 685, which locates Lisu in the region of the Yunnan-Kweichow-Sichuan border country in southeastern China near Lake Lugo and fits with later theories. Some present residents of this area, the Mosuo, have matriarchal customs that accord with the high status of Lisu women. Other Lisu claim to be of Chinese origin, saying their ancestors came from Hunan and Kiangsi centuries ago. Lisu settlements are still found in Sichuan Province. Claiming to be Chinese rather than barbarian, however, could be a self-interested fiction.

Ethnic purity does not exist, and so its absence applies to the Lisu and other migrating groups. The fact that the Lisu, so few in number, have maintained centuries of cultural and linguistic continuity, however, testifies to their culture's vigor and viability. They have survived in China and Southeast Asia, where millennia-long movements have created the most complicated ethnolinguistic kaleidoscope in the world. The Lisu even recount migrations of Han Chinese into their society, such as during wars with the Mongols in the thirteenth century or during the Panthay Rebellion in Yunnan from 1856 to 1873.

When and whence one particular group emerged with language and customs we recognize today as Lisu will never be settled questions. While the 4,000 years mentioned by a Lisu woman in northern Thailand to Otome Klein Hutheesing is impossible to refute, it doesn't pass any historical test.

Four basic theories relate to the origins of the Lisu; these include variations, sub-themes, and mini-plots.

The most all-encompassing, the "Pontic Migration," or north-to-south and west-to-east migration theory, is also called the Heine-Geldern theory. It accommodates the other three and proposes that people from the northern steppes of Russia pushed older groups such as the Mongols southward around the time more western people, such as Scythians and others around the Black Sea, migrated east. The Mongols then invaded (or were pushed down into) China. Kublai Khan, who conquered Dali in 1253 and Pagan in 1287, is the most well-known leader of such a group. The Mongols pushed the Tais and others further south into Southeast Asia. The Lisu and other minorities would be among those whose migrations were thus set off.

Where they set off *from* is a mystery, however, and theories contradict each other. I will cite just a few to illustrate problems scholars encounter when seeking hard evidence on preliterate, stateless people.

In the first theory, perhaps most widely believed, the Lisu come from Tibet. A few still live there and immediately south, and stories Lisu themselves tell point to a homeland further north than their present geographical spread. More than one early ethnography reported that Lisu in China say their name means "have come down from the top [or roof] of the world," a possible reference to the eastern Tibetan plateau.

Indeed, Lisu look like Tibetans. Lisu traditional religion resonates strongly with the indigenous Tibetan Bon (though this could also be said of many other animistic religions), and some women's wraparound dresses and aprons are similar to Tibetan women's. Their language belongs to the Tibeto-Burman group and is closer to it than to the also-related, but less so, Lahu and Akha tongues. All three are classed together with the largest in the group, the Nuosu.

Robert Morse, younger brother of Eugene, was a linguist and scholar born in Tibet in 1923 to American missionary parents J. Russell and Gertrude Morse. He grew up in China with the Lisu, became a missionary, and lived among them in Burma after World War II. Morse came up with a second theory: that the Lisu were pastoralists originally from an area called Chiang, northeast of Tibet, across open land accessible via the Yangtze River. The high Tibetan plateau is too great a barrier from which to migrate directly south, he argued—there isn't any way to get down from it.

Morse supports his theory by citing primary-source Chinese texts at Hwa Chong Ta Sho (now Huazhong daxue, Central China University), where he studied the first two years of World War II. His evidence points to an established Lisu homeland by AD 1200, before Kublai Khan's armies conquered Dali, around Lake Lugu on Yunnan's border with Sichuan. This theory accords with Chinese records placing Lisu forbears along the banks of the Jinsha River (a tributary of the Upper Yangtze), close by the matrilineal Mosuo with whom they share the rare value of feminine equality. Women in this group of Sino-Tibetan speakers, in fact, have even higher status than men, and their culture has been called "the Kingdom of Daughters."

According to Morse, around 1200 the Lisu were enlisted to help Naxi neighbors (with whom they also share cultural and linguistic affinities) just to the south of this area in Lijiang to ward off a Shan invasion from the Northwest. The Shans, also coming along the broad Yangtze valley, had attacked the Naxi at Lijiang on elephants but were thwarted by a crossbow-wielding army of 200,000 Lisu, according to Morse's research. Superior technology enabled them to shoot poison arrows from a distance, causing the Shans to withdraw to Dali. From there they drew up a new strategy—to conquer the Lisu village by village. Morse argues that *this* was the precipitating event for Lisu migrations first west and then south, across the Mekong, and, finally, to the Upper Nu Gorge, where the largest population concentrates today.

Morse's theory is supported by Dr. Joseph Rock, whose research led him to concur that Lisu were former pastoralists and farmers springing from Naxi culture. Variations on this fit with Lisu stories that claim the Lai country, along the Huang Ho (Yellow) River to the east of Tibet and not far north of the Yangtze, is where they first lived in China. Small communities of Lisu live among the Naxi people today in Sichuan, as well as with the Bai, Han, and Yi nationalities.

Theories that sound neat get messed up as more facts are layered in. The Lisu have much in common linguistically with the Yi (formerly called Lolo), a large group of non-Chinese mountain people from an area east of Tibet in the Taliang mountains of Szechwan. A third theory holds that Lisu are an offshoot of this group. Both Lisu and Yi have animal and tree clan names, both hold weddings in the bride's house, and both share the belief that women have seven souls and men have nine. However, these beliefs, as well as one that a black dog on the roof spells bad luck, are just as likely to have sprung from proximity as genealogy. Lisu have always been borrowers.

Linguistics suggests that Lisu groups scattered recently because despite different dialects, Lisu everywhere can understand each other, even if it takes a day or two's contact. Because of linguistic similarities, some theorize that the Lisu, the Yi, and Mosuo groups arose via a mix of migrating Tibetans and aborigines. The Chinese called the Yi "Southern Barbarians," and ninth-century records describe Yi groups that correspond to Lisu categories of white, black, wild, southern, and naked. Lisu could have been part of the Nan Chao kingdom, which existed from AD 737 to 902 and was ethnically Yi or Shan, depending on the source credited. Might they have been serfs and slaves who revolted and consequently formed a more egalitarian society? Pure speculation.

A last theory, not widely held, is that the Lisu don't come from some northern or northeastern "other" place. They emerged quite recently, and their ancestral home is in Yunnan, where most still live. Reinhart Hohler, a German scholar, theorizes that the Lisu migrated both up and down the Salween, Shweli, and Mekong Rivers for only *hundreds* of years and perhaps east to the Yangtze at a particular time. This theory explains why Lisu in the Upper Nujiang gorge wear costumes different from and unrelated to those everywhere else but similar to those of the Nu, with whom they share territory.

Lisu could simply have migrated to or been chased up the Nu by the Chinese into increasingly remote and mountainous valleys—places good for avoiding rulers and, more recently, for growing opium poppies. The Tengchong area is one of the few places where today Lisu are found living in isolation from other tribes. Could it be because this is truly Lisu territory, where they are at home and not encroachers? Lisu villages and houses there are sturdy and have a permanent feeling not found elsewhere. I visited villages near Tengchong in 1997 and 2014, and residents reported that their families had lived in the area for hundreds of years. Evidence offered by a Lisu musician that his village, Shao Hu Ba, was 500 years old was that he could count back generations of named, local ancestors on his *tabiya* to arrive at the number and also that "everyone knows this."

Actually, we will probably never know which theory or combination is closest to the truth. Genetic testing might yield future evidence in this regard, but as a practical matter, the existence and location of a Lisu homeland is likely to remain elusive.

Eugene Morse translated "Lisu" to mean the "loud custom" people. This accords with their reputation in China as merry, talkative, argumentative, and fond of drinking. The "outlaw" people is in accordance with their desire to live "far from the ruler" and is more common in Myanmar today, along with the "wraparound" people. The latter could reference traditional turbans or long belts or women's dresses. Both translations are found in old texts.

Outsiders have called the Lisu by different names: *Li-hsaw, Li-shaw, Lisaw, Liso, Lissou* (varied spelling of same name); *Lu-tzu*; and *Yaoyen, Yeh-jen, Yaw-yin* (these last three variations are all spelled *Yeren* today). Outsiders have also named Lisu sub-groups, usually in an attempt to classify by costume, as in *pfu* or *pae* (white), *ne* (black), *hua* (flowery), or *dja-lae* (brindled) or by where they are from, such as Lushui or Loma Lisu.

It is significant that Lisu themselves don't make such distinctions and that words used to describe them are not Lisu. Some labels, such as the Chinese *Yaw-yin*, are pejorative, translating as "wild people." When asked his or her group, the individual invariably says "Lisu." An adage, *"Lisu nyi, Lisu ma jo,"* means "Lisu two, Lisu not have" and indicates one Lisu identity. It is the business of scholars and other outsiders to argue over classifications.

Because these distinctions are confusing and do not serve my purpose, I simply use "Lisu," sometimes modified with country or area, to describe the geographic locations of individuals and villages.

4

Modern Times

What you eat now is yours,
If you save it, it could become someone else's.
   —*Lisu proverb*

From the sixteenth to the twentieth centuries, Lisu engaged in intermittent fighting with the Chinese over land encroachment, yet most stayed in China through the twentieth century and into the twenty-first—in 2017 over 700,000 were China citizens. Among Myanmar's Lisu (also citizens), today perhaps 400,000 to 450,000, the greatest number arrived from China after the revolution of 1949; they and other minorities are beginning to gain political representation along with majority Burmans. Lisu had been trickling into Thailand before the Chinese revolution, but the displacement it caused pushed the last great migration. About 50,000 live at the southern end of the migration trail in the Thai Kingdom today, where perhaps half are still not enfranchised citizens because of institutionalized discrimination.

The historical record on the Lisu is thin: in 1592 there is an account of Chinese pacification of the Lisu of Yung-ling, who had plundered government salt from Wuchiang. A Chinese retaliatory raid yielded 83 Lisu heads. In 1751 the Chinese began one of many intermittent efforts to control the Lisu in Western Yunnan by settling soldiers and administrators in more accessible villages. There was intermarriage, and descendants, who "became" Lisu, held special positions of power. Merchants followed, selling iron, silver, and salt in return for coffin planks, medicinal herbs, bear gall, stag horn, hides, and beeswax.

Studies by modern Chinese social scientists tell of feudalistic, slave-holding Lisu societies up until the time of communist liberation. These studies don't agree with descriptions provided by Lisu or with their own myths and stories. Such research is suspect because of pressure on Chinese academics to fit research findings into ideological molds; it does not, however, preclude them from being accurate. The Lisu were on the move for the past several centuries and possibly harbored pockets of feudalism or slave-holding, reflecting the society through which they migrated.

The first waves of out-migration from China began around the turn of the twentieth century when Lisu moved into Burma's Kachin and Shan States. An edition of the *Upper Burma and Shan State Gazette*, published in 1900 by the British colonial government, reported that about 1,000 Lisu, scattered in twenty villages, were then resident.

Thailand had no documented Lisu population until around 1910, and northeast India's group didn't arrive in Arunachal Pradesh from Burma until the late 1950s or early 1960s. A few Lisu also settled in Tibet and Laos.

Until the 1970s and 1980s, the Lisu economy was based on shifting, or swidden, agriculture. This was phased out first in China, which banned the practice after the revolution. Although labor-intensive, swiddening lends itself to temporary use because burning land creates intense fertility for a few years. As far back as the 1890s, a key motivation to relocate was the search for good highland poppy-growing land. As the Lisu spread across a wide geographic area in the last century, they located small thatched villages clinging to mountainsides near the top of the range—as far as possible from state control. Particularly in Thailand, they share the rugged upland topography with Akha, Lahu, Hmong, Karen, Yao, and other opium-growing folk, usually at higher altitudes.

The original Lisu religion was animistic, but Buddhist elements, Chinese ancestor worship, Taoism, and other belief systems became interwoven during migrations. Lisu engage actively with the spirit world, and ceremonializing is part of daily life. Rituals involve dualistic logic and combine sets of opposites, seeking to balance forces of nature, ancestors, and the universe.

They also propitiate spirits with animal sacrifices. The earliest Lisu conversions to Christianity occurred in the second half of the nineteenth century in China, but not until the 1930s and 1940s did large numbers convert. Most Christian Lisu came from the Upper Nujiang gorge in Yunnan, China, and practice an American-style, evangelical Christianity.

Lisu migrations from China to Burma and then into Thailand increased with the disruption of World War II and swelled after the communist revolution. Many Lisu, particularly Christians but also ones following traditional practices, left China after 1950 when Yunnan was conquered by Mao's army.

Remnants of the Kuomintang (KMT), the losing nationalist government and army, were among the Lisu's fellow refugees. Former KMT political and military leaders became involved in the burgeoning international opium and heroin trade in Burma and Thailand, which was pushed into those countries after being eradicated in China post-revolution. The trade shifted down into the Golden Triangle of northern Thailand, Burma, and Laos. Migrating Lisu farmers, many of them expert opium growers, settled in these areas looking for new mountaintops and economic opportunities. It was inevitable that the paths of the two groups would cross.

5

Migration

Birds that migrate seldom get fat,
The man that roams is seldom rich.

   —*Lisu proverb*

We left our village in Burma, almost a hundred of us, in the middle of the night and crept over the border into Thailand. We left everything behind, all the animals, because they would have made noise. The British had left, the Japanese were coming, and the Burmese wanted to make us carry things for them. If a Lisu refused, he was shot. It was no fun in Burma anymore! We came to Thailand because we heard there was good land for growing poppies here, and our land wasn't good anymore. In Burma the English taxed us for growing opium, for other things too. The Lahu were their agents, and they added on something for themselves. Then the Burmese tried to make us slaves. So we left, even though over there you could chop down a tree as big as you liked and no one made trouble over it. The Thais treat us okay, even though they don't like us to grow opium.

   —*A seventy-eight-year-old Sin-lee clan member from*
   Dton Loong village in northern Thailand, as recorded
   by Otome Klein Hutheesing in the mid-1980s

Lisu proverbs as well as personal experiences express this people's ambivalence toward migration: when they stay in one place too long they begin to feel hemmed in—yet moving involves costs and dangers.

There are many migrating tribes in Southeast Asia; what distinguishes the Lisu is a willingness to break off in smaller groups compared with others and to establish villages across a wider geographic spread. In this, they are outward-looking and bold. A kin group or even an individual might migrate to resolve village conflict or for economic opportunity. Outside pressures such as wars and insurgencies, however, have also triggered the desertion of whole villages, as recorded above in the interview by Klein Hutheesing.

Nee-shu Ma, a ninety-three-year-old Lisu woman I met in 1997, has been settled in the Yunnan, China, border village of Chang Tang on the Ping Lang River for forty years. She was born across the river in Burma, but fled to escape Japanese soldiers who were conscripting labor there to build roads in 1938 or 1939. During the flight with her family, three of her five young children died or were killed.

Lisu economy, tailored to a shifting agricultural lifestyle, was based on free access to land rather than acquisition through purchase or inheritance. Lisu migrate to find new farmland, to reallocate labor—or to avoid war, conflict, and domination. As the stories above illustrate, the move might be to a different district or to a new country; avoiding conflict is not easy.

Wandering is embedded in their psyches, especially among those who have wandered the furthest from China. Whether prompted by dramatic or mundane events, it has shaped their lives. Even those who are long settled belong to a culture whose traditions, songs, myths, and attitudes were informed over hundreds of years of migrations. This lifestyle serves as a leveler and supports Lisu individualism and non-hierarchical social structures.

China's Lisu population is the most stable today. Since the revolution and by some accounts before, these Lisu migrated shorter distances (but sometimes many times) than those in Burma or Thailand. Reliable information on such a small and scattered group, especially during periods of social and economic upheaval, is impossible to document. Going by anecdote and self-reporting, far fewer of those I visited in the 1990s or in 2014 in the Tengchong and Nujiang areas of Yunnan have moved around than have Lisu in the other two countries. The big exception was in "new" villages settled over the last thirty years by the authorities such as those around Liuku, the capital of

Lisu from further up the river have been drawn down to the Chinese replacement villages such as Tan-na-nu above the west bank of Nujiang. Proximity to a market in Liuku, a paved road, and less steep topography than in mountain villages were advantages Lisu stated in deciding to move there. Author photo.

Nujiang Lisu Autonomous Prefecture. Many Lisu moved there from remote hamlets further up the steep-sided gorge, to land cleared by the government for agriculture. In Liuku, Lisu are the majority population; the dozen I spoke with who had moved there all commented that life is much easier, with access to better farmland, health care, education, and electricity, than in their former abodes. Most had been resettled for at least fifteen years and had paid off government loans on sturdy housing built to lure them from the vertical canyons and tenuous existences of the past. Such resettling continues.

Lisu in Thailand are the most transient. With the exception of a few small groups in northwest India and northern Laos, the roughly 50,000 Lisu in Thailand have traveled the furthest. Land pressure and Thai government anti–forest incursion policies punish minority people, keeping them shifting around and among settlements in Chiang Mai, Chiang Rai, Mae Hong Son, and Tak Provinces. In the 1970s, E. Paul Durrenberger noted a practical adaptation to this: they build houses that can be knocked down and reassembled elsewhere. He contrasted this with other, more permanent villages built by groups such as the Shan—but by 2015 most Lisu in Thailand had also adopted concrete-block construction. This hasn't stopped the Thai government from evicting Lisu from established settlements; in August 2014 it confiscated land from 145 families living in Laowu in Chiang Dao District, jailing farmers who protested the action in their almost-100-year-old village.

While a minority of Lisu from Baumee and Cho-me or from the southeast in Shan State have been settled in mountainous areas bordering China for generations, most Lisu in Myanmar today came from or are descendants of those who left China after the revolution. In 1900 James George Scott, a British colonial administrator and amateur ethnographer, estimated the Lisu population in Burma at just over a thousand. An Indian Army publication reported 35,000 Lisu in 1930, but there is no way to gauge its accuracy. In another army handbook, British army officer and author Major C. M. Enriquez described how he inserted a new verse into a Lisu traditional song claiming "the army is the road to travel" before World War II and enlisted twenty Lisu recruits on the spot at a tribal dance in mountains around Putao.

The Putao Valley itself was too low-lying and mosquito-infested for major settlement until the late 1940s, when an anti-malaria campaign led by the Morse family of missionaries began making it habitable. Energetic evangelizing, land clearing, and agricultural development first drew Christian Lisu to Putao from China. The Chinese revolution in 1949, followed by a dreadful earthquake in Putao in 1950, underlined the Christians' Armageddon message and accelerated the trend. Thousands of traditional Lisu migrated down from surrounding mountains within Burma, and more arrived from China. Many in this group of Lisu took up a new religion and lowland wet-rice cultivation at the same time.

A few Lisu have seen the world from a British Army billet. About 100 were in service by 1930, and in Mesopotamia they served well in spite of fierce heat and "won promotion and distinction out of all proportion to their numbers," according to Enriquez. Lisu in Burma have moved around a lot since they arrived in that country as a result of military, political, religious, and drug-trade–related upheavals.

A Christian Lisu, Eligah Illia, who lived in a small village across the Irrawaddy River from Myitkyina, told me of his extraordinary military career in a 1997 interview:

> I came down from the high mountains to Myitkyina during World War II
> to prospect for gold. I didn't find much, so [I] joined the British Army with
> some Lisu friends. They took us to India for six months' training and then
> told us we were going home. We didn't know what was going on, but as we
> got into an airplane, they handed each of us a big package. Well, it turned out
> to be a parachute, and our first assignment was to re-take Myitkyina, which
> had fallen to the Japanese! Some of the boys really didn't want to jump, but
> after we got our parachutes strapped on the officers hooked their backs into
> this ejecting machine, the rest of us jumped, and before we knew it we were
> all falling and then floating to earth. Some British officers jumped with us
> and told us what to do when we landed. We did it and re-took Myitkyina
> after a few days. The operation was a success, so the British said, "Well done,
> lads. Now you're out of a job." They gave us some money and said to go
> home. So I bought some things and went back up to the border to sell them
> to the Cho-me Lisu up there. I wanted to attend Bible school, but the elders
> wouldn't recommend me; they said because I'd been in the army, I must be
> corrupt. I went anyway because by then I'd decided I wanted to be a preacher,
> not a soldier or a trader.

---■-■---

Movement among the Lisu was so frequently triggered by wars in the twenti-eth century that it has often been more accurate to describe them as refugees rather than migrants—yet it is the moving itself, rather any particular con-flict precipitating it, that they have internalized. Less dramatic events—prosaic mixes of economic and social pressures—are just as likely to prompt a move, as a story told by anthropologist Alain Dessaint illustrates:

> It started when the headman fined two young men for telling stories about a
> widow's sexual adventures. Fat Belly, the father of one of them, was also the
> adopted son of the headman's brother. He complained that the fine was exces-
> sive, that his son meant no harm, and that the story had been spread by other
> people as well. The headman wouldn't back down, the widow and her sup-
> porters were angry. Until then Fat Belly and his son had been thinking about

moving because their opium fields were poor, but Fat Belly had hesitated because his kin, including the headman, were not moving yet. The widow incident pushed him over the edge and they moved several days later. The incident caused trouble within the clan because the headman had been judged unfair.

This started a chain of events, linked to another dispute over the use of a field—in which the headman was again charged with unfairness. When Stupid Squirrel, a poor member of the same clan who was considered the wronged party, complained about the decision, the headman threatened to take away his horse. He additionally accused him of not performing ritual obligations when his wife was sick. The headman's wife stoned Stupid Squirrel's house at night, calling him a dog.

Because his parents had been influenced by Christian missionaries before they died, because he was poor, and because he had doubts about Lisu curing methods, Stupid Squirrel was responsive to offers of help from a Christian Lisu and emigrated with his wife to a Christian village. This in turned shamed several other clan members, and another five of the clan's family groups ended up moving away from the village after the opium harvest. All in all, 80 percent of the village's population migrated within an 18-month period.

Migration is not the only option when a headman is judged unfit or disloyal to his clan—killing may also be resorted to in serious situations. Taking such high-risk actions to solve problems demonstrates Lisu willingness to do just about anything rather than submit to authority, though as a people they are not generally known as particularly murderous or violent.

Opium / Heroin History

Opium was grown in relatively small amounts in China as early as the T'ang Dynasty and in Szechwan from about AD 900. Its cultivation might predate the Lisu themselves in China by several hundred years.

European trade with China began growing in the 1500 and 1600s during the Mughal period; Portuguese traders were the first to import Indian opium there. The British in India took over the trade by 1773, when their maritime empire defeated the Mughals. The British began encouraging opium consumption in China. Warren Hastings, the first governor general of India (1773–85), organized the trade on a large scale, and during his term opium exports grew to one-seventh of British India's total revenues. The empire established a virtual monopoly on Indian opium, and exports to China grew twenty-five-fold from the beginning of the eighteenth century to the beginning of the nineteenth century. Mindful of the drug's effects, the British kept opium as an export-only product and outlawed its use in, or importation to, India. By the early 1800s others, including Americans, entered the trade to China on a smaller scale. China became a society rife with both addicts and widespread casual users.

The British and Chinese fought two wars over opium during this period, with the British winning both. Free trade was their justification, but securing access to the immense Chinese market for British-controlled Indian opium was the actual cause. Since 1729, the Chinese had been trying to curb opium smoking and importation, with little success. The first Opium War, from 1839 to 1842, was triggered by the emperor's decision to destroy Indian opium confiscated by the British. The Chinese lost, and the British extracted a $21 million indemnity from them, about a third of which was reimbursement for opium destroyed. The British won these concessions in the name of free trade—ironically, to import a monopoly-produced, illicitly sold narcotic to a country where its use had been banned for over 100 years. The Chinese then lost a second war, from 1856 to 1858, but as a concession were allowed to put a small tax on imported opium. This war marked the beginning of an almost 50-year period of de facto legalization of domestic cultivation and importation of opium in China.

These wars opened up tremendous trade opportunities for the British. From 1811 to 1821, they exported about 340 tons of opium a year to China; from 1829 to 1839, their annual opium trade to China reached 1,841 tons. In the decades after the wars, this grew a peak of 6,500 tons in 1880.

The defeated Chinese responded in the 1860s by allowing more opium to be grown domestically to stem imports and resulting capital outflows. Peasants were often forced to grow opium instead of rice, and Sichuan and Yunnan, far from the weakened central government in Peking, were favored cultivation areas. By 1875 a third of Yunnan's cropland was devoted to opium; it was second only to Sichuan as an opium-producing province. The opium market experienced unprecedented growth, spurred by competition between foreign importers and the Chinese government's counter-efforts.

The Lisu, who lived in Southwest Yunnan, were not yet major poppy cultivators at this time. Although some sources say Chinese traders had introduced the Hmong, Kachin, Lisu, and other hill tribes to the crop by the 1850s, it was the reversal of poppy policies, beginning in the 1890s in England and then in China in 1906, that forced the newly illegal crop into the highlands. Chinese middlemen introduced it on a massive scale, profiting from the market created by 8 million Chinese addicts. By this time, earlier policy promoting opium cultivation in China had become successful, at great social cost. By 1900 China's domestic opium crop reached 22,000 tons a year. "There is an opium pipe for every house in China but an opium pipe for every person in Yunnan," according to a Chinese saying in the late nineteenth century.

In 1905, just before opium prohibition in China, geographer George Forrest wrote an account of his October to December journey along the Nujiang gorge, inhabited mainly by Lisu. Opium poppies flower in this period, yet he fails to mention them among Lisu crops, which he describes in great detail.

By 1911, however, the British Counsel at Tengyue (today called Tengchong), about 50 kilometers west of the Nu, described increased cultivation of the opium poppy in the "tribal area" to the north—from 27,000 acres the year before to 43,000 acres that year. Around the same time, there are several descriptions of the ban on opium production in the plains and the devastating effect this had on Chinese peasants. The price tripled within a year or two, and a class of corrupt officials sprang up to profit from the newly contraband trade. This change to an opium-based economy occurred quickly and had far-reaching consequences for the Lisu.

Opium consumption in China reached 22,500 tons a year by the early twentieth century, seventy times what it had been in 1800. The poor soil and high mountain terrain of the Lisu, not yet under Chinese control, was ideal for poppy growing. Chinese officials' and soldiers' crop suppression tactics didn't work in the wild mountain people's inaccessible territory. Lack of roads and outsider ignorance of the areas made it possible for Lisu and other mountain cultivators to defend the new, profitable crop.

While the growth of new addiction among the Chinese slowed as a result of the 1906 ban, by 1920 almost all Lisu had become expert highland opium cultivators; few, however, had become addicts. By the 1930s it was estimated that 10 million Chinese used opium regularly. Since it was

Lisu woman in northern Thailand scores opium pod,
1996. Author photo.

no longer grown by Chinese peasants or imported on a large scale, the
Lisu and other highlanders, particularly the Hmong, must have been the
main supply source.

The Lisu were not left to poppy cultivation for long, however, and
"pacification" measures beginning in the early twentieth century caused
the first exodus of Lisu from China into Burma. Although the measures
were developed ostensibly to bring them under Chinese political control,
in fact harassment of Lisu and other minorities had more to do with
Chinese officials' relentless informal taxation or rake-off of profits from
the illegal trade.

Beginning around the same time and up until around 1930, Lisu from
the Kengtung area of the Shan State moved south into highland areas of
Chiang Mai and Chiang Rai Provinces in northern Thailand in search of
good poppy-growing environments, as well as to escape Burma's taxes
and legendary banditry.

The communist revolution in 1949 abruptly halted China's massive
opium trade. Traders, dealers, and in some cases addicts were jailed

or executed. With no way for consumers and growers to connect, the Chinese market collapsed and the trade shifted suddenly to the "Golden Triangle" area of Burma, Laos, and Thailand. By the early 1950s, fleeing remnants of the defeated Chinese Nationalist army (the Kuomintang, or KMT) had fled to northern Burma and Thailand and quickly took over the business. Heroin was beginning to outpace opium as the most internationally traded narcotic, with greater profits. Larger supplies of raw opium used to produce heroin were needed, and the KMT pressured hill farmers such as the Lisu and Hmong to open new poppy-growing areas in the Golden Triangle. Many Lisu living in Burma were pushed into Thailand for this purpose.

Lisu's involvement with the drug trade has always been as pawns of powerful forces. First, they were enticed into cultivating poppies by traders and corrupt Chinese officials at the end of the nineteenth century; after 1950, pressure came from the KMT. By then, the KMT had become an agent of the US Central Intelligence Agency (CIA), paid to assist in America's project of stopping the spread of communism. Regardless of whether agents and politicians in Washington were aware of the KMT's drug-related activities, American funding was used to cement KMT control of the opium trade. For a full account of this history, see *The Politics of Heroin* (1972) by Alfred W. McCoy.

According to McCoy, the KMT and Thai police (also CIA clients) proved more adept at organizing opium production and marketing than in sealing Burma/Thai/Chinese border areas against a feared invasion by China. While Cold War policymakers in Washington focused single-mindedly on halting the spread of communism, they either failed or refused to see that one by-product of their actions was to help build a truly international drug market.

This was a crucial moment for opium growing in the Golden Triangle where Lisu and other cultivators lived. Then as throughout history, decisions of governments more than criminals often determine the direction of the illegal trade. The new Chinese government effectively stopped opium cultivation and trade beginning in the early 1950s. This left Iran as the major supplier of opium, with Southeast Asia a growing competitor, until 1955. Then Iran, too, took the politically and morally bold decision to abolish poppy cultivation.

As McCoy details in his meticulously researched but still controversial work, China and Iran were not the only countries making important choices: "In the 1950s the Thai, Lao, [French colonial] Vietnamese, and American governments made critical decisions with the unintended consequence of increasing Southeast Asia's opium production to feed the habits of the region's addict population and transforming the Golden Triangle into the largest single opium-producing area in the world."

The Thai police, with Thai military cooperation, used CIA-funded weapons, other equipment, and cash to develop Bangkok into the opium-trading capital of Asia by 1954, according to McCoy. When Iran dropped out of the market in 1955, it created a huge void. Dreams of profits buried any qualms corrupt Thais or the KMT might have had over the social consequences of expanding the opium trade further into their own region. Working together, they wove an economic web of steady markets overseen by middlemen, good prices, and protection from government interference to support poppy cultivation. It is not surprising that Lisu and other highland farmers began turning more fields over to profitable poppy cultivation in this era.

Subsequent twists and reversals of government policies twenty or more years later again caused convulsive upheaval among the Lisu and other farmers at the bottom of the food chain whose economies had become opium-dependent. In Burma and parts of Thailand, opium poppies are still cultivated; here as elsewhere, it is farmers, addicts (including prostitutes, many of whom are underage), and societies that bear most of the costs while government-protected criminals reap most of the profits.

The pejorative neologisms of nacro-state, narco-capitalism, and narco-economy are now well understood to have international causes and consequences and are used to describe situations in Mexico and West Africa and, in the 1970s, Columbia. Such terms had not yet entered the mainstream in the 1950s and 1960s as the history related above unfolded. Even the term "War on Drugs" unveiled by President Richard Nixon in 1971, although involving other countries, was primarily thought of as a *domestic* policy. But the true dawn of the modern multinational narcotics trade occurred in the Golden Triangle in the 1950s—complete with political backing of governments, drug cartels, high finance, and borderless reach—as first described by McCoy in a doctoral thesis on Southeast Asian history at Yale University in 1972.

International efforts to stop poppy cultivation have a history of misdirection, political interference, and poor implementation. The net results today are exponentially larger and cheaper supplies of heroin, methamphetamines, and other illegal substances than before the US-led "War on Drugs" began. This has occurred both in the Western countries that have spent billions waging that war and in markets closer to production.

In the process, hundreds of thousands of occasional and regular opium smokers turned into heroin addicts across Southeast Asia. Some of the farmers banned from growing poppies such as the Lisu, unable or unwilling to come up with viable economic alternatives, have become involved in more lucrative aspects of the drug trade, which today revolve more around methamphetamine production as governments suppressed opium cultivation in the Golden Triangle. Among small farmers in Myanmar and northern Thailand, this is particularly true. In economic terms, they have moved up the value-added ladder from being poppy growers to employees, mules, or small-scale middlemen. Many Lisu have died in drug-related violence, especially in Thailand and Myanmar.

This has had a negative effect at the village level on minority groups experiencing the repercussions of the huge multinational trade. A local story connects the dots:

A well-established Lisu opium-producing village with a population of 250 near Chiang Rai had 2 opium addicts, a few casual users, and 6 Chinese addicts in the period 1979 to 1989. By 1995, after poppy growing had been sharply curtailed and Thailand hailed as a US partner in drug suppression, close to 20 heroin addicts lived there. Thievery, a minor problem in the past, became common, and several people contracted AIDS through needle sharing. The Lisu handled the situation in a way that demonstrated both how removed the village is from the Thai legal system and the decisiveness of tribal justice. Over a period of less than a week, 4 of the addicts were murdered; the rest fled. The authorities were not notified, and they did not interfere. In its more than fifty-year history, no one remembered such a traumatic rent in the village's social fabric occurring, yet they accepted with resignation the brutality of the problem's resolution as a necessary evil.

The story of government/military/police involvement in the drug trade, interspersed with intermittent eradication activities, is a tedious tragedy involving greed and corruption. It continues today, and some Lisu, whose culture values agency, action, and risk taking over the passivity of victim-hood and addiction, have left their villages to join the perceived winners of the War on Drugs.

6

Identity and Cultural Flux

Lisu two, Lisu not have.
—*Lisu proverb*

Cha-tsu-mai, a wizened old soul permanently doubled over, nonetheless climbs quite nimbly down the bamboo ladder from her loft to chat with Otome Klein Hutheesing and me in an interview in northern Thailand. She is seventy-seven years old, born a Han of the Tong-ja clan in China.

At thirteen she walked from China through Burma to Thailand with her aunt with the intention of collecting and returning home the bones of that lady's husband, a fatal accident victim. Said bones were located near Chiang Rai—functioning well within the body of the still-living husband. He had recovered sufficiently from his accident to marry a Yao woman and settle with her and their baby son in a Lisu village.

"My aunt was very angry at first, but then her husband apologized and said, 'If you don't mind, we can all stay together here.' I quickly became a Lisu girl. The dogs would chase me when I wore my Chinese clothes, so I changed them, and soon I was speaking Lisu and worshipping Lisu spirits along with my own ancestors."

Within a few more years, she married a Lisu man from Mae Morn and moved there. When her own son was eight, he wanted to go to school, but the village didn't have one (in 1975). So she went to a neighbor, a Christian Lisu woman, whose son attended school in Chiang Rai.

"She said she couldn't help unless we become Christian," Cha-tsu-mai remembers. "I said, okay, let my son become Christian. But the woman said, 'O-o-oh-h-h no, it doesn't work like that, the whole family must change.' And so we did. And then we Christians moved to this village, Huay Khai, and now all but four here are Christian. It's an easier life. When you are sick, you just go to the doctor and pray a bit, you don't need to sacrifice chickens or pigs. And we don't worry about bad spirits bothering us."

Although Lisu ethnic and religious identity is distinct, it is not immutable. In addition, ethnic groups are not closed, as the above story illustrates. Tribal minority groups in China, Burma, and Thailand are not homogeneous, and because of proximity they borrow beliefs and practices from each other. Cha-tsu-mai appears to have maneuvered through three identities in her lifetime: Han Chinese, traditional Lisu, and Christian Lisu.

Living close to and among so many different groups over time and across a great geographical spread, Lisu people and culture adapt according to neighbors and circumstances. This is particularly true in Thailand, where one mountain is often home to three or four hill tribes. At the same time, Lisu culture is distinct.

To try to figure out how this can be directly tackles the question of what "Lisu-ness" consists of.

Language, as well as dress, customs, and cosmological and political organization, are "carriers" of culture. Lisu culture has so far weathered physical migration, inward and outward ethnic migration, and political upheaval in several countries, even as it changes.

Historically, migration, intermarriage, and change in identity for economic, political, and other reasons created a permeable boundary around Lisu culture and spiritual life. This is true of all migrating hill tribes of Southeast Asia. Yet there are patterns. The Lisu seldom intermarry with Karen, whom they don't esteem highly, or Hmong, whom they do. The most common non-Lisu unions with other highlanders are with Akha, Lahu (with whom they share Tibeto-Burman languages), and Haw Chinese. They also have married into the majority populations of China, Burma, and Thailand.

Over the last hundred years, large numbers have either converted to Christianity or added Buddhist practices and Chinese ancestor worship to a more basic animism practiced in the remote Upper Nujiang gorge. Marxist ideology has caught on with some. The depth of these changes is arguable. The Lisu's situation—a small and widely scattered group—is unusual. Their culture has interacted, adjusted, and survived in ways uniquely Lisu as they've looked out at the world from various niches over time, across thousands of miles.

Although small in number, Lisu are a dominant group, and outsiders—such as Cha-tsu-mai—who marry in are usually absorbed. The exception is when Lisu marry people from the majority population and move to the city. Lisu men often marry outside to women who don't carry as dear a bride price as Lisu girls, and these women usually develop Lisu identity within a few years because custom is to live patrilineally. In northern Thailand in the early 1970s Durrenberger found more young married couples, however, living in or near the bride's mother's village in a social formation he calls "sister clusters." There are also many Lahu men and women who wear Lisu clothes, speak the Lisu language, and claim Lisu identity—who nonetheless worship Lahu ancestor spirits.

Particularly in China, people have integrated into Lisu groups during different periods for various reasons, including many from other minority groups (such as the Chin Haw and Yi) as well as the majority Han Chinese. My visit with Klein Hutheesing to the Lisu village of Tsur Khur, in Nujiang Lisu Autonomous Prefecture in Yunnan Province, illustrates this.

The village has a smorgasbord feel—housing styles include mud brick, wood panels, bamboo, timber slabs, and even log cabins. The people's names, especially nicknames, were unusual: Taco, Chutee, Mee Mee. We met a family whose members had become nominal Christians in the past three years. "We're Christian, but we don't do anything about it," was how they characterized their religious practice. (Note: "doing" is more important than "believing" in the Lisu worldview.)

They live in a Lisu village, speak Lisu, consider themselves Lisu, and take part in traditional customs such as feeding the first rice of the year to a dog. About a half hour into the conversation, however, I learned that both husband and wife were Han Chinese who had moved to Tsur Khur because of the fertility of the land. Over the years, incrementally, they "became" Lisu.

This wouldn't be different from a couple from Moscow moving to Afghanistan and gradually becoming absorbed—if the Lisu were not such a tiny minority. The facts that Yunnan is historically more a part of Southeast Asia than of China and that the pressure of being Chinese has often proved great offer some explanations.

A key, then, is that Lisu society, although small, is *open* to new members. Lisu society, with its flat social structure and emphasis on independence, is easier to join than more hierarchical communities, even or especially in small areas where they dominate.

In the spiritual realm, fluidity and pragmatism are also the norm. From the Lisu Christian's point of view, the fact that he is no longer an animist hasn't altered his cultural identity. He considers himself to be as Lisu as any and resents any implication to the contrary. Hindus, Christians, and Muslims share the Indian identity, Christians and Jews the American outlook, so why wouldn't the Lisu culture, spread out as it is, also have religious differentiation?

This becomes obvious in Myanmar, where the majority of Lisu have converted to Christianity and organized in unprecedented ways that some might judge "un-Lisu." Self-preservation under difficult circumstances appears a strong motivating force. The first concrete example I encountered in the 1990s was in Mogok, an urbanized ruby mining area 200 kilometers north of Mandalay. There, missionary Bobby Morse introduced me to David (Ngwa-za) Fish, a third-generation Lisu Christian who had collected traditional Lisu proverbs and songs over the previous thirty years. He shared these with me, and the pithy Lisu sayings he collected head most chapters of this book. Fish is the chairman of a local preservation committee in the Mogok area that includes Christian, Buddhist, and animistic Lisu. His English was excellent; for once I didn't need a translator: "Christians, because we have a written Lisu language, can record traditional things, like songs and sayings in danger of being lost. This is especially important in areas like Mogok where Lisu are often ruby miners instead of farmers, and we've been caught between military factions and had a lot of political and economic pressure to integrate into Burman society," he told me. By 2014, Christian Lisu in Myanmar as stewards of traditional culture had become entrenched. The Lisu "Cultural Unity Movement," led by Christians, is well-organized every place they live there.

Most of Thailand's and many of Myanmar's (non-Christian) Lisu honor the Buddha with a small image near the family spirit shrine. Whether this is

David Ngwa-za Fish, right, a third-generation Christian in Mogok, was an early leader in the Lisu Cultural Unity Movement in Burma. Pictured here in 1997, as of 2017 he has been collecting Lisu songs and proverbs for almost forty years. He provided me with the Lisu sayings that begin most chapters of this book. Author photo.

out of politeness to their hosts or because they resonate with the animistic style of Theravada Buddhism practiced in these countries isn't clear.

"Oh, our own spirits are the main ones," or "the Thai policeman (or other official) gave me the Buddha statue," or even "the spirits are all related" are typical Lisu responses to my questions about the commingling of Buddhism with traditional religion in Thailand and Burma. Some have become Buddhists, but it is difficult to accurately gauge what percentage or the "purity" of traditions practiced.

Along migration paths, the Lisu absorbed beliefs and practices of many with whom they've shared mountaintops and markets. The most northern group in the Upper Nujiang gorge did not worship ancestors sixty years ago; only more recently have some adopted the practice. In China today ambitious people, including Lisu, aspire to join the Communist Party—membership in which requires repudiating God and religion. In 2014, I encountered members of a rising Lisu political class who were agnostic or atheist. Because in the Lisu worldview what you *do* is more important than what you *believe*,

Urbanized Lisu living in Mogok, Myanmar, participate in the gem industry. Here, many Lisu trade gems (particularly rubies) at an informal market by a Buddhist temple in the 1990s. Author photo.

such fluidity does not require as big a leap as it does in more belief-based cultures. The irony is that Lisu have become Christians, for which the term *faith-based* was coined. I did meet Christians and animists who closeted themselves, returning to church or tabiya only after they had retired from government service, pensions safe in hand. Many borrowings are strictly local and idiosyncratic: a Lisu shrine in the Dansha area of Yunnan had a Tibetan Buddhist dorje in a place of honor; another included an ancient ax dug up when the farmer was clearing his field.

Lisu who stay in their own villages but become Christian retain and uphold *illi* Lisu (custom) more than those who don't consciously forsake religious tradition but live among majority lowlanders. While isolation slows down assimilation and preserves the traditional, the desire for benefits offered by modernization appears to be universal.

The quest for cultural or religious purity has been and always will be doomed. Change, integration, and reorganization affect the Lisu as they do all people. The variables are rate of change and specifics. The process is relentless, and Lisu are not exempt. When not looking at an "exotic" small group such as the Lisu, this doesn't seem tragic.

People reading this book left their tribal huts generations ago, and most don't feel the worse for it; uneasiness over the assimilation of remaining ethnic minorities could represent projected grief at our own loss of belonging to smaller, more intimate societies—mixed with a dollop of nostalgia about life in small communities that most of us have never experienced.

National and global integration, embodied by the rise of the Internet, are phenomena that everyone, including Lisu from tiny villages, are affected by just as they are subject to world market prices of opium or sugar. My anthropologist father-in-law Walter Goldschmidt lived with the Sebei on Mount Elgin in a remote corner of Uganda in the 1960s, where the economy was cattle- and barter-based and investment and debt meticulously kept track of in a shared memory network of oral tradition. He recalled that Sebei "records" could be extracted from the heads of twenty-year-olds, who told him that "no one had any money" thirty years before—in the period of the Great Depression.

We might like to imagine the sense of belonging and fitting into a traditional village, but how long would most of us last if confronted with its realities? Knowing that my great-grandfather defaulted on paying the first-born calf from a heifer your grandfather used as partial payment of bride price for my grandmother and that this debt has been passed down to me (now, with interest, I owe you six calves) makes modern debt service seem less baffling.

7

View from the Village

When you shout, it echoes down the valley;
When you pull one vine, the whole jungle shakes.
   —*Lisu proverb*

A TEMPORARY ENCAMPMENT

"Which village (*tya-gua*) are you from?" A straightforward question, but when asked the young Lisu girl in northern Thailand looks perplexed. Her confusion lifts when the query is refined: "Where is your house?"

Tya-gua is the Lisu word for stay, place, to dwell, or to live. In China, the words *tsai-tseu* connote the same and in Myanmar, *taun-gya*. For the Lisu, attachment to a particular place doesn't fit their reality or stir the same emotions it does in settled people. A village is but a temporary encampment; when a group migrates, they say "we close the mountain," not "we leave our village." As villages become more permanent, this is changing—however, the temporary feeling inside Lisu houses was still palpable in 2014 in all three countries. They simply don't "nest" in the way other people do.

Lisu villages offer a mixture of the appealing, the unappealing, and the haphazard. They are sited higher up the mountain than other communities and until quite recently were inaccessible by road. When one approaches a Thai or Burmese Lisu village along a hillside path, the first sign might be

Approaching a Lisu village, one often encounters a rest bench or shrine along the trail. These are built as part of healing or other ceremonies. Author photo.

woven bamboo trays full of old clothes, broken utensils, other bits and pieces. These are in various states of decay, remnants of ceremonies to chase away bad spirits and remove reminders of them from within village boundaries. A few benches along the path, some fresh and some old, or perhaps a rest house constructed of split logs, with bamboo walls and thatched roof, are evidence of ceremonies of a different kind—to call people's lost souls back into their unwell bodies.

The thatched village, pleasant to look at from afar, is not laid out in an orderly fashion. Houses are strung along a steep, erosion-gullied laterite hillside. Twisted paths running between houses turn into mud when it rains. Snarling dogs often ward off approaching strangers. Pig pens and piles of building materials and farming equipment take up space underneath and adjacent to the house.

A blacksmith's hut was formerly universal in most villages, but by the 1990s it was less so. Usually small and open, it contains a piston bellows, hearth, and anvil. A blacksmith is considered something of a magician and healer,

A blacksmith's hut was formerly universal in Lisu villages, and all men had blacksmithing skills. This image was taken in northern Thailand in the 1970s by anthropologist E. Paul Durrenberger.

but not every village has one. Older men can smith their own rakes, hoes, knives, and gun parts, though this skill is diminishing among the young.

No Lisu builds a house directly in front of or with its roof aligned with another—the roof alignment would make it too easy for spirits to hop from house to house, and having a structure in front would block the spirit path to the altar. Such beliefs are built into the physical village.

Lisu are fond of and use products from trees and plants, and many plant small kitchen gardens, flowers, and vines adjacent to or near their homes. Prosperous families are apt to live nearer the top of the village and poorer ones at the bottom. The headman's house is often around the "center," although this doesn't exist in a symmetrical sense. Lisu dualistic beliefs are embodied in everyday sayings, such as "top of the village, bottom of the village," which simply means everyone.

Their hamlets have charm. In the late afternoon, children playing, strutting cockerels, and colorfully clad women are likely first impressions. A group of older boys might gather by a rest house or bench, singing and joking. A hunter returns from the forest with his long barreled musket or crossbow slung over a shoulder. The overall beauty of Lisu and other mountain settlements is often lost in photographs. They look dustier and sparkle less than in reality. Photos flatten out their verticality, and it is difficult to catch the gestalt. Only when you are there, perhaps seated on someone's porch and looking out over surrounding mountains, can you fully appreciate the scene.

Day begins early. Crowing roosters, snuffling pigs, barking dogs, and infant cries punctuating the night pick up tempo as dawn approaches. The women are up before light, and the thunk, thunk, thunk of the rice pounder (today apt to be gasoline or electric powered) hulling the day's supply signals that dawn mustn't be far off. Rice pounders were traditionally human powered and often doubled as afternoon courting sites. Animals are fed, the fire rekindled, and cooking begins. The head of household binds his baby granddaughter to his back with a long wide cloth that makes a comfortable sling for her to look out over his shoulder at the mountains and sky coming to life in grades of pink and gold and green.

After a breakfast of rice and vegetables, workers of the household set out to their fields, often an hour or more walk. They carry packets of rice and chili sauce to eat later with field produce. At harvest time, many sleep in field huts for days at a time to maximize working hours and guard produce. Most of the year, in fact, the village is deserted of working-age people during the day, with only a few old people and young children about.

By late afternoon and early evening, people drift back. Food is prepared, and the family gathers for a smoky meal around the fire or perhaps in the porch area in the hot season. Daughters-in-law serve and eat last themselves. If there are guests, the men and women eat and socialize separately—but usually informality, chitchat, and doing tasks such as sewing or repairing tools take up the balance of the day. The family retires early, but the night's silence is not infrequently broken by the howls of dogs or a shaman calling his spirits.

———————————■-■———————————

The temporary feeling of Lisu villages, and the relative lack of attachment to place exhibited by people living in them, are reinforced by the absence of larger-scale art or permanent public infrastructure. Benches, rest houses, and bridges used in soul-calling ceremonies are pleasing to look at when

Lisu children play in a village on a steep slope in northern Thailand in the 1970s. Like most, it has the feeling of a temporary encampment, in the process of being built or torn down to move somewhere else. Photo: E. Paul Durrenberger.

fresh but are just as likely to be rotting away. No committee oversees civic affairs. There is nothing like the large carved village gates or giant swing of the Akhas or heavy carved ceremonial figures or fine paintings of the Mien in Lisu villages. Their material talents tend toward the portable and practical, such as clothes making, basketry, mat weaving, wood carving (mainly for weapons such as the sling bow and crossbow), and tool, musical instrument, and jewelry making. Artistic expressions are also portable—music, singing, dancing, and storytelling.

Villages are sited on mountains or hillsides with fertile soil: defensibility, availability of water and labor, and perceived freedom from evil influences are traditional requirements. Market opportunities and proximity to a school are newer measures of desirability. Lisu prefer well-forested areas because they depend on the forest for building materials, food, medicine, and herbs. "Their villages are always isolated on a very lofty ridge or on the sheltered side of a peak, and as often as not are hacked out of dense forest," Sir James George Scott wrote of Burmese Lisu settlements in 1932. Such areas are becoming hard to find, and as villages become more permanent, surrounding resources diminish.

In every country, however, when a new site looks like a strong possibility, a divining ceremony tests whether it is free from disease and other evil influences. In one, rice grains are placed in the shape of a star, with a blade of grass in the center, representing a tree. If this isn't disturbed overnight, the site is deemed safe.

In a story regarding the suitability of a potential Lisu village site in northern Thailand, an advance group of Lisu performed the above-mentioned ceremony in what appeared an ideal setting. However, the omen was not good; in the morning the star had been scattered. The place was so pretty, however, that the men decided to camp out another night and try again. They offered extra prayers and offerings to local territorial spirits, asking permission to live there. However, in the morning the star had again been disturbed, so the Lisu moved on. That day, however, they ran across a Lahu shaman, who claimed good connections with local spirits. When they told him about the site and their test results, he offered to go back with them and intervene. They did a new test, new prayers, and new offerings—and received a positive result. The Lahu shaman, having proved his influence, moved to the new Lisu village and promised to help protect the people. The village gained a new shaman, and the Lisu added a few Lahu spirits to their pantheon. E. Paul Durrenberger ran across another situation in which a Lahu shaman allowed behavior a Lisu nepa had warned against—in this case, he told them it would be okay to dig up a ruined old pagoda they came across to look for possible valuables in its foundation.

In Thailand, the ideal village setting is more than halfway up a ridge with a stream on the other side, at an altitude of between 4,000 and 5,000 feet (1,200–1,500 meters). Lisu prefer higher altitudes than Lahu or Akha with whom they often share mountains, and they settle in places other groups wouldn't consider prime. Some Lisu prefer not to overexpose themselves to water because the water spirit can be capricious or even malicious. An elaborate and rickety system of bamboo aqueducts around the mountain was sometimes devised to deliver water.

If they lack this concern, they just go down to the water source. One Thai Lisu told Durrenberger the only way not to offend spirits would be to stay in bed all day, and no doubt there was probably at least one spirit who wouldn't like that either! So he follows Lisu custom and performs requisite rituals as a sort of insurance, hoping he won't need it. Such skepticism is common, yet it doesn't seem to limit ritualizing. In general, Lisu choose a place that allows them political independence yet isn't too far from a market town where they can purchase provisions and sell cash crops. For security, they like proximity to another Lisu village and for access to cheap labor, a few nearby Lahu, Akha, or Karen villages.

In different parts of China, criteria differ. Around Tengchong, villages are sited in greater isolation from other groups, on lesser inclines, and at lower altitudes—often snuggling into foothills bordering small valleys at altitudes of 2,000 to 3,000 feet (600–900 meters). The valley floors are devoted to wet-rice cultivation and pastureland. There, Lisu like proximity to water; we visited several villages with streams running right through them or located on rivers. Around Liuku and further north in the Upper Salween Valley, however, Lisu live at great altitude; their villages frequently nest on incredibly steep mountainsides. A tip off the porch of one of these homes can mean a fall of several thousand feet.

In Burma, Lisu also traditionally sited villages at 5,000 feet (1,500 meters) or higher, according to early British military and geographical sources. According to Major C. M Enriquez of the British Indian Army, Burma Rifles, who reported on Lisu who had migrated to Burma from China: "They live for a generation or so in some high, cold and barren spot, until they have cut down all the jungle available for *taun-gya*, and then begin to cast about for new forests to devastate. Those who move very far south into warm climates are noticeably inferior to those who live on mountaintops." More recently, Lisu have moved into lowland areas as malaria has been eradicated. The Putao Valley and the area around Myitkyina are two such places.

There are two Lisu house types: one is built directly on flat ground, often cut into the hillside, with a dirt floor and woven bamboo panel walls and thatched roofs. This is called *micha-he* and is the main style found in Thailand. Often, it can be broken down and moved. In Burma, traditional Lisu more often live in this kind of house, while Christians, who immigrated south from China's Upper Salween area, favor elevated houses on posts with split bamboo floors, called *ketche-he*. These houses also have thatched roofs. In other areas, such as Tengchong, the micha-he has wood plank walls instead of bamboo panels and often a tiled roof and feels more permanent.

Materials from the forest are used to make both house forms: woven bamboo or wood walls, split bamboo floors (for the ketche-he), wood frames and stilt posts, and grass thatch roofs. Earthen-floored houses are warmer and sturdier at high windy altitudes, stilted ones easier to clean. Lisu women are tidy but not fussy housekeepers; they do a major clean just once a year. "Too much cleaning makes the spirits angry," one woman in northern Thailand explained to Klein Hutheesing. Those with stilt houses keep their animals penned downstairs; pigs and chickens quickly consume edible refuse swept through cracks in the bamboo floor, and anything spilled doesn't require much cleanup.

Lisu build dualistic ideas regarding male and female, north and south, east and west, heaven and earth into their houses. The back wall of the Lisu house is against the upslope (north, nobility or heaven orientation) of the hill with the family *tabiya* (altar) at its center, facing the entrance and the downslope (south, people), where the pigs also live. The shelf for the oldest ancestors is on the left (signifying male and bigger), and one on the right (female and smaller) is for the parents and grandparents of the head of household. Directly in front of the altar is a male area, where women don't sit or work.

Houses are built as large as needed for the people living in them at time of construction; a room or a wing is added if the family grows. Basic space division seldom varies. The main bedroom is next to the altar, to the left or east (male) side as one faces the door. Sleeping platforms for unmarried males are to the left of the main bedroom and for unmarried females to the right or west (female) side.

A matrilineal pillar, called the mother post, is also on the right side. This is where the senior woman of the house communicates with ancestors during the maize festival. Because the Lisu woman joins her husband's clan at marriage and women aren't as involved with ceremonializing as men, the area around this post is usually her place to work. She sits and mends here, lounges with friends, or ties the innumerable decorative "tails" to the post as she stitches them for a daughter's New Year's outfit. The water jar and fire are also on the right-hand side of the house, where cooking is done. This is the area in which the Lisu woman performs her most important labor: giving birth. Near delivery time, a special cot is constructed, built almost at ground level so that after the birth the woman can benefit from the "mother-roasting" fire that is kept burning for seven days.

*Lisu houses in Thailand always include a matrilineal
pillar where the senior woman of the house communicates
with ancestors and works. Author photo.*

If a son-in-law lives with the family, he often builds a separate sleeping hut
for himself and his wife behind the house, to the right. In this case, although
he is a man, he takes the "smaller" side since his lineage spirits are not the
main ones worshiped in the household.

When building houses, men do the work involving wood and bamboo and
tasks that require climbing. Women gather bundles of grass used for thatch
and throw them up to the men attaching the roof. Since a woman's genitals
(even her trousers) should not be above a man's head, women avoid doing
work in which there is a likelihood of this occurring.

With one door and usually no windows, Lisu homes are dark and smoky.
Ground-built ones have a high threshold at the single door and a hard-packed
mud floor that keeps the home cool in hot weather. Such a floor is prone to
dampness and chill in cold, wet weather, and families often huddle around
the fire on mats. Some houses, especially raised ones in Burma / Myanmar,

Typical raised bamboo house found in Myanmar and sometimes also Thailand. This Thai Lisu house can be broken down and moved. Photo: E. Paul Durrenberger.

have two fireplaces. Smoke drifts up and out open eaves, fumigating bundles of dried corn stored above on its way out.

An empty feel pervades Lisu homes, with few cozy touches such as pictures on the walls or other decoration. Often, tools or supplies such as rope, piping, or fertilizer, related to agriculture, are piled up in the east (male) corner. Tiny stools, a light woven table that is taken away when not in use, and beds comprise the furniture. Sleeping platforms or beds are low and multipurpose; often, bedding is rolled up during the day. Space within the house needs no markers because it is already divided up in every Lisu head according to ceremonial needs and where each sex does his or her activities.

I noticed this bareness in all three countries. A Burmese man explained to me, "The Lisu are not attached to things like we are." This appears true even when they become rich. The home of Joseph, a Christian ruby miner I visited in Mogok in 1997, was free of art on walls or curtains on windows, though he was said to be the richest Lisu in the world. His house was large and modern, built of teak, marble, and other stone. I thought of Joseph when I visited a new Lisu amber millionaire in Myitkyina's urban/rural outskirts in 2014. Shoehorned among modern houses, tiny farms, and traditional Lisu bamboo houses, his house was built in lavish Chinese style. Additional new floors with exterior walkways and shiny stainless-steel balustrades were being added to the original construction in a seemingly offhand manner. Workers at noisy machines created clouds of dust as they cut and polished amber in a workshop next to his front door. In addition to scant furniture and a huge flat-screen television, big plastic bags full of more amber and twenty-four-packs of sodas lined the walls. Comparatively rich Lisu homes in China are also bare, although a few Chinese decorative touches, such as designs on interior woodwork or, more often, murals with Lisu-inspired motifs, are now painted on outside walls. Old popular prints of Mao, now thirty or forty years old, adorn some homes.

The immediate vicinity of the house is also where work and visiting take place. This is often on a low split bamboo-floored platform also used to dry rice. Nearby pens of woven bamboo fencing, south of the house, keep pigs, cattle, and horses contained. Until recently, pigs still freely foraged during the day, coming home only to eat and sleep. Animals frequently became sources of contention when they damaged neighbors' fields or gardens.

Every house has a stilted granary close by, and many clans, including those whose family spirits don't like particular cooking smells, have a separate cooking hut. The spirits of the Secho clan don't like garlic, and clans that worship the candle spirit avoid both garlic and onions. Shamans also generally dislike the wafting smell of these two ingredients, which are, however, loved by most Lisu.

In villages in China, Lisu often abide where their parents and grandparents lived and died. They look more permanent, particularly in the Tengchong area near the Burmese border in southwestern China. Wood, stone, and tile building materials in such communities bespeak affluence, permanence, and Chinese influence. Houses have earthen floors, as in Thailand, but are often built as timbered, two-story affairs. A perplexing lack of stairways to the top floors—a ladder is put up when needed even here, where they are well settled—is a vestigial remnant of the temporary quality of Lisu homes elsewhere. Many also have a large second building, with a top story used as a granary or open storage area to keep gigantic winnowing baskets and other farming equipment. In addition, large corn drying racks usually grace the area in front of every Lisu house in China.

In the Dansha area in the 1990s, many Lisu were prosperous, living in wood houses that included Chinese elements such as courtyards and tile roofs. Villages were close to fertile fields and often sited as low as 2,000 feet (600 meters) above sea level. Author photo.

In the Dansha area of Tengchong, houses are larger and finer than Lisu houses I visited anywhere else. Here, connecting wood walls between rooms create private courtyards and a more Chinese aesthetic. The timber trade in this area has made many Lisu relatively rich, and the valley soil is fertile. Thick twig fences or stone walls line village pathways, creating a different and sturdier feel of public infrastructure than the low, disintegrating bamboo boundaries found in Thai and Burmese villages or to the east in the Nu valley. But here, as in all Lisu villages, the unit is the household, and "community spirit" as we think of it in the West is unknown.

SOCIAL ORGANIZATION AND SYMBOLIC SIGNIFICANCE

Durrenberger suggests that self-protection is the main reason the Lisu gather in villages—the instinctive reaction to a history punctuated with raids by bandits, tribal enemies, and government authorities. This could be true, but Lisu villages are not stockaded. There are few reports of walled settlements in Burma and China in the past.

Earth-floor homes are dark and smoky, with one door and no windows. The hard-packed mud floor is cool in hot weather but prone to dampness and chill when it is cold. Author photo.

Leadership is difficult to maintain among the independent-minded Lisu, and village headmen come and go. There are many stories of headmen who were killed or against whom even their own kin turned. The Lisu generally despise authoritarian behavior and will not tolerate it. Leadership must be earned—not demanded, imposed, or passed on from father to son. In Myanmar, the Lisu word for headman translates as hunter/trapper; in Thailand, thick-skinned man. (The Thai word commonly used translates as village big man and in China, simply big man.) The terms might refer to qualities required of leaders in varied circumstances.

Headmen in Thailand, called *pu-yai ban* (Thai language), are considered foreign ministers to Thai officialdom and not necessarily Lisu leaders because they are usually on the payroll of the Thai government. In parts of Burma their role is stronger, as they have come under the influence of more hierarchical Shans and Kachins, as well as Christian leadership. In China, an informal group of elders might be more influential in one village, a headman in another, or a party official in still another.

One or two clans normally dominate a village, but it is not simply divided along clan lines. It is more accurate to describe the village as a collection of households organized into affiliation groups of three to seven families. These generally consist of other kin but not necessarily clansmen, as sometimes a group of married sisters will form the core living matrilineally. As previously noted, Durrenberger called the phenomenon "sister clusters," observing that often more than one clan was involved. Sometimes, the group includes members with ties other than kinship. These households cooperate economically and socially and often migrate together. They do not compromise Lisu independence, however, as individual households can and do change affiliation to another group or move away without the others.

Affiliation groups are the sub-units making up a village and have as much to do with affinity as obligation—they are a hallmark of Lisu social structure. Among most Lisu, it is to this group of family and friends, rather than to clan, that allegiance is felt. In this regard, the Lisu are notably less clannish and inward-looking than groups such as the Hmong or Akha. Belonging to a successful group is more important than clan membership, since no clan is considered better than another.

Ceremonializing, working in fields (each family cultivates different fields, but within affiliation groups labor is traded), collecting food and herbs from the forest, visiting back and forth, and the easy laughter, banter, and singing Lisu are known for usually take place within these smaller groups. This is not to say the village is unfriendly or that socializing outside of the affiliation group doesn't take place. An outside visitor of many days could easily fail to notice this social patterning, which is, however, distinct and observable once you know the governing rules. The other key to Lisu social structure is the strict set of guidelines restricting with whom men and women may speak freely or nurture intimacy in any way (see Chapter 9, Book I, chart on sexual talk). Combined with affiliation groups, this ordering of relationships forms the core of Lisu socializing.

Every individual in a Lisu settlement, however, fits into some kind of kinship category. Thus everyone is a son, daughter, sister, brother, cousin, father or mother, grandfather or grandmother—and is addressed as such. Within this system there is shading and a more fine-grained kinship distinction than in Western societies.

Clan and personal rivalries are a reality; Lisu are competitive. This leads to behavior akin to "keeping up with the Joneses," which isn't as concerned with harmony as with excelling. Striving has led to a number of Lisu growing quite rich. But volatile inter-family disputes and village factionalism have also been known to end in migration or even killing, including patricide and fratricide. "Warlike" and "wild" were words often used by early ethnographers to describe the Lisu, particularly those coming from the Upper Nu Valley.

There are few village-wide events. In Thailand and parts of Myanmar, several men visit Apa-mo's (village guardian's) house every fifteen days. Intervals between visits may vary (in 2014 Apa-mo's house was visited monthly in Dton Loong, Thailand), and the fortnightly pattern could be borrowed from Shan Buddhists in those countries who visit the temple on full and dark moon days. Rules of conduct and the quest for myi-do (repute) keep relationships and activities in check and on task and are more important than "church attendance." Making a living and attending to household chores take up most people's time, and Lisu pride themselves on industry. If a woman marries within her own village, for example, she should not visit her parents' home *too* often as it would not be fair to her husband's family, who has compensated her father for her labor by paying a bride price. Her pride is at stake, and too many visits will cause gossip.

Lack of community events does not, however, stifle village communication. As the Lisu proverb states, "News of flowers is carried by the wind, but gossip is carried only by men." Privacy is unknown among the Lisu. Unlike societies where one goes into a room and closes the door before imparting a secret, Lisu are more apt to venture deep into the forest or to a wide-open field to share a confidence. The reason becomes apparent during marriage negotiations, when the "village telegraph" picks up the most sensitive signals. Scraps of intelligence regarding price and questions such as "how much are they asking" or "has he come down yet" pass from household to household; it's not unusual for neighbors unrelated to the drama to accurately predict the final deal because an established market exists.

The New Year's celebration is one of the few true "public holidays" in the village, when for a few days everybody drinks, dances, and follows the Lisu banjo and gourd-flute music from house to house. Any Lisu and any outsider,

Men visit Apa-mo's house, here at the New Year in northern Thailand. Author photo.

for that matter, may join in. Social barriers come down and village boundaries expand. This is the special time for gaining repute, expressing Lisuness, and nurturing age-old customs. The holiday functions as a marriage market.

No organizing committee orchestrates events, however, and there is no central stage. The celebration moves about the village, created by every Lisu for every Lisu. The holiday has an ephemeral nature, with song and dance evoking a sense of place that doesn't normally exist, a ritual place where Lisu custom is affirmed and renewed.

━━━━━■-■━━━━━

A young Lisu mother sings as she washes clothes by a thin stream of water pouring from a split bamboo aqueduct. Her washing spot is shared with four other households in the village of thirty low thatched homes on the side of a mountain.

> My older sister, my younger sister one place,
> Father, his younger brother one place.
> In my father's home there is no trouble,
> There is no custom to stay in father's place.
> I separated from my siblings,
> My sadness is endless.

The New Year celebration is the closest thing to a public holiday in Lisu villages. Music, dancing, and following the pipes contribute to bringing down social barriers and to creating a marriage market. Author photo.

There might be a ritual element to the woman's sadness; fetching a good bride price, marriage, and moving away to have a family are significant events in every female Lisu's life. These are the means by which she gains repute, and every Lisu woman looks forward to having children. However, as in many cultures, when daughters-in-law move into their husband's families, the transition can be rocky.

On the red earthen path that leads away from the village, perhaps on a different day or a different year, two Lisu men indulge in a parting song as they close the mountain and move on.

> Your father has no country
> You will be missed in your birthplace
> The elders are told a child has gone,
> Gone to the other world.

In these songs and others, the village is more a poetic reference or constructed idea—a place one has left or is about to leave—rather than *this* actual village in the present moment. Klein Hutheesing collected the above

songs and argues that in Thailand the idea of "village" symbolically represents world or country where blood relatives dwell. In song, the village is
sentimentalized as the lost, longed-for homeland. The woman's songs tend
to be sadder than the man's because she is more likely to be separated from
her family and birthplace.

The Lisu man might have to complete some years of bride service in his
wife's village as part of the bride price negotiation, but generally he returns
to his father's village with his wife and children when the obligation (often
a few years or less) has been fulfilled. If he is the eldest son, he generally
lives in his father's house. Even if the husband is poor and had to promise to
stay with the wife's clan group until his father-in-law dies, he may eventually
re-join his blood relatives if he desires. Sons-in-law often feel uncomfortable
in their fathers-in-law's homes because they cannot worship their own ancestor spirits there. That is why when living matrilocally is a long-term proposi-
tion, the younger couple will normally sleep in a separate hut or build their
own house.

DISPUTE SOLVING

Robert Morse described the scene: eighth son, a man in his thirties, sings
out his grievance in a heat of versification. Beseeching the council of three
old men directly on some points, on others he plays to the rag-tag jury of
neighbors gathered to see how this dispute, the talk of the village for weeks,
would be settled:

> My sweat has fallen as I weeded, as I hoed
> Till shadows grew long, I walked tired on the path
> The grass is slippery and burns my feet.

He holds a small bundle of sticks, each roughly six inches long, and one at
a time lays them on the ground with a flourish as he completes each major
point of his argument. His archaic style of poetry is the language of Lisu
dispute solving, learned from watching countless cases argued.

Eighth Born said the opium field was given to him (to plant the following season) by a departing neighbor in exchange for help with moving him
to a new village. After he had cleared and planted it, however, another
villager, Nu-sa, claimed the field because its last user was his son-in-law. By

now the local land spirit and bad-talk spirit must be offended, and everyone would suffer.

When it is Nu-sa's turn, his case is also conducted in a sing-song dirge: How could he know Eighth Born had cleared the field? It is around the other side of the mountain. He did it quickly just to take advantage of the situation. He lays one stick on the ground in a ponderous style to convey the weight of his argument.

Unlike Eighth Born, a lazy man who smokes opium, Nu-sa has been very busy in his fields. Down goes another stick. Son-in-law moved and took his daughter away; the use of the field should rightly be his because the bride price was quite low. Besides, bride service was not performed diligently, although everyone knows his daughter gathers lots of vegetables and is full of repute.

By the time his argument is finished, all of the sticks lay on the ground.

Back and forth, the elders and villagers listen attentively. General nodding occurs at indisputable points; twitters greet other, less–universally acknowledged ones.

In a social setting such as a Lisu village, full of strong-willed egalitarians—without much central authority—how do people resolve disagreements? Lisu in different environments have tried a number of approaches that generally rely on negotiation and consensus building. The ad hoc "trial" scene described by Morse took place in a village in Yunnan in the 1940s.

Morse didn't recall details of the judgment, a compromise over land use one party thought unfair that precipitated a small-group migration to a village further up the valley.

The traditional Lisu way of justice is probably as fair a system as can be found. The elders confer, and the dispute is usually settled on the spot. Villagers act as a check by bearing public witness to both sides' stories. The elders help negotiate a settlement, which is paid in liquor, rice, livestock, or labor. The loser might also have to feast the village. This last element discourages frivolous suits. Particularly tough cases sometimes take a day or more to settle, Morse recalls.

No system is perfect. Clan or clique allegiance as well as prejudice (such as against opium smoking) can get in the way of justice. This is one reason why most Lisu villages are dominated by only one or two lineages. The council of elders, never a formal body among the Lisu, is apt to consist of one or two clan elders representing the two disputing parties and the village headman, who get together only when a dispute won't go away. The typical successful Lisu headman avoids getting dragged into quarrels in any official capacity— he doesn't want to suffer the consequences of unpopular decisions.

The headman of Dton Loong, a long-established village with eighty-two Lisu and twenty-two Akha households, in Pa Mai Daeng District an hour's drive north of Chiang Mai in northern Thailand is a good example. A smiling goat clan member in his mid-forties, Alay Pa waves aside my apologies for disturbing him one rainy season afternoon in 1997.

"I'm used to it, you are the fifth today." Most visitors seek assistance in bureaucratic matters: obtaining a signature for a child's school enrollment, conferring over an unusually high utility bill, asking for a certificate of residence in the village. This latter item is one of dozens of pieces of paper required by the Thai government from minority people seeking citizenship. A harder one to secure is a birth certificate because most Lisu women do not give birth in hospitals. The headman receives a small or large gift (such as whisky, cash) for each favor, depending on degree of difficulty. He is chosen because he speaks Thai well and is perceived to have diplomatic and problem-solving skills. His role is like that of a minister to Thai officialdom, a small but necessary cog in district and county bureaucracy.

When I asked if his loyalty to his village or to his allegiance group is greater, Alay Pa doesn't agonize: his group, all goats, is more important.

How can he pretend to be fair, then, in helping settle disputes between members and non-members of the goat clan?

> This is a small village, and before a dispute comes to my front door I've heard all about it. If my lineage member is in the wrong, I try to get another older kinsman who is close to him to talk him out of making a complaint or else influence him to apologize and bring the wronged man a bottle of whisky. I get the middleman to let the fellow understand I know he's guilty. For the sake of the group he shouldn't come to me with the problem because I'll have to say it out loud, and that will make both of us look bad. If the other guy is in the wrong, I do the same for him, with one of his senior lineage members.
>
> But we usually get along, and I don't spend much time on these kinds of matters. We must all agree before we go ahead with something big for the village, like electricity or a school, and this is my main job: getting people to agree.

The headman of Dton Loong, Alay Pa, is a member of the goat clan who acts as a go-between for Lisu and the Thai government; 1997 Author photo.

Alay Pa seems to be a natural consensus builder. Several people meander in or peak their heads through the open window of his concrete house during our interview—each receives a nod and a smile.

In the case of disputes, he consults with clan and village elders only in "serious" matters. Divorces don't fall into this category, and he grants them readily because "the arguing couple will just go to the District Office and get one there if I try to talk them out of it." The feeling that the Lisu are usually the losers, guilty or innocent, if Thai authorities are consulted motivates them to solve their own problems or submit to small fines for minor offenses, such as letting one's pigs run loose. The headman levies these, but as punishable offenses have already been determined, he is only the administrator.

Quarrels increasingly arise over land use in Thailand. Land is becoming scarce and less fertile, as villages such as Dton Loong, Doi Laan, and Doi Chang become permanent. The Lisu belief that argued-over land brings nobody any good because the resident spirit will be offended and bring bad luck to everyone motivates people to solve disputes. However, that belief developed in the days when land was freely available, and it doesn't work as well now that the pressure valve of frequent migration has been removed.

Arguments over runaway brides or brides who return home before the marriage is consummated still occur. Alay Pa says they are becoming less frequent as the time between "engagement," when the bride wealth is negotiated, and marriage, when ideally it is paid off in full, is now often six months or less. In the past, marriages were arranged by parents years before the children grew up, and the boy's family would pay the bride price in small installments over a long period. A girl who refused to go through with the match at the appointed time was sure to stir gossip that she had been seduced in the meantime. Disputes still occur over marriage payments and problems over returning the bride price.

Durrenberger observed that among Lisu everything is negotiable, even kinship terms. Most offenses are mundane: my pigs damaged your field, your wife took calabashes from my garden without asking, your dog bit my child. Even sexual offenses such as extramarital affairs are argued and settled, and damages are calculated in pigs, opium, or cash. If one person recognizes that he is wrong, he can admit guilt by bringing a bottle of liquor to the injured person and begin discussions with "what do you want to do about this?" Or a third party may serve as a go-between in negotiating a settlement. Once an agreement is struck, both parties have entered a contractual agreement, and each expects the other to uphold the terms. Prestige and honor demand it. When there is no settlement, however, there are no expectations. This system is different from Thai and Burmese social interactions in which there are many expectations, but generally they remain understood rather than stated, tacit rather than explicit.

Individuals settle most disagreements without recourse to headmen or councils or elders. The Lisu social order is based on independence; for it to function, people must be accountable and honorable and they must abide by negotiated decisions. Disputes that aren't settled invariably fester: they lead to feuds and were perhaps the most common triggers of migration in the past. Since whether to stay or move on was a constant theme of Lisu village life, it is often the unresolved dispute that lends final weight to the "move on" side of the argument. The alternative to settlement or migration is an appeal to lowland authorities. This is considered more dangerous even than migration or a festering feud: police don't understand Lisu custom, always ask for bribes, or even jail both parties.

PART 2

Being a Lisu

8

Childhood

When an infant says Ba-ba first, Father will be tired; when it
pronounces the word Ma-ma first, Mother will be tired.
  —*Lisu proverb*

Lisu child rearing, particularly infant care, isn't complicated: when a baby
cries, pick it up. If it's hungry, feed it. If not, carry it around and comfort it
until it stops crying. The traditional Lisu saying above indicates that males
and females are equally qualified for this task; in fact, anyone older than three
or four will do.

Children are highly prized, and singing to, rocking, and amusing infants
is second nature to Lisu—grandfathers and mothers, brothers and sisters are
almost as likely as mothers to hoist the baby onto their backs in a cloth sling
and carry it around as they go about household and village business. This
practice continues until the child graduates to being one of the carriers itself,
at four or five, of a new baby sibling. Cleaning the baby after it has defe-
cated, however, is women's lot. "You can't trust a man to do this job well,"
commented a Lisu woman in northern Burma. Another in China concurred,
"Men are no good at it."

When a Lisu infant in a village in northern Thailand sucked its thumb,
anthropologist Klein Hutheesing reported its mother wasn't bothered.

Little girl with baby strapped on her back, early 1970s in northern Thailand. Photo: E. Paul Durrenberger.

"Wu-sa (Lisu sky god) has put honey on it. She will stop when she's older," the mother stated with confidence.

Mothers breastfeed infants for about two years, and girl children sometimes sleep with their parents until puberty. When babies first move on to solid food, rice—pre-chewed at first with some vegetable or banana—is given to them. They are fussed and clucked over and encouraged to eat so as to grow "big as a pumpkin" (or a gourd), much as infants are everywhere.

Having children is a universal life goal of Lisu men and women. In China, where strict family planning limits even rural couples to two children, in the 1990s most Lisu I interviewed reported that they had three, four, or five offspring. Mao made an exception in the case of minorities, especially those living in frontier areas, and remains popular with them because of it. The Lisu in all three countries often state the number of children born into the family, directly followed by the number who died. In Myanmar this was painful—it was common for a couple to have had twelve children and five, six, or seven deaths. Only once in the 1990s did a Lisu man report "no deaths" after mentioning the number of his children to me.

Klein Hutheesing reports that women in her study village, Doi Laan, pitied her because she has no children and encouraged her to have a baby when she was younger. Her concern, "but what about a father, mustn't I find a good father for the child first?" was flicked aside. "Lisu, *eka-lai* (foreigner), Thai, it doesn't matter, anyone will do," she was told.

She also notes that adults seldom play with children: an insect might be pointed out to distract a baby's attention or a stone put in an empty can to make a rattle for a toddler. Childhood games are learned from the backs of older brothers or sisters. Learning by doing is the Lisu way. Children follow the flute-like instrument with a gourd at one end or the Lisu banjo, they watch, and they finally join in at New Year's dances—there are a lot of different dances, but no one teaches the girl or boy her or his special parts.

Durrenberger comments that growing up Lisu involves graduating from one kid gang to the next—with small, medium, and large the approximate classifications. Wild bands of boys (the groups become sex segregated at around seven or eight) are encountered careening down rocky lanes in Lisu villages following a runaway bicycle wheel rim or motivating it over the crest of a hill with their sticks. I saw the same homemade toy, a small wheel attached to the end of a stick, in villages in Thailand, China, and Burma.

To the Lisu way of thinking, after everyone cuddles and carries a baby for its first few years, it becomes the father's duty to "raise" the child. Traditionally, this doesn't involve much work; the main job is to teach Lisu custom, *illi* Lisu. Values stressed are "work hard," "take care of your repute," and "know about shame." Beyond that, boys are let to run free while girls are watched over

Lisu women find babysitting boring and prefer fieldwork, even in Thailand's steep terrain, according to Otome Klein Hutheesing. Photo: E. Paul Durrenberger.

more closely. In addition to being industrious, the Lisu girl must be modest and build up her repute by carefully observing society's restrictions on her behavior (see Chapter 9, Book I). Training starts at age seven or eight and intensifies at puberty.

Since a key way wealth is distributed and redistributed among Lisu is through bride price, everything possible is done to ensure that the little girl doesn't become a wayward young woman. Visiting too often, singing with the wrong partner, or engaging in any other behavior deemed "loose" decreases her suitability and thus her price.

Great pride is felt by a girl and her family when she fetches higher-than-usual bride wealth. Indeed, a man cannot ultimately be judged a successful father until well into middle age—and only if all of his daughters have brought good prices and settled into marriage and not one has run away from her husband. Running away is not uncommon, however; girls share equally the Lisu independent spirit. Bride wealth (or at least a portion, depending on how long she tolerated the marriage) must then be returned. Typically, this causes problems because the money has long been spent.

From the age of five or six, children are expected to help out. Bringing water in long bamboo containers and washing clothes are their special chores. They go to the fields with both parents from infancy and learn by watching and doing. This is changing as Lisu children go to school and there is greater integration into the lowland economy. Babysitting, according to Klein Hutheesing, is a relatively novel occupation for Lisu women, who find it boring and prefer to work shoulder to shoulder with their men in the fields.

In Burma, Helen Morse (Eugene's wife and Bobby's aunt) remembers that Lisu always had children plant beans, squash, and cucumbers because tender young hands help these crops grow sweeter produce.

GIRLS: TO WORK EARLIER AND PLAY CLOSER TO HOME

The Lisu don't dwell on childhood memories and consistently fail to recall in detail how they experienced their own growing-up process. As a result, there is little to nothing to be found on this topic in ethnographic literature.

Margaret Morse, daughter of American Christian missionaries Eugene and Helen, was born in a Lisu village in Putao in the far north of Burma and moved with her family at age eight, in 1965, to settle an uninhabited, undemarcated area along the border with India called Mue-pa, or Hidden Valley. She learned English as a second language at four or five and lived as every other child in the community. Her recollections are probably the closest we can get to what life was like for a young Lisu girl before roads, electricity, and other modernities began changing their way of life.

She told me of her earliest memories: waking to the smell of wood smoke and watching and listening to the birds as they flitted in and out of the house. She could see through the slats to the grass roof where birds and sometimes snakes nested.

Gathering fallen fruit on frosty mornings from the *jed-sdee* (chinquapin) tree was one of her first tasks. "It wasn't a job, more like a contest among the children because the one who got up earliest was able to gather the most fruit that had dropped the night before," she remembers.

By the time she was eight, rain or shine, she would carry water from the ravine. Using a basket slung over her forehead she filled two or three bamboo tubes, about a meter in length and 8 centimeters in diameter, with water. "They were very heavy. We didn't have shoes, only rubber slippers for Sunday, and in winter it would be very, very cold, 40–45 degrees, and slippery. My feet would go numb and would hurt so much when I thawed them by the fire. But Lisu children don't complain, so I couldn't either. I didn't want to be called a sissy."

Margaret walked about a half hour to school by the side of the river with her sisters and Lisu friends. Again, this was a rain or shine activity. She, like other Lisu children, would take rice wrapped in a banana leaf to school for lunch, or when food was scarce, she would go without. After school she and friends would each take a large basket and machete and forage in the jungle. They collected certain plants, including *yeh-zhe-mo*, a kind of weed that pigs and sometimes people eat. In the rainy season, they also collected fragrant mushrooms. Catching termites occupied children's attention as well: "Depending on how hungry we were, we would eat them alive or take them back home. They didn't taste bad raw, and we needed the protein. But they were much better toasted by the fire, with the wings singed off."

Back home, she'd make one or two more trips to fetch water or else collect firewood. Homework (not a problem most Lisu children had to deal with in the 1960s) was to be done before dark, when only light from the fire and a few homemade candles would illuminate the house. "I think we went to bed quite early," she remembers. Special events, such as holidays and weddings, were always timed to coincide with the full moon. "It was so bright, you didn't need candles. I remember singing all night, or at least until the moon went down, at parties."

At harvest time, everyone was needed to work the fields, so school was dismissed. Margaret also recalls a time when she was older when the school needed a new roof. All the children, boys and girls, had to collect bamboo and Seu-bow leaves. "The vines had huge thorns and the leaves, little stickers. We were quite competitive and would go into the jungle after school to find and gather it. We braided it into big thick ropes and tied them up with bamboo string. We strapped enormous bundles of them onto our backs, and I remember they were forever getting caught in the underbrush and on low branches on the trek back home."

Life wasn't all work. Girls played a variation of jacks, called *leh-po*, with five rocks. There are ten levels of difficulty, in which the girl has to perform increasingly difficult movements, such as weaving her fingers together, clicking her thumbs, and so on, between the time she throws one rock in the air and when she attempts to pick the others up.

Lisu children, both boys and girls, are expected to help out. This girl is taking a break from a construction project. Author photo.

Another favorite was *sho-lo-qua*, a team game involving several levels of skill. A round, flat seed from the *adge-dta-dta* tree is tossed at a target, which is another wedged seed sticking up from the ground. First the seed is tossed with the hand, next from the top of the foot, then from between toes, ankles, knees, and other body parts, ending with letting it slide off the top of the head.

Both girls and boys make flutes and pop guns, which use little hard fruits as ammunition, but making dolls from sticks and building little houses for them is mainly a girls' amusement, Margaret recalls. Lisu children have a form of "paper, stone, scissors" that they call "knife, hammer, and tweezers," as well as a version of "eenie, meenie, minee, mo" to choose the order of players. A game of endurance, called *na-do-chi-pa*, is similar to the Russian kick-dance krazachkis. "A group of girls starts dancing and one by one drop out when exhausted. The winner is the one who keeps kicking the longest, perhaps a half hour or forty-five minutes," Margaret told me. Girls favored most of the games mentioned; boys would play them up to age five or six, when they begin their own set of diversions.

BOYS: RUNNING FREE AND LEARNING TO SURVIVE

Tommy Morse, Margaret's older brother, also learned English late; he, however, doesn't recall as much of the work side of childhood because his earliest years were spent in the Putao area, where agriculture and trade were more established. Children's (and adults') lives were easier there. Unlike his siblings and cousins, he wasn't interested in schoolwork—instead, he ran with a group of Lisu pals whose main entertainment was hunting. His skills in this area proved essential to the family's survival when they resettled in Hidden Valley when he was thirteen.

"Growing up Lisu differs from family to family, just like growing up anywhere," Tommy says. "But Lisu are keen hunters, so most boys learn these skills so they can supplement the family diet. Lisu have fought the Chinese, Tibetans, Burmans . . . so knowing how to use weapons is basic to survival. Boys do quite a bit of work for the family by the age of ten, and by fifteen [they] are expected to work like an adult." While in Thailand today there isn't much forest cover left in which to practice such pursuits, in Burma and China, Lisu are still keen hunters.

By the time a Lisu boy is five or six, he has made his first "sling-bow," a kind of cross between a slingshot and a bow. Made of bamboo, rattan, and jute, it looks like a bow 2.5 to 4 feet long, but in the middle of the bowstring is a small woven rattan pouch, from which rocks or clay balls are shot instead of arrows. Called a *nye ma poer*, it requires a horizontal orientation to shoot instead of a vertical one.

"We'd hunt for hours, and [we] learned about animals and the forest from observing and from the experiences of older boys," Tommy says. His family appreciated the small game—rats, porcupines, birds—with which he began supplying the cooking pot starting at around age eight.

By his early teens the Lisu boy graduates to a small crossbow, or *chyeh*, which takes more skill and strength to use and involves poison-tipped arrows. By practicing all the time, adept boys can shoot a mouse from 20 feet. Made of wood or sometimes bamboo, a hemp string, and a bone trigger, this is the traditional hunting and defense weapon of the Lisu, as well as a symbol of Lisu manhood. A basket and bamboo quiver toolkit always accompanies the crossbow and is slung over the shoulder. In addition to arrows, Lisu hunters carry a small knife with a curved blade called an *a-tha-liq* and either a flint or matches, which must be kept dry, as well as the constrictive poison, *dto*, for their arrow tips. The poison is aconite, powerful enough to kill smaller game even if the shot wouldn't otherwise have proved fatal. The area the arrow has pierced is cut away, and the rest of the meat is safe to eat.

"We would practice with moving targets," says Tommy, "starting with rolling things on the ground and then throwing things up in the air. We got pretty good. I remember taking our dogs out to help us sniff out civet cats. Dividing up, we'd cooperatively hunt them down. We'd parade the trophy around the village and collect an egg or something from each house as a reward for catching the hen killer. We wouldn't eat the cat unless we were really hungry—but [we] used its skin,"

Tommy recalls most fondly an after-harvest Lisu boy tradition that took a bit of preparation. They would collect banana leaves and use them to cover a makeshift frame they built to half encircle a harvested field. This created a meter-high green wall to hide behind. They cut holes in the wall about 5–6 inches in diameter about a foot above ground level every 2 meters. For two or three days they'd put a little grain through the hole on the outside of the fence. Then on the third or fourth night they would collect blankets, knives, crossbows, candles or flashlights, and food and make camp headquarters and a fire at the far end of the field away from the wall.

"We'd make the rounds quietly. We'd take turns shining the light through the hole and shoot whatever was on the other side. A small kind of porcupine was the best. We'd shoot dozens of them. When we each had a bag full of critters, we'd bring them to the fire, pull out the quills, burn off the hair, and scrape the skin with a knife. Then we'd wash and gut them at the stream. We'd roast them over the fire, along with taro roots, and feast on it all, along with a few greens and pickled bamboo shoots. We'd camp out the night and take any leftover game home to our families."

Their village in Putao had a river with an island on it. Tommy and his friends would spend most of the summer there, trying to catch fish. Spokes from an old umbrella served as the basis for a spear gun, and they also fashioned goggles to better see underwater. "The Lisu are incredibly ingenious when it comes to make-do inventions; they can copy an idea and then come up with something that works, made of materials they find around," he says.

By age fourteen or fifteen this stage of boyhood is over, and as young men they take on greater responsibilities. In addition to hunting for larger game, such as deer, guar, wild cows, monkeys, and tigers, they begin to develop new interests.

Teenage boys and girls start to get together again, traditionally around the village rice pounder: this looks like a wooden seesaw, with one end the pounder, which hits the rice placed in a mortar. Girls take turns standing on one end, using their weight to operate it, and winnowing. When no boys are present, according to Margaret, "It was all girl talk: who had her period, who was growing breasts, and, of course, who liked so-and-so." But when boys were around, the atmosphere changed dramatically to one of courtship. The boy would sit next to a girl he liked, and they would talk and sometimes exchange secret letters. "They were beautiful, flowery love letters," Margaret remembers (written in missionary-introduced, Romanized Lisu script). "Of course, we'd have to hide them from our parents!" In Thailand and China today, each family or allegiance group is more likely to have a gas-operated rice pounder, and young people find other places to meet, such as at wells or clothes-washing spots.

Sex-segregated teen groups collecting food in the forest sing as they work, usually folk songs, sometimes generating new lyrics as they forage. Margaret recalls how one group would start singing and then another, unseen and perhaps across a small valley, would answer, and they would engage in responsive, antiphonal harmonies. The Lisu love of singing and natural talent to spontaneously create two-, three-, and even four-part harmonies has been

While operating the village rice pounder (like this one in Thailand in the mid-1990s) was teenage girls' work, it was also a traditional courting spot, where girls and boys began to get together again after somewhat sex-segregated childhoods. Author photo.

noted by many. This talent seems to develop just in time for courtship, and many a romance blooms between young singing partners.

Still seen and heard at planting or harvest times are boys and girls, or men and women, in adjacent rows or fields, singing back and forth to relieve the tedium—filling the valley with song. Childhood might be over, but the Lisu relive it in music that harkens back to youth and the village of their fathers.

9

Men, Women, Courtship, and Marriage

If you want riches, cut two fields,
If you want trouble, marry two wives.

If you're late in planting, your fields turn to bird feed,
If you marry and have children late, you won't reap the benefit of their strength.
—*Lisu proverbs*

NEW YEAR CELEBRATIONS: SETTING THE STAGE FOR ROMANCE

A good time to observe relations between Lisu men and women is during New Year celebrations in Thailand, China, or Burma. The Women's New Year the first lunar month is generally the main festival, with the smaller Men's New Year the following month. Not only is this period significant in terms of reaffirming all things Lisu, but for four or five days the village crackles with sexual energy. Dancing is almost nonstop. Liaisons, proposals, and marriages flow from the Lisu New Year like music does from flutes (*djeulae*), reed pipes (*fulu*), and wood lutes (*tseubeu*). Days of singing, feasting, and drinking have their effect, and the Lisu's rigid system of sexual etiquette (compared to that of the Lahu, Hmong, or Akha) is a bit likelier than usual to slip. The exception is in Christian villages where traditional New Year celebrations were muted for years but which are today being revived via cultural preservation movements.

The New Year is when divorced people, widows, and disaffected spouses indulge in greater sexual banter than usual or even slip into the forest for a fling—but this is only a sideshow. The main event is the age-old marriage market, which moves into top gear. Boys who have observed this or that girl over previous months or years take the opportunity to approach and make their admiration known—perhaps visiting and serenading her after dark. Lisu girls, who have refined the coy downward glance to a high art form, are at their maidenly prettiest.

Of all the images of Southeast Asia's hill tribes, photographs of young Lisu women in Thailand, Myanmar, and China, resplendent in New Year's finery and ancestral silver, are the most abundant. Visiting and even would-be tourists become smitten knowing nothing beyond this colorful representation of feminine beauty and potential fertility. The reputation of Lisu women as the most beautiful of the hill minorities is mostly earned over the New Year period. Not only looks and outrageously colorful costumes but also their distinct shy pride, along with confidence in the women they will soon become, are on full display. New Year is the time Lisu nurture and increase their myi-do (repute)—and nowhere is this more obvious than among the young beauties arriving at ceremonies and dances in groups, where they arrange themselves to best advantage. In *Peoples of the Golden Triangle*, Elaine and John Lewis comment that a clear example of the Lisu desire to be first and best is seen in the way village girls compete, with great family support, to create the most resplendent New Year's outfit.

Having a beautiful, hardworking, modest virgin to parade at New Year celebrations presents one of life's great opportunities. Getting one's daughters well married for a good bride price is a prime life goal of every Lisu parent—and fathers especially harbor the blame if this is not accomplished.

Boys and men tend to arrive later at gatherings not of a strictly religious nature, and they pay less attention to dress than do girls and women. Yet in 1998's New Year celebrations in the northern Thai villages of Doi Laan and Doi Chang, about half of the males donned traditional black velvet, silver-studded jackets, worn with wide blue knee-length trousers and leg guards. Males distinguish themselves with their musical and dancing ability, as well as in song and through display of Lisu-style bravado. This has a humorous edge and often features outlandish storytelling or poetic recitations.

Wearing pounds of ancestral silver is no longer a part of New Year's celebrations in China; the Red Army confiscated ethnic minority silver during

Lisu girl in Shan State, Myanmar, 1989, is dressed for New Year celebration—a time when liaisons, proposals, and marriages flow like music from the lutes and pipes in several days of singing, feasting, and drinking. Thai Lisu women wear the same style of clothing. Photo: Richard Diran.

Lisu women's dress varies widely across geographical spread. Styles migrate with people, as this young girl (above) from around Myitkyina, Myanmar, illustrates with her Upper Salween–style, Chinese Lisu attire. The woman (top right) who lives in Mogok, Myanmar, wears an outfit similar to ones found further south in China. I also met women in Burma wearing clothes indistinguishable from those worn by the woman (bottom right) reading the Bible in a church near Tengchong, China, but with a different head covering. Thai Lisu women wear the same clothes as those worn by women in parts of the Shan State (see photo p. 101), Myanmar. Author photos.

"the Great Leap Forward" of land collectivization from 1958 to 1962. This hasn't dampened Lisu enthusiasm, however, for their favorite holiday. An inversion of bride stealing was described to me by a Lisu woman living by the Nujiang in 1997: at the height of the revels at a northern Lisu New Year's celebration, a group of six to ten unmarried girls swoop down on a boy one of them likes, carrying him off to a sand pit on the bank of this raging cosmic river. They bury him up to his head after first thoughtfully covering his head with a scarf so he doesn't get sand in his eyes and mouth. The girls then surround the "grave" and cry crocodile tears. The most convincing weeper is the girl who likes him most.

Around Tengchong further south, there is an additional Lisu tradition of sword-ladder climbing after the New Year, on the first day of the second lunar month. This ritual provides young-bloods with the opportunity to show off bravery and skill and seal the affection of one whose attention was recently caught. Each of the fifty-foot ladder's seventy-two "steps" is actually an upward-facing sword blade. While it is the job of the village shaman to be the first to climb it barefoot, other men are welcome to follow him. Usually, it is those of marriageable age who take up the challenge, as well as an additional feat of walking across beds of hot coals.

Knowing custom and passing it on to youths is an important function of traditional celebrations. Gatherings at the shrines of Apa-mo (village guardian) and I-dama (local land spirit), as well as household rituals and feasts, unfold in an unrehearsed manner. No single stage manager but a random pitching in characterizes such events: one person collects a sprig of a certain bush used to sprinkle blessing water, another begins the song, still another decorates the New Year's tree planted in front of the house or prepares an offering. Younger boys never forget to bring firecrackers. Lisu girls notice which young men show interest in keeping custom; this augers well for a future head of household.

GENDER ROLES, COURTSHIP, AND SEXUALITY

Although details vary, the way the sexes relate, as well as courtship and marriage customs, are similar in most Lisu communities across the three countries. The pattern is set and the rules learned within the family group—girls must know about *sha-taw* (shame); boys should be resourceful, protective, and clever. Both must be hardworking. Everyone grows up with marriage and children as life goals—offspring bring joy when young, labor when older, security in old age, and sustenance and honor when one passes into the spirit realm. Not having descendants to provide one with offerings and worship in the land of the dead is a lonely and frightening prospect to Lisu (and many other traditional peoples). Not everyone lives long enough to become an ancestor, and dying before one has children is a sad fate.

Many ethnographers have commented that Lisu woman enjoy higher status than other hill women and that they control the household's money. By contemporary standards the segregated sex roles of Lisu men and women do not bespeak equality if "sameness" is the standard—but Lisu women occupy respected positions, and, when questioned, their men always affirm female equality. After childbearing age, women gain even more respect. They are often entrepreneurial and appear to have more scope for self-determination than women in other tribal groups with whom they are compared.

Lisu are closest to the Lahu in this regard and both groups use chopsticks, which Chinese ethnographer Shanshan Du notes "only work in pairs," as the sex metaphor. But when Thai Lisu speak about what behavior members of each sex should practice to increase repute, the model for females is most often the elephant, while for males it is the dog. Each fulfills *myi* (potential, or name) in a gender-specific way.

Elephant and dog analogies were investigated by Klein Hutheesing, whose work with the Thai Lisu focuses on sex roles. When she asked a woman why the Lisu adopted the elephant as a symbol for females, she was told "don't you know elephants are shy? . . . When they fornicate, they do not want anyone watching." So the Lisu woman aspires to gain elephant repute, *h'a-ma myi-do*: to be shy, modest, tenderhearted, and aware of status. In China, the elephant metaphor is also often used by Lisu; here this might have been influenced by folklore portraying the elephant as bashful and moralistic. In one folktale an elephant has intercourse in the water so she cannot be observed; in another she kills a servant because he committed adultery. In Indian-Tibetan Buddhism the elephant represents crop abundance and fertility, as well as longevity and royalty. Lowland Thai refer to elephants and femininity in a specific way: women are compared to the animal's hind legs, which Thais note do the heavy lifting. The animal's strength and size don't take away from its femininity to the Lisu, who equate bigness with fertility potential. Women joke about "big vulvas that make big children come out" and comment on the relative sizes of women whose deliveries they have witnessed. Lisu use of this metaphor is more egalitarian than the Thais'.

The Lisu man in all three countries strives to be as bold and adventurous as a dog, and they have hundreds of dog stories. The dog is a common symbol in Chinese peasant myths as well. The dog is a trickster, a guide, or founder of lineages. In Lisu myth, Wu-sa revealed through a dog where people could find the first rice to plant. The Lisu often mention that a dog accompanies Apa-mo and sometimes refer to the dog as guardian of their culture. According to a Lisu folktale reported by Durrenberger, man has an intimate connection to dogs: at the time of creation, dogs had men's genitals and men had dogs'. This caused problems for the men because they couldn't take care of their fields with all the time spent copulating when females were in season and time wasted stuck together afterward. So the people went to the creator and complained, suggesting that a swap be arranged with dogs, which have the leisure for such sexual habits. The wish was granted and explains why men work all day in their fields and dogs can spend so much time copulating.

Thai Lisu have a complex system regulating freedom of sexual speech with members of the opposite sex within the clan (see table on p. 106), also reported on by Klein Hutheesing. It is permissible to engage in sexual banter or (for older women) even lewd behavior with non-clansmen and some family members, while it is taboo to mention anything to do with sex to others. This taboo is strictly observed and never spoken of, and yet it extends to cover anyone in the company of those with a restricted relationship. For example, when in the presence of a pregnant woman and her father, father-in-law, brothers, sons, or male parallel cousins (sons of her father's brother or mother's sister in the same generation, who are considered siblings), it would cause shame to everyone if someone asks if she is hoping for a boy or a girl. A woman should not sing, dress, comb her hair, or look in the mirror while in the presence of any of these menfolk. But with one's cross-cousins (children of one's father's sister or mother's brother, who belong to a different lineage) and other marriageable people, it is permissible to discuss intimate matters, joke, or fart.

Males have a corresponding set of restrictions. Maintaining such taboos require vigilance and awareness of others' relationships, as it is not just one's own that must be monitored. Furthermore, a friendship between two people may change after years of easy camaraderie—when, for example, a woman marries a relative of her brother-in-law, he shifts into the "brother" position and she must "become shy" with him.

Sexual talk chart

A Lisu Woman May Not	A Lisu Man May Not
talk about intimate matters with:	
her father	his mother
her father-in-law	his mother-in-law
her brothers	his sisters
husband's older brother	younger brother's wife
parallel cousins	parallel cousins
sons, sons-in-law	daughters, daughters-in-law
brothers of her parents	sisters of his parents

In permissible company, sex talk, puns, and suggestive behavior are not unusual. Older women will even tease men and overtly appraise penis size. This sort of play, however, reaches its peak in single-sex company, particularly of women. While young girls may be present, it is those past child-rearing age who indulge in the raciest discourse. The male organ is called a spade and the female's, a frog. Women like play-acting both parts (using large white radishes or clenched fists for the man's role) for the amusement of other woman and perhaps to instruct younger ones. Those who excel in this kind of play are called "penis-talk experts," according to Klein Hutheesing. Speculation about men's organs is common, although size is valued for its perceived ability to make big children, not good sex.

Lisu women reporting to her indicated that they do not find sex an enjoyable activity in itself. They speculated that this could be because they "don't work at it, like men" and have no peak to their sexual feeling. Lisu women told Klein Hutheesing that what they like most about sex is its reproductive potential. They do not generally take off their clothes to have intercourse but simply lift up one baggy trouser leg to accommodate partners. Women sometimes tease each other about dried semen on their trousers—if in the wrong company, this causes acute shame. Teenage girls sometimes lie together in bed, openly touching each other's bodies and joking about their scents. Breasts are not taboo or titillating, merely pleasure giving, and even through their teen years, some boys and girls lie with their mother and play with her breasts.

When women refer to their own organs, it is usually in association with blood and babies. An elderly woman will tease a younger one already burdened with many offspring: "Your vulva has so much blood, it goes 'blop-blop' and wants more children."

Lisu mothers in Thailand usually give birth in a squatting position, on the right side of the house, in a low cot built for that purpose. Some Chinese Lisu and many in Burma build a separate birthing hut. One or more women assist, and a long cloth is hung from the rafters for the woman to pull against when it is time to push out her baby. Mother-in-law can be counted on to remind her not to scream out in pain, as this is considered shameful. Although by Western standards of hygiene the Lisu setup leaves much to be desired, relatively high rates of Lisu women and babies survive childbirth, and many herbal and other folk remedies common in China assist with pregnancy and birth. The mother is not allowed to consume food or drink regarded as "cooling" during labor, as Lisu believe this will make the birth difficult or impossible. There is some knowledge of germs, and care is taken to ensure that the knife or scissors used to cut the umbilical cord is clean and free of rust. New mothers are allowed to rest for a month and are fed special, nutritious food—particularly chicken. The "mother-roasting" fire is kept burning for five to seven days or up to a month in cold weather. During its first seven days of life, a baby is not yet considered human and it is taboo for outsiders to visit. On the eighth day, however, Apa-mo is informed (as he is in the case of a new foal or litter of pigs)—but with a child a pig is killed, prayers are said for protection, and a naming ceremony is held. The afterbirth is buried under the fire or placed high in a tree in the forest. Unlike some other groups, Lisu do not consider multiple births bad luck or evil.

Lisu women do think menstrual or birth blood is offensive to Apa-mo and give this as the reason they are not permitted to visit his shrine. They don't see their bodies as unclean or inferior but rather that their blood and earth power could neutralize Apa-mo's power. Visiting his shrine would thus be a breach of etiquette, an offense tied to Lisu dualistic beliefs placing females (associated with body, blood, and earth) in opposition to males (associated with soul, spirit, and sky). Occasionally, older women, particularly healers, are allowed to visit Apa-mo's house.

In a different context, if a female wants to abuse another, she will lift one trouser leg and tell the other woman to eat or lick her frog. If two women are fighting and the husband of one happens to be there (which isn't uncommon in a Lisu village, where there is no such thing as privacy and neighbors drift in to witness a hot argument), one might hurl the ultimate insult: "You, I let your husband eat my vulva." Such expressions are learned at an early age, according to Klein Hutheesing, who has heard toddlers as young as two or three babbling "let me eat your vulva." While there is a male equivalent, also an insult that men use among themselves, it is more common for a man to say "you, eat my wife's frog" if he really wishes another man ill.

Lisu girls and boys grow up in a society that combines earthiness and knowledge about reproduction, on one hand, with restrictions and taboos on the other. The normal sexual tensions develop with adolescence, and not too long after that, the search for a mate begins.

------------■-■------------

As indicated in the maxim that begins this chapter, Lisu traditionally marry young. They are generally monogamous and have children early. Avoiding shame and building repute in adolescence is motivated by the desire to make a good match. The stress of always having to worry about shame is relieved after marriage, particularly for women, although it is replaced by the stress of living with the husband's family. Even so, a Lisu woman from Doi Chang in Thailand, Ami-zah, reflects a typical attitude when she told Klein Hutheesing, "Life really begins after marriage; before that, we know nothing of life."

Until forty or fifty years ago, most marriages were arranged. Bride and groom were promised to one another as young as age five or six. The marriage took place when the boy was nineteen or twenty, soon after the girl began menstruating at sixteen or seventeen. Virginity was valued and guarded; sometimes a prospective bride would move in with the family of her husband-to-be as young as age ten or eleven for safekeeping.

The importance of the marriage alliance among the Lisu is chiefly in terms of clan relationships and distributing wealth and labor—unlike in societies where land and inherited wealth and position are the key issues. In the past, there was more emphasis on lineage in China than in Burma or Thailand, where distribution of resources is more heavily weighted. The former system of arranging marriages left scant room for courtship yet lots of time for trouble to develop. Particularly in the Upper Nujiang region of China, it was not uncommon for extended feuds or even inter-village wars to result over recalcitrant brides, runaway brides, or those stolen before they were delivered to the rightful family. The epithets "eloper" or worse, "bride-stealer," stuck once applied and could ignite decades of animosity. Shame, the return of down payments or installments of bride wealth, and the amount of fines or other penalties were disputed for generations.

Today, most Lisu claim marriages are based on love and the belief that no girl should be forced to marry against her will. But in all three countries, there are considerations beyond love. Durrenberger makes the interesting assertion that Lisu, like everyone else, generally marry whom they are supposed to marry, whether by arrangement or not. But the Lisu will skirt or bend the rules when a couple is set on marriage. "Oh, but there was love" is the typical way Lisu parents explain away any leniency on their part in negotiating a good price for their daughter.

In a typical courtship, a boy will first notice a girl and watch her for awhile before advancing. She will most likely be from a nearby village, and he may take the precaution of finding out whether she is from a different clan than his and thus marriageable. A girl must not appear interested or sexually aggressive in any way if she wants to be considered a good prospect. Hardworking boys with repute and inventive tongues are considered the most attractive. Ability as a hunter, especially skill with the crossbow, increases a young man's allure.

The boy might hang around with a group of others by the village rice pounder in the afternoon when a girl he likes is there with friends. This notorious courting spot is disappearing in Thailand and China but is still in use in some mountain areas of Burma in the Shan State. There is usually some part of the village, however, where young people can gather that is public enough to preserve propriety.

Courtship advances during fieldwork. Members of sex-segregated teenage work groups observe each other and sing with those in adjacent rows or fields. Sometimes boys spontaneously come up with romantic or suggestive verses, which the head girl might counter with the versified equivalent of cold water. As is the case everywhere, Lisu boys enjoy making girls blush or fume. Singing and music are favored activities—the main courting tools. Groups of boys will sit around singing in the evening, perhaps on a bench in a well-traveled lane, and serenade the neighborhood with sentimental or humorous love songs. If a girl walks by, they might substitute her name for the inevitable "darling" or "you" in the song:

In a beautiful glade
I met my darling.
Then a white dove
Startled my love
And she jumped into my arms, oh my!

Lyrics in Lisu love songs aren't different from those the world over; it is the way they are sung, the harmonies and inflections, that make them distinct. The following two were popular among Lisu in Burma:

When I see your face
And your body, so like a flower
You make me feel
We will live forever.
When the moon shines at night,
It's shining for you and me
When the wind blows gently,
It's blowing for you and me.

In addition to New Year's and fieldwork, opportunities for group singing or duets occur in the rainy season when people work inside, during feast preparation, and at village-wide feast days.

Chinese Lisu say "singing is as indispensable to life as salt." This can be taken literally when its importance in courtship is considered. In that country, customs have changed since the revolution, and within some groups, girls are allowed relatively more freedom. After a "dressing ceremony" at age fourteen, girls are said to move from childhood to adulthood. They may participate in social activities and can play the bamboo flute, sing, and drink alcohol in public. They are also reported to engage in sex before marriage, although Chinese parents still often choose their children's life partners.

In the time-honored dance, understandings are reached and marriage plans begin. In Thailand and Burma, when the girl accepts a small gift from the boy to "put a flower in her hair" (three or sometimes thirty silver rupees are traditional), it is time for bride price negotiations. The couple often exchange small gifts. I was told by a man near Tengchong in China in 2014 that in his area "when a boy sends rattan to a girl (to make knee bracelets), it means 'I

love you,' and if the girl sends gators back to him, it means 'I love you, too.'"
Go-betweens begin positioning themselves.

When plans do not develop in what parents consider a timely fashion or if
the parents strongly object to a match proposed by the son, another approach
kicks in. A Lisu mother in China reported that she traveled around to several
villages with her thirty-year-old son a few years ago when he was dragging his
feet about getting married. The son said he trusted his mother's judgment and
married the girl she recommended, who turned out to be a good choice. "Only
women can know about the right girl" describes the typical Lisu attitude.

Often, in the period between when a girl and boy develop serious feelings for one another and the official engagement, tensions develop between
their families. The man's lineage considers itself the "tree," with women
being "leaves." The threat of having a leaf "stolen" makes the bride's family
unhappy, even though on another level they have been planning for it. Lisu
are no more rational than people anywhere.

But if a boy and girl have "arranged" their own marriage without help
from the mother, a custom in Thailand and Burma comes into play soon
after. They set the date for their elopement, or what Klein Hutheesing calls
their "quasi-elopement," because typically everyone knows what is going on.
Two go-betweens chosen by the boy, or sometimes a party of them, will
visit the girl's home and ask to take her away for the night. The mother may
let her go, but reluctantly, or posture as if she disagrees. After the girl has
"fled," the mother will cry out so that everyone in the village hears, "daughter, come back," three times. Most neighbors know which daughter is being
called and with whom she will be spending the night. The big question then
becomes "how much?" Or sometimes the couple will disappear to a field hut
for the night, and the go-between will visit the bride's parents the next day to
let them know a man, not a tiger, has taken her.

Lisu are supposed to marry outside of their own lineages—to do otherwise is considered incest. A Lisu women joins her husband's clan upon
marriage, but families can and do go through contortions and clan swaps
from the father's to the mother's or a step-parent's to get around particular
matches being ruled taboo. In such cases, the potential groom must pay
a fine to the bride's father on top of bride price. The groom is also fined
if the girl he wants has a still-unmarried older sister. However, if she is a
bit older or has already been unsuccessfully married, his side will use it to

advantage. While virginity is valued, the rules have relaxed somewhat, as they have some places on clan intermarriage. A Burmese couple living on the outskirts of Myitkyina told me in 2014 that there and around Putao, the rules were more lax than in Mogok, where the wife was from. Christian and urban influences have a role in this. While everything else appears negotiable, paying bride price itself is not. The practice has survived and is still the norm (see Book II: Contemporary Sketches). Only the poorest Christians report dropping the practice, but Burmese Christian Lisu make up the majority and most women, young and old, whom I asked told me exactly how much they'd fetched.

The ideal is marriage is between cross-cousins. Family name carries more weight than genetics in this system, which is common across Asia. Among the Lisu and many other groups, each person belongs to a patrilineal line. That means one's lineage is the same as one's father's—intermarriage in which is forbidden. This differs from the Western kinship system, where the main distinction is between siblings and cousins. The Lisu don't make this distinction; instead, they differentiate cross-cousins from parallel cousins, who are of the same generation and considered siblings.

NEGOTIATING BRIDE WEALTH

"My girl's a little bungler, she often burns the rice," the bride's mother sings from her seat by the fire. Beginning the final phase of the marriage negotiation, go-betweens hovering, representatives from the two families face each other across an open hearth. The raised bamboo house where the drama unfolds is perched high above a tributary of the Salween River in Yunnan in Southwest China. The mother's opening line does not really disparage her daughter but is rather typical Lisu bargaining, an attempt to lull the other party into giving up something before realizing it.

"Don't worry, we're as fond of her as [of] our own daughter; step by step she'll become a good and able housewife," the groom's father counters. In chant and response, elders from both families hammer out a deal that is generally favorable to the bride's father. This could take a day or several days, depending on the complexity of the arrangements. The final details will be predicated on whether Father needs money or labor most—but whatever is lacking, the marriage of a daughter will improve his situation. Toasts and cross-toasts of rice liquor accompany the bargaining along with pronounce-ments of new kinship alliances. Members of both sides soon become intoxi-cated. Durrenberger says that after his first session in Thailand, he explained that it was "not custom" for anthropologists to drink on such occasions. One or more of the main parties, he says, often pass out or "rest" for a time. Someone else, a go-between who might be an aunt or uncle, takes over until the swooner comes to and continues negotiating.

Among Lisu scattered across Southwest China, Burma, and northern Thailand, this is life's most crucial deal—the way to distribute wealth and to forge or strengthen social and economic relationships. Payment of bride price has a leveling effect on Lisu society and for generations kept most fam-ilies within a fairly narrow range of wealth. This is important to the egali-tarian Lisu—people for whom being as good as anyone else is a cherished value. Beyond gifts and other exchanges, where and with whom the young people will live will be decided—for the length of the bride's father's life or at least until the groom's family has paid off the bride price. The girl's father has the right to demand that the couple live in his village, and he will enforce this if he needs labor more than cash. More often, he will ask a higher price in exchange for relinquishing the demand; usually, the couple ends up living with or near the boy's family within a few years of marriage. In the past these obligations could go on for generations, and it was not unheard of for a widower to be paying off his wife's family thirty years after the woman died.

Beyond cash, silver rupees, horses, cows (these two items more fre-quently in the past than today), or other payments, a key area of negotia-tion is kinship terms: who will call whom by what name after the marriage takes place? Relationship adjustments required by marriage are not taken lightly. If a husband does not want to call his bride's older sibling or par-allel cousin "Older Brother" because he, in fact, is older, this is negotiated beforehand to avoid trouble.

All relationships have economic implications, especially for the bride's father. The go-between team's first announcement of the business at hand—"Old Man, your daughter is no longer your daughter—will typically be responded to with something like "you must be kidding, I brought her up better than that. She wouldn't hang around with trash like Third Born." This is ritual posturing; the father has very likely been expecting such a visit and been planning his strategy.

The traditional payment for go-betweens (who might be men or women at different stages of the negotiation) is liquor, and they will always turn up at the father's house with a few bottles and some tea. As they go back and forth in preliminary negotiations before the families sit down together, they, and often everyone else involved, get drunk in non-Christian families. This usually includes a gaggle of older men or women, drawn into the drama. The role of these elders is crucial, since almost every proposal made is initially branded incestuous. This increases the fines the boy's family must pay—and it is the job of the old men or women on both sides to draw up (conflicting) genealogies that families haggle over for several hours or sometimes a day or two. Often, just when a settlement seems within reach, her side will raise a fresh objection, and a new chart is drawn in the dirt to show why the marriage couldn't possibly take place. The ancestors would be offended because so-'n-so's great-grandfather's brother was married to the daughter of the prospective bride's great-aunt. Anyone who has witnessed these negotiations comes away impressed—both with the amount of genealogical information stored in gray (and usually drunken) old Lisu heads and also with their skill in retrieving it at the optimum moment.

But since the boy's father must supply liquor to all parties as well as kill a pig to feed them every day of the negotiations, he is motivated to strike a deal and be done with it. The dice are not in his favor, and everyone knows it. Negotiations and periods of payment are not as drawn out as in the past, but it might still be six months to a couple of years between the go-betweens' first visit and when the marriage feast is held. In the meantime, the couple has probably begun to live together.

Traditionally, most marriages take place after the New Year and opium harvest, as this is when families are the most flush. To get married without having a wedding feast and ceremony, when the bride officially leaves her father's lineage and joins her husband's, is shameful. But often the new couple or the boy's parents must defer this ceremony, as the bride's father's demands take precedence. When the celebration takes place, the Lisu sing: "The silver has been paid. Our hearts are satisfied. Father and his older brother are content, so there is nothing to hinder it now: let's be merry!"

The final amount paid after all the haggling is often predictable, based on factors of the bride's age and previous marriage history, as well as fines the boy's father must pay. This indicates that price isn't as tied to local markets as it is to kinship and relationship building. Bride price is sometimes called a "milk fee" and is regarded as compensation to the parents for their efforts at nurturing the girl who is about to go off and join another lineage—contributing her labor and repute to it for the rest of her life. The younger she is, the more her parents are losing, and so they must receive more. The crucial importance of potential new labor alliances through marriage is discussed in Chapter 12, Book I. The Lisu never refer to a woman as having been "bought." The term used is always "she has been paid for."

In Burma, a standard price forty years ago was 200 silver rupees, but in the 1990s most Lisu were poor and the boy's family often simply paid for the wedding feast, especially among Christians. In Thailand, the price in 1998 was usually between 10,000 and 20,000 baht. In China at that time, 2,000–3,000 yuan was quoted as a good price; this amount has risen dramatically because birth restrictions and the aborting of female fetuses have resulted in serious sex imbalances today.

For the Lisu woman, however, whatever bride price she fetched is forever remembered. She may be sixty, seventy, or eighty years old, and she will always recall the exact amount her father received, whether she lives in China, Burma, or Thailand. The amount, usually a standard one, is often stated with pride—it shows she is equal to others. There are exceptions, when no price is paid because of unusual circumstances. True elopements or daughters without a father are a few of these. Some, but not all, Christians have replaced bride price with a "gift exchange" that is a nominal amount, still favoring the bride's side. It doesn't appear that the practice is in decline; in villages visited in 1997, 1998, and 2014, brides were still being negotiated over with vigor.

Anthropologist Edmund Leach's reduction of all possible kin relationships down to bride givers and bride takers is still relevant. Brides are associated with fertility, negotiating for them with Lisu custom. Klein Hutheesing reports that in northern Thailand, in a traditional wedding song from Burma, a marriageable girl is compared to a "wet-rice field." Thai Lisu grow dry mountain rice exclusively, but Lisu who moved to Thailand from Burma remember cultivating wet rice, which they have done since the 1950s.

> Do not say I sell the girl because I am poor.
> It is the ancestors' way to consider the girl.

In town they sell wet-rice land, don't they?
You will say that the father has sold the girl,
that the mother had wet-rice fields to sell.
In town, people sell and eat wet rice fields.

10

The Household

THE PLACE FOR FAMILY AND WORK

Whenever two cups are kept together, they will rattle.

Don't argue if you want knowledge,
Don't be lazy if you want riches.
—*Lisu proverbs*

Implicit in the Lisu elder's traditional instructions to the newly married couple is the understanding that when people live together, there will be disagreements. Getting along and working hard, however, are the keys to wisdom and riches.

Among the Lisu, custom has the final say in most things. It is custom for the man to be the head of the family and for the wife to control the money. It is custom to honor ancestors at the family altar. It is custom for each child to be named according to birth order, that is, First Born, Second Born, Third Born, and so on. And it is custom that the man's domain of the house is in front of the altar and to the left and the woman's to the right. These customs, and others particular to each clan, are learned and internalized. Conversely, when Mother or Father says "there is no custom" in an emphatic way about something, such as speaking in a disrespectful tone or sleeping when one should be weeding the vegetable patch, a child soon learns the behavior is to be avoided if he or she doesn't want disapproval or, when older, a slap.

The cooperation in which Lisu families engage to make a living draws them together, and on a day-to-day basis most households are busy and productive. There will always be divorces, squabbles, and family feuds—but among the Lisu, it seems that serious disagreements are more often reserved for those outside household and allegiance groups. As a tiny minority who has always lived on the fringe of larger societies and within a flat and unconnected social structure of their own, the family is the unit that matters.

In all cultures, it is in the earliest intimate settings that a person soaks up his or her values. In the case of the Lisu, every child is cherished, and all members of the household cooperate in feeding, caring for, and amusing young children. They show amazing tenderness and patience and don't display irritation when ones old enough to walk, say three or four, insist on being carried. Beyond that, to have shame, to know and honor one's obligations, and to work hard are the lessons to learn to be successful. Since the gregarious Lisu like to visit, gossip, sing, and joke as they work, children learn that it is also important to enjoy life and to tell amusing stories.

But work could be the single-most-important value—the main requirement demanded of the individual in this egalitarian system. Since status and wealth aren't inherited and all clans are equal, it is up to each individual to prove he or she is as good as anyone else. One does this by developing one's *do*, productive potential or power—in other words, by working. The Lisu don't tolerate laziness. Children begin working early and are expected to make significant contributions to the family. Although most Lisu children attend school now, the work requirement has only been slightly modified. In the past, infants and children accompanied their parents to the fields where they learned the essential skills. During harvest time today, classrooms are often empty of Lisu students old enough to work.

Opium addicts are despised because they are idle and therefore poor and unable to meet ritual obligations such as reciprocal feasting. Although one of the first things Lisu do when they move to a new area is plant marijuana for its useful hemp fiber, they seldom smoke it. There are spiritual and survival issues at stake. As one Lisu woman explained to Durrenberger, "It is not possible to be a lazy Lisu. If you are lazy, you would have no pigs; with no pigs, one could not make ceremonies to the spirits and then you would die." Traditional Lisu work very hard to support themselves and their pigs; Christian Lisu work equally hard to sell their pigs at market to gain riches.

DUALISM IN DIVISION OF LABOR

House, field, and jungle are the main places of work. Increasingly, men spend time in lowland towns marketing produce. Men and women work equally hard in the fields, but sometimes at different tasks. Most household jobs are more apt to be done by one sex than the other but not exclusively; for instance, childcare and cooking are generally in the females' domain, but men cook in field huts and sometimes at home. They are always the roasters of any game they have killed, and they frequently carry babies around.

The Lisu divide all that exists into pairs of opposites, beginning with male and female. This is so thoroughly internalized that most Lisu could not communicate it; observers must know it and look to see how it manifests.

Nevertheless this system, in which even months are categorized as male or female (with a few combination months), also separates space, including the house, into male and female domains. Similarly, most work, including agricultural tasks, is assigned to one or the other sex. Klein Hutheesing thoroughly investigated this phenomenon in Thailand and reported the results shown in the table on page 120.

She notes that rainy months are mostly female, while the hot season is men's time. There are domestic and commercial parallels; for instance, clothes making gets done indoors by women during the rainy period, and men are kept busy participating in markets during the first few months of the year after the harvest season.

Women take care of the domestic animals and know them best, but men will cut banana stalks to feed them if no woman is available. The Lisu are not sentimental about domestic animals except for their horses, which they name and grow fond of. Horses are prestige items, and it's a sad day when the necessity of parting with them for cash arrives. Trucks have replaced horses in many places today. Small pigs are tamed by children, and individual animals are known by characteristics but not named. Piglets are often used as hot water bottles in cold weather.

FOOD, FEASTS, AND LIQUOR

Within the household, it is the female, often a daughter-in-law, who does most meal preparation and collecting of edible forest products. Her space is

Month	Activity	Gender
January	tree felling	male
February	preparing fields	male
March	firing the fields	male
April	maize planting	female
May	rice planting	female/male
June	preparing poppy fields	male
July	breaking maize cobs	female
August	sowing poppies	male
September	cutting maize stalks	female
October	cutting grass for roofs	female
November	harvesting rice	female/male
December	harvesting opium	female/male

around the stove, on the right side of the house, where the vegetables and water jar are kept. When she first moves into the household, her cooking ability is a matter of intense interest. A new husband confided that his wife's tendency to over-salt had him worried, and a couple of older women were overhead discussing their respective daughter-in-laws' rice-cooking talents. Pounding the daily rice is traditionally the job of daughters.

The Lisu eat lots of vegetables, both raw and cooked, mainly produced in their fields and gardens. Diets vary according to location, but rice, pork and vegetables are staples everywhere. Pork fat is used as a flavoring in many dishes, and chili is both mixed in and served as a condiment. Chicken and pork are often stewed or roasted with a sour fruit called *amu-gwa*. Eggs are eaten in small quantities, as are fish and game when available. All Lisu consider bamboo worms and bee and wasp grubs to be delicacies. They collect whatever roots, greens, and mushrooms are available from the forest to supplement what they grow and raise themselves. Rattan shoots are very popular in Myanmar, but I wasn't offered them in Thailand or China.

Lisu food is delicious and completely distinct from national cuisines of the countries in which they live. Mint, ginger, onion and sesame are characteristic tastes. A gelatinous starchy jungle root is used widely as an adjunct to rice. Rice porridge is cooked with chicken for old people, and new mothers are fed extra meat, often chicken cooked with star anise and white pepper.

The Lisu make a fresh and zesty tomato sauce, similar to Mexican salsa, that is popular in Thailand, Burma, and China. Tomatoes, onions, coriander leaves, and chilies are combined with ginger in this dish, which accompanies most meals. Pounded rice is formed into cakes, called *papas*, which are cooked in a variety of ways, sweet and savory. As a dessert, they are sliced and deep-fried, then served hot with a dipping mixture of sugar and ground sesame seeds. Papas are traditionally important at New Year's rituals in every country, when they are called ancestor cakes and wrapped in leaves. In the Upper Nu area, one of these is used as a target in a crossbow competition; the tiny bundle is placed at the end of a stick four or five feet tall on the edge of a cliff, and the men take turns trying to hit it.

Liquor making is mainly women's work and is associated with fertility. Men make the large barrel from a tree trunk harvested in the forest and hoist it when required, but getting the flavor right is considered a female art. Not all households attempt it because the process is arduous, resource-heavy, and financially risky. Those who use the activity to earn cash are often disappointed—the traditional Lisu necessity of offering hospitality to guests can see profits consumed by an overabundance of visitors to the liquor maker's household. Liquor is made from fermented rice or maize, and the best "liquor medicine" recipe is hotly discussed in the runup to feast days, when testing and comparing among neighbors intensifies.

On such days, women and men eat separately, and men and children (up to the teen years) are fed first. Again, it is daughters and daughters-in-law who serve food and liquor, and as they gather in colorful groups they may be heard grumbling that the best bits are gone before it is their turn to eat.

Clothes

The distinctive dress for which the Lisu are known is equal parts cultural identity and personal pride. Making clothes was entrusted entirely to female hands, although store-bought clothing, including in traditional Lisu styles, is worn day today. Lisu women will tell anyone willing to listen how much time this takes (or took) even as T-shirts, sarongs, and jeans increasingly populate family wardrobes. Clothing repair and laundry are also mainly women's work, although little girls and boys are taught to launder at a very young age. In the past, most Lisu wore clothing of homespun hemp cloth—black, or white with a thin blue horizontal stripe (in China), and more blue and red (in Burma/Myanmar and Thailand)—and clothes were hand-stitched. This is infrequent today, and sewing machines and store-bought cloth have had a huge impact, first in Thailand from the 1970s and in the following decades elsewhere. In China, the thin blue stripe is now printed, not woven. In Myanmar, Lisu everyday wear tends toward sarongs and T-shirts instead of traditional dress. In addition to convenience, the heat at the lower elevations they now inhabit necessitated this change of wardrobe. Because cloth is purchased rather than hand-loomed, Lisu traditional outfits are becoming more brightly colored and are often made of synthetic fibers.

This is particularly true in Thailand, where relative affluence combined with Lisu competitiveness spur young women to create the most beautiful costumes possible, particularly for the New Year celebration. The basic Lisu outfit there continues to evolve, with girls using machine-made strips for the yokes of their outfits and adding more tassels to their maidenly tail ornaments. Patterned chiffon, bright velvets, and polyester prints are now more common than the solid colors of the past.

There are variations of Lisu women's dress across the group's wide geographical spread: twelve distinct costumes in Myanmar alone, whereas Thailand's smaller population sticks more to one style. Only a few will be described here, as most boil down into two types.

Lisu women in the Shan State, Myanmar, and in Thailand (who are by far the most photographed) wear a tunic—knee-length in front and mid-calf-length in back—traditionally blue in color, which crosses over the chest and is held together by a wide black velvet belt over knee-length baggy black trousers. The tunic's chest panel is of a contrasting color, such as green, and the sleeves are usually red. The yoke is made of a circular piece of black cloth to which borders of many different colors are over-sewn. Leg guards or gators, also usually red, are embroidered at the bottom and complete the basic outfit. Older women sometimes wear aprons and large black turbans—generally, their outfits are more subdued as they don't want anyone to say they aren't acting their age. Even with all the other changes, most women own and wear traditional dress regularly, even if store bought, and are still engaged in clothes making in Thailand.

At New Year and other celebrations, younger women wear black velvet vests clasped with silver buckles and adorned with great numbers of silver buttons. A magnificent pair of pom-pom–tipped tassel tails loops over the back of their belts, with 100 or so delicately hand-stitched strands. These tassel tails bob tantalizingly at the rear with any body movement. Layers of heavy silver necklaces cascade down their chests. Silver earrings with yarn pom-poms hold multiple strands of fine silver chain that pass from ear to ear, dipping down to sway under the chin and frame the face. Wide silver bracelets with beveled edges and rings are also worn. Black circular headdresses have hundreds of strands of multicolored yarn folded around the front that trail, shoulder-length, off the back.

Variations of this outfit, not as fancy, are worn in southwestern parts of Yunnan and by the Baumee and Lushui Lisu in mountainous border regions of China and Myanmar. In these areas, most Lisu no longer have silver jewelry with which to adorn themselves but make do with multiple strands of tiny plastic beads, some of which are metallic stand-ins for silver.

Tengchong-area Lisu women in China wear a stunning version of this outfit without a yoke. Instead, colorful squares of cloth are sewn into panels down either side of the chest that extend over the shoulders into a large sailor-type collar that falls freely to the waist in back. The back part of the tunic is bordered with panels of colored cloth and cowry shells. This outfit doesn't have a long lower front panel to the tunic; instead, a knee-length apron, also decorated with cowry shells and cloth applique, is worn belted over black baggy trousers to cover the front of the body. A smaller set of tails without pom-poms at the end folds over the back of the belt. In addition, women and men from these parts wear about a hundred rattan fiber knee rings above their leg guards, which gives them a look unlike Lisu elsewhere. Their headdress is circular and black, as in Thailand, but festooned with a fringe of fine metallic chain instead of yarn, and it is worn regularly, not just at festivals.

A more simple, Chinese-looking version of this style is worn by "White" Lisu in both Myanmar and Yunnan: it is black or dark blue with several borders around the sleeves and hem and at the point where the tunic crosses the chest to fasten on the right side.

The style of outfit worn by northern Lisu from the Upper Nu Valley couldn't be more different. A hip-length black velvet tunic is worn over a long-sleeved blouse and long flowing skirt made of yards of white homespun hemp or cotton printed cloth with hundreds of tiny blue stripes and pleats. A diagonal sash with white medallions of conch shell crosses the chest, and a delicate headdress of orange and white beads hugs the head. Many strands of orange and white "ancestor" beads complete the outfit that is also accessorized with huge round loop earrings of silver or brass and many bracelets.

Lisu men's outfits are more conservative and vary less from country to country. The traditional black cross-the-chest–style jacket is now usually only seen at feasts and festivals, though, and men have taken to wearing the ubiquitous T-shirt or knit sport shirt with a store-bought jacket when it's cold. In all three countries, however, Lisu men wear still wear wide Chinese-style knee-length pants and leg guards of various colors. In the Nujiang region around Liuku, some men (called Black Lisu) wear long jackets made of homespun hemp, and women wear long vests made of the same material, over dark blue shirts and loose black pants. In Thailand, young men's pants are blue and older men's, black. At New Year, Thai Lisu men wear the traditional jacket but in black velvet and decorated with silver buttons. Unmarried men also wear a set of pom-pomed tails.

Men still usually carry shoulder bags, which show off the Lisu women's weaving and stitch-work. Today in China, this is often their most obvious cultural marker. Many are workbags, simple and unembellished, and have a rattan strap worn across the forehead. The Lisu do not have as fine a tradition of stitchery, embroidery and weaving as the Hmong, Mien, or Karen. Most shoulder bags in Thailand are woven of white or unbleached cotton homespun and have vertical stripes of various colors. In the Nujiang gorge, bags are often bright yellow, with delicately embroidered black and red "ears" attached to the bottom corners. A similar color scheme is found on the finest examples of young men's courting bags, which are beaded and elaborate. A multicolored yarn mane at the bottom and silver dangles at the top characterize such bags.

Children and young people wear the same clothes as adults. Exceptions are caps mothers make for babies and small children. These employ a unique style of triangular folded patchwork with many borders. Entrepreneurial Thai Lisu women have adapted this style in making cushion covers, small purses, and other items they sell in Chiang Mai and at other tourist destinations.

THE HOME/JUNGLE/FIELD CONNECTION

While women (and often children) are in charge of collecting food from the jungle, including animal fodder, men usually harvest building materials growing there. In the case of the Lisu, this almost always means bamboo.

The man is the one who cuts the bamboo and then makes and keeps in repair fences, aqueducts, pigpens, and the like. This work is considered somewhat dangerous, and strength is required to split long bamboo poles and also to "weave" the typical fencing found in Lisu villages. Men are also the chief basket weavers.

Klein Hutheesing reports that Lisu women are not comfortable in the jungle, will not go there alone, and prefer well-worn paths when collecting kindling. The first time a woman carries a new baby through the jungle, she will smear soot on its forehead and pierce a needle through its bonnet to frighten spirits away. The jungle is a place of intense spirit activity and falls under the male's work domain. Men are more at ease there and will camp out while hunting gaur, boar, deer, or smaller game. The crossbow is a key symbol of Lisu manhood, which fits the Lisu's dualistic system whereby male principles of spirit/sky and wild are placed in opposition to female ones of earth and domestication. Even a Lisu ruby miner in Mogok, Burma, proudly displayed his crossbow, stating, "Every Lisu man must have one" while admitting he hadn't shot his in years. Women are not allowed to shoot or kill wild animals, although they slaughter chickens. Snakes must also be killed by men, since they are wild and often spirits in disguise.

Men communicate with spirits, and when doing dangerous work such as felling large trees to open new fields or to use for building materials, they ask for protection. A Lisu man will not balance on a slender scaffolding 30 feet above the ground, wielding a huge ax, without first having communed with the tree spirits. Today there is increased danger: beyond falling, he could be arrested for illegal cutting and be thrown in jail.

Moving to lower altitudes with warmer climates is one reason Lisu men and women began dressing like the majority population. But other cultural markers survive: men still harvest forest materials and weave the household's baskets.

Before clearing or burning a field, the Lisu farmer holds a ceremony to warn animals and ask the territory spirit to prevent accidents. Bowing three times, making outward and downward motions with his joined palms, he delivers this prayer in a staccato fashion before lighting a field prepared for burning:

"Today, in this place, I am going to burn. You, gentle ones, great spirits, announce this to every living thing: ants, crickets, every kind of animal.

*Basket weaving, as shown by this man in Da-goo Sheetza village in Putao Valley,
is a male task. Author photo.*

Today I cannot live without burning. I live in the land of the king, so I have to
pay taxes. And now, if there are animals that can fly, let them fly. If there are
animals that can jump, let them jump. If there are animals that can crawl, let
them crawl. Today I am going to burn, I cannot stop it."

11

Cosmic Views

The day of death is unknown,
Thieves don't carry torches.
   —*Lisu proverb*

All ne-pas are liars.
   —*Lisu Christian saying*

SPIRITUAL AND PHYSICAL WORLDS CONVERGE

I knew I was in trouble with Apa-mo. I saw him in a dream; he was wearing white and had long white hair and a beard and looked very old, very kind. But I had done something wrong, and he was angry.

So the next morning I sacrificed six chickens, three hens, and three roosters in Apa-mo's house and called him. I offered him the chickens and asked for his help in following Lisu customs. I gave him my respect and apologized for offending him, and I also asked him to help the people in the village make their crops.

There is only one Apa-mo for all the Lisu. I think the Chinese Apa-mo is the same one, too. Maybe the same one for all people, I don't know.

Abu is the *mur-mu-pa* (village servitor or priest) of Doi Chang, a mixed Lisu/Akha village in northern Thailand, and the teller of this story. His normal speech is a kind of relaxed chanting, and he looked out from under a silver brush of hair with large almond eyes and laughed easily as I interviewed

In Thailand the ne-pa, or village shaman, is the link between the visible world of men and the invisible world of spirits. Photo: E. Paul Durrenberger.

him. He and the *ne-pa*, or shaman, serve the spiritual/medical needs of the Thai Lisu village, and any man is deemed qualified, as no special gifts or talents are required.

While non-Christian Lisu are usually classed as animists, in fact their religious practices comprise many influences. These are arranged and modified to fit their location, perceptions about how the world works, and what humans should do about it. In the cosmic area, as in most others, the Lisu defy pigeonholing—but *doing* is more central to religious practice than is *believing* anything in particular.

The Lisu mur-mu-pa's job is to take care of the shrine to Apa-mo, the grandfather or guardian spirit. Apa-mo's house is the first permanent structure built after settling in a new site in Thailand and usually among non-Christians in Myanmar. The custom could come from southern Chinese

Lisu, although it is not practiced in China today. Any family that moves to the village subsequently sends a male representative to Apamo's house to announce its arrival and ask for protection. His shrine is sited in a grove of trees on a hillside above the village. It is a simple high shelf containing offering cups for every clan in the village plus four cups for the four directions and is encircled by a large stick-fence enclosure. Two smaller altars are placed behind it, on the upslope of the hill, to the right (less powerful side) for Apamo's helpers and to the left (more powerful side) for the big and small hill spirits. Directly behind, further up the slope, is an altar to the more powerful great area spirit. Behind that, outside the stick compound, is a shrine to the big landowner spirit. This spatial arrangement conforms to the Lisu belief of the relative power of above versus below and left versus right.

In addition to keeping the shrine swept and the offerings fresh, the Thai mur-mu-pa calculates the two worship days of the Lisu Chinese-based lunar month and collects money or offerings from each household on village-wide holy days. He is chosen by Apa-mo through a random toss of coins, cowry shells, or split hollow twigs: in three separate throws the same configuration of one head (open side up) and one tail (open side down) is always reached. It is part of the dualism, or logic of polarities, permeating Lisu life. Such beliefs are found in Chinese Taoism and in many other indigenous religions. In Abu's case, he tried the test several times but always got the head-tail combination while other men present kept getting two heads or two tails. He was reluctant but said that a chosen person may not refuse to serve and that he could not move away from the village without first convening with the men and choosing a new priest in the same manner. Since communal worship of Apa-mo is one of the few village-wide activities, it is a binding force.

In contrast to the mur-mu-pa, the ne-pa is the link between the visible world of men and the invisible world of spirits. The ne-pa's role is more dramatic and requires specialized skills. In Thailand, he is charged with curing medical malaise as well as putting to right misfortune thought to have supernatural causes. He contacts the spirits directly through channeling or possession during séances to determine which, if any, is responsible for the problem. In China, practices and names for healers differ, and most don't enter a trance state.

Ceremonializing is a constant of life, not attended by any particular reverence. Lisu joke about their gods and spirits and tell stories on them not unlike irreverent Christians with their variations on "Jesus walks into a bar . . ." The spirit world is ever-present, and there is no sharp divide between it and the human world—and thus little distinction is made between physical and spiritual problems. The Lisu have an easy, bartering relationship with spirits. They show respect but are not overawed. As anthropologist Durrenberger pointed out, "Lisu have no philosophers, theologians, or full-time religious specialists of any kind. Theirs is a practical religion . . . concerned with the everyday."

While Apa-mo and the mur-mu-pa are fixtures of Lisu village life in Thailand ("No Mur-mu-pa means no village," according to Abu), they might have been graphed onto the Lisu cosmological setup along migration paths. Almost all information about mur-mu-pas and Apa-mo comes from academic investigations of the Lisu in Thailand, where most studies of the Lisu were conducted in the twentieth century.

There was little detailed information available on Lisu spiritual practices in China or Burma before then, although in a mid-1990s visit to Myanmar I met Lisu who recognized Apa-mo in the Tengchong area. Early, non-academic sources on China and Burma tended to bundle the entire subject of animistic religious practice among many tribes as "primitive spirit worship" without detail or analysis. Coupled with the isolation of these two countries in the last half of the twentieth century and the lack of access to remote and off-limits areas where the Lisu live, there is a dearth of information on religious practices.

In China, several groups of Lisu I interviewed on a trip with anthropologist Otome Klein Hutheesing in 1997 to the recently opened Guyong area were unfamiliar with Apa-mo and the mur-mu-pa's role. They did have an "old friend" spirit who seemed to have some commonality with Apa-mo. Their village healer is called a dashipa or sometimes a *ne-gu-pa*, not a ne-pa, and he does not enter a trance state or have spirits "ride" him, as in Thailand. I interviewed several Chinese Lisu dashipas in 2014, who all told me that ne-pas practice "the dark arts." It is possible that communist teachings and biases against superstition and witch doctors maligned the ne-pa's role in Chinese Lisu society or that the role itself changed during migrations. In Thailand, a dashipa, if known at all, is considered a junior, or assistant, ne-pa.

Several old Christian men living in Myanmar around Myitkyina who had migrated from China in the 1920s and 1930s reported to me that Lisu in the

Upper Nu did not worship ancestors, Apa-mo, or I-dama, the big territorial spirit known in Burma and Thailand. Other sources confirm this. These men were conversant with a pantheon of animistic spirits including the creator–sky god Wu-sa and Moo-sin-ee—the biggest spirit of trees and rocks invoked by Lisu in the old days to help defeat enemies.

Thai Lisu and many in Myanmar consider Apa-mo (literally Grandfather, with the honorific mo added) the oldest Lisu ancestor. He figures large in daily life, although he is not senior in the overall pantheon of Lisu spirits. Perhaps Apa-mo originated within southern Chinese Lisu groups that migrated to Thailand and gained importance along the way as a protector because of frequent establishment and abandonment of villages. Or, he could have been borrowed from the Shans in Burma, who also have a village guardian. In Myanmar, Apa-mo's shrine is called My-o-fang, a Chinese name. Southern Chinese Lisu might have suppressed memory of Apa-mo as a result of communist campaigns to repress religion. It seems clear that he didn't originate among Nu Valley Lisu. More study is needed for conclusions to be drawn.

The mur-mu pa is always a man, and women are not allowed in Apa-mo's house. When I asked why, a group of Lisu men in Thailand conferred noisily—from the oldest to the youngest, each contributed to the discussion until consensus was reached and a spokesman explained, "It is not custom. It wouldn't be polite, and women don't want to go there because they learn from the older ones not to. Maybe if they go, they will hear a man praying for sons. A woman wouldn't want to hear about that if she doesn't have any sons, only daughters."

Durrenberger, who studied Lisu religion in Thailand, concluded that the ban on women in Apa-mo's house fits perfectly into dualistic logic—because women would neutralize the power of spirits with their earthboundness. The Lisu divide everything into pairs of opposites. Thus: woman, seven, earth, right, moon, human, and body are placed in opposition to man, nine, sky, left, sun, spirit, and soul, and so on. Depending on whether one wants to balance (neutralize) or increase the power in any given situation, either opposite or like forces are combined. This logic also applies to Lisu curing.

Apa-mo guards the village from bad influences but doesn't rule or own it. He is approachable. Unlike other lineage spirits, he is grandfather to all Lisu and doesn't belong to any clan. He also differs from non-lineage spirits in that he is benign, a member of the family. A bit stern, he is nonetheless held in affection as the upholder of Lisu custom, morals, and etiquette. He reflects how the elder Lisu is supposed to behave: give directives, protect, or punish when someone gets out of line.

Apa-mo's main job is maintaining clan customs in the village. In these duties, he is sometimes helped by two territorial spirits: his brothers Yi-da-ma and Xwa-seu, who he consults as "lawyers" or "assistants." One old Lisu man told me that before, in China, there weren't so many thieves and troubles and that Old Grandfather used to manage without the help of these two.

The morning after a child is born, its father or grandfather visits Apa-mo's house to let him know about the new family member. He offers meat from a freshly killed pig and asks for blessings and for a name for the child. Similar offerings are made at the household shrine. A prayer is said, as the following recorded by Klein Hutheesing:

> This morning we tell you a new child is born. We come to tell you. You who take care of the altar, come receive. You who speak and banish bad spirits, you who can drive away bad things, come eat your fill. Big and small, come receive. You who take care of the altar, give blessing. Let her have blessing in the future. In the future, let our work be good, let us be able to keep pigs. We ask a name from you. Let her have a long life until her hair is white, her eyebrows long. Let her labor be good. I cannot pray more. Tell us a name, come receive.

The name is divined by cowry shells but is a secret and is not used. Instead, Lisu go by birth-order names, First Daughter, Third Son, and so on, as well as nicknames.

Likewise, when a sow or a horse gives birth, Old Grandfather is informed. His blessings are also asked before a long trip, and in the case of crop failure he is consulted about what sacrifices to make. One man, planning his suicide, told Apa-mo and asked his forgiveness beforehand. Any Lisu man who has committed adultery must confess to him and offer sacrifices. Naughty children are told Old Grandfather will be angry with them.

Lisu mur-mu-pas don't receive special rewards or status. But on the first day of the New Year, the people come to his house to play music and dance to say thank you. The servitor has no ostensible political power and has to take care of his fields like everyone else. Claiming reluctance for the office goes with the job; every mur-mu-pa I spoke with felt it was a burden but didn't want to incur Apa-mo's anger by refusing to serve when chosen. A mur-mu-pa in a village near Chiang Rai was recently excused from duty when he landed a job in Taiwan. Each Thai Lisu village has just one servitor, although it might have two or three ne-pas.

In addition to Apa-mo and other spirits, there is a creator sky god called Wu-sa, or Wu-sa-pa, to whom traditional Lisu do not address prayers because he is considered too remote to contact and unpredictable. Having created the world, he lost interest in it, somewhat like the god of Enlightenment-Age deists. Wu-sa, however, does strike out (most often with lightning) like Old Testament Yahweh to punish bad characters. He is also overlord of the dead. Wu-sa writes on each person's palm how long his or her life will be and how it will end. Although Wu-sa is generally considered unapproachable and impossible to bribe, one occasionally hears of "letters" written to him asking for prolongation of life when a sick person hovers near death.

Christians have embraced Wu-sa as their top and only god. They do not bother, in the sense of "doing anything about," other spirits in their traditional pantheon, though they keep track of them as common references.

Klein Hutheesing reports some evidence among Thai Lisu of a god senior to Wu-sa. When an infant sucks on its thumb, mothers in her study village would say "it doesn't matter, Wu-sa-pa-mo put honey on it." Wu-sa-pa-mo gives the Thai Lisu rain and is said in a mythical past to have shown the people, through a message to a dog, where rice grain was planted. At the new rice ceremony today, the dog is given rice first. Even Christians in Burma tell the story, altering it only in that the Lisu found the rice grain in the dog's ear themselves.

Lisu practices present a bewildering number of elements. The world is alive with spirits and imbued with their forces. They hark from many traditions. Showing all spirits respect is considered prudent, and new ones encountered are easily embraced and fit into a capacious pantheon—often, it seems, out of politeness. Spirits' existence is doubted by some, but even skeptical Lisu attend to customary rituals. Individual beliefs vary; it is what you *do* that counts. Lisu custom is to act *as if* spirits exist. "Whether or not we believe it, it is custom," was a response to many of my questions regarding the credulity of those performing ceremonies. A practical result, not what you believe, is the issue. Rituals are perceived by most Lisu to be effective, and there seems to be an overriding feeling that one should do these things to keep up appearances, rather like some people go to church.

Families maintain a household shrine, or tabiya, which is dedicated to the ancestors of the male head of the family. While women might tidy the altar or prepare offerings, the area directly in front of the altar is not for them to sit in or use. In China, where tabiyas exist, they usually hold twelve ancestor cups and are above a sideboard-type structure—in a lower position than in Myanmar or Thailand, where they are set or sometimes hang about four feet above the floor. However, placement of shrines on the upper, or hill, side of the house, opposite the door, was identical in all three countries. The lower position could be explained by the fact that both during the Cultural Revolution and in periods prior to it, the Chinese outlawed religious practice—in 1997 Lisu in Tengchong County told me they had only reinstated tabiyas within the last ten years. Many Chinese Lisu have not revived the practice of having tabiyas in their homes.

In Thailand, the number of cups on the tabiya varies according to clan, with a larger shelf placed to the left for more remote (and powerful) ancestors and a shelf on the right reserved for the parents and grandparents of the household head. In Myanmar, shrines had either three or four ancestor cups. In all three countries, Lisu exhibit an engaged, if matter-of-fact, relationship with spirits.

Occasionally, the spirit of a lonely dead person will call out to a relative. Spirits with squeaky voices, spirits without heads, or short white steamy ones who look like children are seen in the forest by Lisu men. Women seldom report such sightings, but they avoid going to the forest by themselves or lingering there because it is regarded as habitat for men and spirits.

Ba-chu-ma has long fangs, hair matted with lice, and breasts so long she tosses them over her shoulders. In remote areas people sometimes run across and are injured by tigers and furry wild spirits called Kaw Ne. Spiritual causes in the other world are seen by Lisu as effects in this one.

Members of the hemp, buckwheat, and wood clans are often said to be infected by the vampire, witch, and were-animal spirits. These people can't help it; they do not wish to be evil. However, when they take on the evil shapes, they like to eat human flesh and harm others against their own will. Lisu say they received this punishment for not following Lisu custom. Men and women can become witches, vampires, or were-animals; since this is contagious, it runs in families. Such people cannot be killed because the evil spirit will then enter the killer and he will become infected. Most Lisu will not marry into these clans, which have become isolated. People from these lineages are, understandably, more apt to convert to Christianity.

There are so many spirits to consider—especially in Thailand where Lisu have traveled the furthest. They fall into four main groups, outlined by Durrenberger.

Members of the first group are the only offendable ones: those associated with productive forces such as fields, land, paths, trees, water, and political divisions—such as villages, provinces, townships, and mountains. The belief that arguing over fields will bring bad luck to both parties and possibly to other people's fields in the area is based on these spirits' quickness to take offense. This usually leads Lisu to negotiate and settle rather than quarrel over land issues.

The second group is helpful. They are soul-calling spirits, the spirits of the rest house, the bridge, the two tables, the three tables. These spirits are called when one's souls have gone missing. Soul loss is considered a common cause of illness in many cultures and is discussed in the next section.

The third group of spirits consists of people who have died a bad death, such as by gunshot, childbirth, drowning, or accident. These souls don't go to the land of the dead but roam the earth, hungry. People need not offend these spirits for them to strike, so there's nothing to do about them until they do. Then, offerings are made, and they are asked to please go away.

The last group is less powerful: the spirit of malicious gossip, the spirit of calamities, and the sickness essence. They are dealt with in the same way as bad-death spirits.

The Lisu are interested in spirits for practical reasons: they need to know which one is responsible for this or that misfortune and what is required to right the offense. They also seek permission of certain land spirits before opening a new field or planting, and they thank others at harvest time. Their discussions about spirits invariably center on such pragmatic concerns. The typical Lisu attitude is one of wanting to be invisible to spirits, not to annoy them. This is recognized as impossible, however, because spirits, like people, are capricious and take offense even when none is meant.

Buddhist elements have been co-opted by the Lisu, such as the candle spirit, which is worshipped by several, but not all, clans. Other Chinese additions are ancestor worship and propitiating heaven, earth, and kitchen spirits. Worship of Kwan-yin, the Chinese goddess of mercy, is on the rise among Lisu in Thailand and Myanmar. Lahu customs are kept in some Lisu villages, as in building a house for the hill spirit. Lisu with Lahu background, in fact, almost constitute a sub-group, except that most are completely absorbed into Lisu practices. This is in contrast to the Akha, who also live in Lisu villages. Shan Buddhist customs, such as rest house and bridge building for spirits, are popular among groups in many locales.

The success of all enterprise depends on the Lisu being on good terms with ancestors and other spirits—well-being in this life is connected to contributions made to the well-being of ancestors. To ensure this and to overcome sickness, one makes appropriate offerings and follows Lisu custom. What is appropriate varies from family to family. If an ancestor was an opium smoker (rare but not unknown), the mother of the house offers the first bit of opium processed to him or her; she also has the knack of choosing the right pig or chicken to sacrifice. The man typically exaggerates the size or value of the offering and generally becomes expansive in his requests for supernatural aid. Thus, if he is clearing a field, he will ask not just for success in this venture but also for freedom from accidents and sickness for his family, the acquisition of silver and gold, and a bountiful harvest.

Especially around the New Year, the mur-mu-pa or ne-pa will prescribe special ceremonies to find out if someone should construct a new house, bridge, or bench, for example. Healing ceremonies are held as needed throughout the year.

With so much communication with spirits interwoven into daily life, it is notable that Lisu are not preoccupied with an afterlife. They don't perceive a sharp break between this life and the next because spirits are quite similar to people. They have emotions and shortcomings. Spirit bureaucrats must be bribed, and spirits sometimes lie; they must eat, and they participate in markets.

CALENDAR OF THE THAI LISU YEAR

(not all celebrated in all countries)

- *Ku-shey*, the New Year, sometimes called the Female New Year, falls on Chinese New Year and is the most important Lisu holiday and religious celebration. It is the time both to thank Apa-mo and other spirits for the harvest and to show off wealth in the form of silver in costumes and jewelry. Dancing, drinking, and visiting go on for days. Sometimes villages celebrate on a series of different days. This lengthens the holiday, allowing Lisu from neighboring villages and further afield to attend each other's celebrations. Held in January or February after the important harvests, it is the most auspicious time for courting, when young men attempt to see as many girls dressed in their New Year's finery as possible (see Chapter 9, Book I). A wave of engagements takes place each year after this Lisu event. Children who have the left the village as a result of marriage or other reasons always try to come back to their father's house to celebrate New Year.

- *Eu-yi-pa*, the Second (Male) New Year, is held thirty-eight days after the first and is possibly a Chinese carryover.
- *Mwa-ha-tdu-vu* is five months and five days after the New Year. It is the time to ask Apa-mo for good luck and for families to leave a woven "boat" or tray with old things, clothes, and other items associated with sickness on a path outside the village. This sends away the old and the bad and invites in the new and auspicious.
- *She-ha-chu-pak-ew-a*, or the Small New Year, is celebrated seven months after the New Year. It is also called the New Corn Festival. The Lisu say thank you to Apa-mo for looking after crops. A typical offering would be cooked ribs, two ears of corn, and two cucumbers. After the ceremony at Apa-mo's house, a ceremony is held at the household shrine as well. Plants and flowers are arranged there, and offerings of cucumber and pumpkin are made. This is the time when the entire village leaves a large "boat" filled with old things outside the village boundary. Each household makes a little "boat," which is put into the big one. (Individual "boats," in fact, are placed along paths outside the village after sickness or whenever people want to rid themselves of bad luck.) Those children or others who left the village to live somewhere else and didn't make it back at New Year always try to come back for the Small New Year.
- Ten months after New Year, the Lisu call Apa-mo to ask him to take care of crops and provide a good yield. In Thailand, one male pig and five chickens (two male and three female) are typical of village offerings.
- At least once a year, usually when the main crop is planted, Lisu make offerings to the forest guardian spirit of beeswax, tea, tobacco, rice, and sa paper flowers and umbrellas. These last two offering items are usually associated with Buddhism. Buddha's spirit is a "foreigner" compared to Apa-mo, who is family.

LISU CURING AND DEALING WITH SPIRITS ON A DAILY BASIS

The night is broken by a howl; the Lisu shaman is calling his spirits. The spirit comes down to "ride his horse" and shouts "people, why have you called me?" The words come from the shaman, but not in his usual voice. Facing the family altar of a simple dirt-floor house, bent over at the waist, he appears to be bobbing slowly up and down, chanting, palms pulled together in front of him holding a bundle of burning incense sticks in the dim light. He is in a trance, possessed by a senior lineage spirit who has been called to the séance. A man, one of several men and women gathered around the house, answers the spirit: "We have a problem and need your help."

Actually, they have more than one problem. The Lisu man in the scene above described by Durrenberger tells of them in no particular order. A pig has gone missing, a woman is sick, someone's son is acting crazy and doesn't want to take care of his fields.

The shaman, speaking in a sing-song, rhythmic voice, using language people have to strain to understand because it includes archaic and unknown terms, remains in the trance for about thirty-five minutes as four different spirits come down to "ride" him. Each identifies itself and advises the people on how to right their misfortunes. Some advice is contradictory, as the spirits appear to confer with each other and to call down successively more senior ones to offer solutions. Finally, the shaman says through the last spirit possessing him that "my horse is tired now, I will go back." This is the signal for two young men to stand up and catch the shaman as he falls backward out of the trance, insensate for a few moments before he gathers his wits and sits down quietly to drink tea.

Attendees draw around the fire to discuss what they have learned. The shaman doesn't participate; his part is over—and in any case he doesn't remember what happened. The woman who has fallen sick is being attacked by a bad-death spirit, the soul of a person who did not go to the land of the dead because of the violent manner in which he died. The remedy is to offer the spirit something and send it away. In this case, the woman's husband must offer a pig the next day, and plans for a feast are made. The runaway pig, however, will come back tomorrow if its owner makes amends to the spirit of the stream whom he inadvertently offended. A chicken is sacrificed that evening at a makeshift altar, and the man apologizes. The case of the son isn't so clear; one spirit said he is being called to be a shaman, another said he is simply crazy.

The Lisu shaman calls his spirits in northern Thailand, early 1970s.
Photo: E. Paul Durrenberger.

In day-to-day lives of the Lisu, religion's main function is to help solve problems without obvious solutions. Not much distinction is drawn between illness and other problems. The first strategy is to try to find out if there is a natural cause behind the misfortune—such as an "eating mistake" or a broken bone—or a supernatural one. Spirits are considered supernatural, an invisible force like electricity, whose effects are nonetheless real and ultimately also "natural." In the case of illness, symptoms will be the same whatever the cause, so Lisu employ herbal medicines, patent medicines, and other means available to bring about a cure. If natural medicines don't work, it begins to be assumed that the cause could be supernatural. Only when a specific therapy is demonstrated to be effective can a diagnosis be stated with certainty.

While there are few village-wide holidays or other communal religious activities, a day seldom passes without some sort of curing or séance such as the one described above. These vary from soul calling and stick and leaf soul-bridge ceremonies to more elaborate ones that involve large bridges or rest houses and small or village-wide feasts. Holding a feast is a political as well as a religious act—it shows you are as good as anyone else, fulfills reciprocal obligations, and builds myi-do (repute.)

In the Lisu universe, men have nine souls and women, seven. This belief is integrated into daily lives in which productive forces, spatial concepts, nature, people, and things are always coupled as negative and positive polarities. Above is to below, as heaven is to earth, as strong is to weak, as man is to woman, and so on. A main cause of illness is that one or more souls have strayed, causing the person to be sick and to feel out of balance. This system is shared by many groups, not just Lisu. The soul might have left on its own accord because of dissatisfaction with the human condition, or an offended spirit might have captured it. A person weakened by soul absence becomes vulnerable to further attack from natural or supernatural forces, akin to a weakened immune system. The wandering soul could offend a spirit while it is away, so every attempt is made to call the missing soul back and to bind it to the body to make it whole again.

In addition to soul loss, a person may be made sick by a spirit he or she has offended, or, as in the case of the woman mentioned above, one can be sickened by a spirit who simply wants to extort a bribe in exchange for going away. Spirits bite, intrude objects, or in the case of some, such as the witch spirit, invade bodies to make people ill. Serious illnesses often have multiple causes.

The bad-death spirit is another known to attack without provocation, as is the spirit of malicious gossip. This spirit, having heard bad talk about someone from many people, will cause misfortune to the maligned one or his household.

A group of old Christian Lisu in Burma who migrated from the Upper Nu Valley recalled spirits from their childhood: in addition to Moo-sin-ee, who is easily angered and known to be capricious, Ju-go-ne, the spirit of the road, can cause people to get lost. Di-ne and Ne-khu, two lesser spirits, were known as biters. He-kwa-ne, in contrast, is a benign house spirit who doesn't require offerings.

In the Lisu world, it is men, not women, who concern themselves with spirit communication (man is to spirit as woman is to earth in Lisu cosmology) and who act as go-betweens. Klein Hutheesing observed, however, that even though Thai Lisu women profess not to know about spirits, they are always doing something about them. She describes women as nurturers of these forces, as it is the woman who prepares food or sacrifices to be made to them. She knows which spirits demand live animals and which cooked animals, as well as what to place on the offering tray: raw or cooked rice, water or liquor, tobacco, tea, joss sticks, or a bit of boiled chicken or pork. She knows when to appeal to which spirit. However, when questioned more closely about this or that one's qualities, is it male or female, what does it look like, and so on, a woman's typical reply is, "How should I know? I've never seen it."

But when it comes to soul absence Lisu woman often know what to do, especially in day-to-day cases thought not to involve spirits and when children are affected. Although women don't conduct large ceremonies and do not visit the village shrine for fear of neutralizing its power, it is not uncommon to see a woman, holding a rolled-up turban in one hand on which she balances a boiled egg, moving about the household area, pleading with a missing one: "Oh, soul of Ami-zah, please come back." This is the woman's specialty, and when a child has been frightened or bitten by a dog or is sick, it is usually Mother, in her domestic realm, who does something about it.

Since soul absence is either the main cause of, or else accompanies, so many supernaturally caused diseases, Lisu have a collection of ceremonies to call the soul back. Durrenberger describes the experience of soul loss: "You wake up in the morning and all you can see is pig shit. You don't want to go to work, you had bad dreams in the night and have no appetite—so you suspect one of your souls is missing." If it seems like a serious case, the first remedy is to hold a soul-calling ceremony, in which family and other clansmen and friends gather. Each takes a turn at calling the missing soul.

According to Durrenberger, "One person could make an elaborate speech or poem, going on for some time: 'look at your fertile fields, waiting for you to work their rich black soil, look at your beautiful children and your wife, they miss you, see all your pigs, see your green fields, listen to us call, and return, soul of *Alei-pa*.' He then ties a small string around the affected person's wrist if the sufferer is younger, or neck if he is older. The next guy up might simply say, 'We love you, we miss you, come back.' Either way, by the end of the ceremony, most people begin to feel better," Durrenberger explains, adding, "wouldn't you?"

If the ceremony doesn't yield a cure, they try something else. A shaman is consulted, and a second, third, or, as the situation dictates, a fourth or fifth opinion is elicited from lineage spirits regarding the cause of illness. Spirits, like humans, are often mistaken and can and do lie. They might consult a shaman from another village, the way Western people bring in a specialist, if the family member isn't responding. The thighbones and livers of chickens and pigs sacrificed to bring about cures are examined to yield oracular signs. Many men, not only shamans, can interpret such evidence. If symptoms persist, they try other medicine or perhaps get a shot if the injection doctor from the lowlands happens through the village.

It's not so different from trying aspirin, then Tylenol, a chiropractor, and maybe meditation or biofeedback to get rid of a nagging pain.

A larger soul-calling ceremony, which could mean building a bamboo or wood bridge and invoking its spirit to accept an offering of a chicken or pig in exchange for the missing soul, might be performed. The symptoms and illness are drawn over the bridge and removed from the village. From inside to outside (the illness leaving the village) and from outside to inside (the soul returning to the body), the Lisu always deal with polarities, or sets of opposites, which their therapies attempt to manipulate and balance. As a last resort, they will take the person to a hospital in the nearest city. If the person is cured there, the Lisu will know the illness must have had a natural, not a supernatural, cause.

Lisu also conduct ceremonies to counter poor crops, insect infestation, lost pigs, or adultery. Everything is interconnected, underlying causes can only be natural or supernatural, and the basic principle of working with polarities is applied if a supernatural cause is suspected. Lisu negotiate to settle scores with spirits as they do with humans. Christians in Burma report prayer

A bridge is built so that symptoms or illness may be drawn over it and away from a village in northern Thailand. Photo: E. Paul Durrenberger, 1970s.

ceremonies to be effective in stopping locusts from eating their crops—the two systems aren't as far apart as they might seem.

The ne-pa, ne-gu-pa, or dashipa, who like the mur-mu-pa is chosen by the spirits, is also normally reluctant to take up this role in all countries where Lisu live. According to Durrenberger, who surveyed the people in his study village, not one person wanted his son to become a ne-pa. Although the ne-pa collects small sums or gifts for his work, they are not thought to compensate him for all the effort and time it takes away from his fields.

In Thailand, the first sign that spirits have chosen a man to be a ne-pa is that he begins to exhibit abnormal behavior—having fits, not working, wanting to put his hand in the fire, or bashing his head against trees are examples. The following description of how one becomes a ne-pa is condensed from a monograph Durrenberger wrote on Lisu religion:

> The man must have lineage spirits to become a ne-pa, since these are the spirits who take care of the shaman. Some Lisu have no such spirits because the great-grandfather of the present generation was not Lisu. In such cases, Lisu will determine [if] a man behaving bizarrely is simply mad.
>
> But if he has lineage spirits, if his odd behavior continues over several months, and if he sickens when he eats foods forbidden to shamans such as onions and garlic, it begins to be assumed that the man has been chosen. Séances are held to confirm it, and the news spreads to older shamans who come to initiate and train the neophyte. He is taken into the jungle, and the older shamans drive off bad spirits and hold a special ceremony with beeswax candles, crushed beans, and bamboo cups, to induct him. The new shaman's lineage spirits take turns "riding" him, but spirits of other lineages are prohibited, although, typically, they will want to try. Following the initiation, the new shaman seeks further training from a senior shaman of his own lineage. During such sessions, in which both senior shaman and neophyte are possessed, the Lisu say, "the spirits of the senior shaman instruct those of the junior one."
>
> If other villagers are present at such sessions, the spirits will repeatedly ask them if the neophyte's behavior is appropriate and if he is speaking intelligibly. A shaman may not just utter gibberish. Beyond giving up certain foods, the shaman must observe other restraints: he cannot drink much liquor, smoke opium, kill monkeys or other animals, depending on his lineage. If he indulges in proscribed behaviors, his spirits will thrash him.
>
> One spirit always stays with the ne-pa, gives him power, and guides him in doing service for the people. The Lisu say this spirit is analogous to a person who tends horses. The shaman belongs to his spirits in the way a horse belongs to its owner. Besides all the ceremonies, diagnostic, and curative skills

such as handling coals and blowing water and oil into fire, he must learn techniques to chase away bad spirits. His job is dangerous, he gains little status or wealth from it, and because of all the spirits he may anger along the way, "it's easy to die" for the man fulfilling this role, one shaman told Durrenberger.

-----------------■-■-----------------

Other village specialists, such as medicine women and incantation men, take care of other problems. In the case of medicine women, the knowledge of herbal medicine is passed from mother to daughter. Only after the mother dies will the daughter install the medicine spirit in her house and begin practicing her healing art. There were five women recognized as healers, called *ne-mas,* in Klein Hutheesing's village. They call ancestor and household spirits as needed. In other villages and in Burma, these women are sometimes *ne-chi-ma jua-ma.* Incantation masters learn healing prayers from other masters and invite the Incantation Spirit to come live in their houses. In China, there are men called *dashipas,* who are like junior ne-pas, as well as medicine women.

When ne-pas and medicine women, injection doctors, and lowland hospitals are unable to cure the patient and the person lies dying or has just died, there is a custom to follow: with prayers and other encouragement, family members urge his or her souls to leave quickly and not to linger on earth. Klein Hutheesing describes a recent death of a young woman with AIDS, in which her father asked her to let go of life and not worry about her family. He stated down to the baht how much money they had in the bank to take care of themselves. "And that's thanks to you," he said, patting the former sex worker's hand as he gently coaxed her into the next world.

The Lisu prayer for the dead is sung to urge souls to join the rest of the dead and not hang around among the living: "Today you have died. The sky takes your strength, the earth takes your bones. To die is your Grandfather's custom, you must follow this custom. Wu-sa made you die, the time is right. Wu-sa makes the sky take your strength, he makes the earth take your bones. Your Grandfather and Great-grandfather also died like this, so you must also go there. Do not be lonely for this life—go straight to the land of the dead." The song continues for several verses, describing the path to the land of the dead and cautioning the person not to stray from it.

The Burmese Christian Lisu David Ngwa-za Fish, who grew up in the Wa State and collects traditional Lisu songs and proverbs, told me of a soul-sending song that was effective but so powerful that many singers were afraid to perform it. The singer's souls accompany those of the deceased's to the land of the dead, where they are left—and then the singer has to sing his own souls back to this world. Making a mistake means his souls could be lost. He says Lisu call it "The Song That Break's Open Hell's Gates."

————————— ■-■ —————————

The day of death is unknown,
Thieves don't carry torches.
   —*Lisu proverb*

For life's major passage, from life to death, Lisu funeral rites vary depending on how the person died. If a child dies, no special ceremonies are held, and its grave is not marked since children's souls have not been completely formed. If the person died young or had a bad death such as by gunshot or in childbirth, the body is cremated rather than buried. But the Lisu usually bury their dead after the corpse has laid in state for three days. Family members place seven or nine pieces of unbroken husked rice and seven or nine pieces of silver (depending on whether the deceased is a man or a woman) in the dying person's mouth or in the casket to ease his or her way to the land of the dead.

In Thailand, after the body has laid in state in a casket to the right (west) of the family altar if it is a woman and to the left (east) if it is a man, prayers are said, and a wake is held at which the men gamble, play a checkers-type game, and perhaps drink, they say, "to forget." The coffin of a female is carried out to the right through a hole broken in the bamboo wall and that of a man through a hole made to the left, when it is removed for burial.

Lineages have different rites and practices, but the idea is always that when someone dies, he or she becomes a spirit. "The sky (more powerful) takes your breath, the earth (less powerful) takes your bones," is repeatedly stated, and the person is encouraged to join the ancestors and continue increasing the clan's *do* (power) by looking after all earthly descendants. In return, the living promise to remember the dead person with prayers and to feed him or her with offerings.

A guardian spirit attends the grave, which is located in the forest, not in a burial ground shared with others. To determine if the spot is appropriate,

*A guardian spirit attends a forest grave, in this case a burial mound that
will disappear within a few years, 1970s. Photo: E. Paul Durrenberger.*

an egg is tossed, and if it breaks, the place is acceptable. A flimsy twig fence
is built around the burial mound, which the family attends for ceremonies
at the anniversary of the death for the following one to three years. By that
time, the low mound becomes overgrown and, along with the twig fence, is

reclaimed by the forest. The person finds a home again on the family altar when his or her male grandchild becomes a head of household.

In China, some village leaders were buried in Chinese-style monuments but with Lisu clan decorations on them. These monuments are set in burial grounds above the village in a site similar to that of Apa-mo's house in Thailand. While this practice was reserved for a few Lisu, the newest such monuments I saw were more than fifty years old. Most people today are buried randomly in the forest.

Impact of Christianity . . . Just One More Influence?

In China and proportionately more in Burma, Lisu have converted to Christianity in large numbers. While definitive statistics do not exist, scholars and missionaries agree that of Myanmar's roughly 400,000 Lisu, 75 percent to 80 percent are Christians. Most of these Lisu come from around the Nujiang gorge in Yunnan, China, and entered Burma within a few years of the Chinese Communist revolution in 1949 or are the descendants of those Lisu.

Christian missionaries, both Protestant and Catholic, began working in China during the nineteenth century. However, it wasn't until the 1920s that Lisu began converting in large numbers. Thousands of Lisu took up the evangelical Protestant style of Christianity offered by missionaries, and today perhaps half or more of China's 700,000 Lisu are Christians; this proportion is on the rise but impossible to measure accurately. Christianity continues to grow in both countries, although foreign missionaries were expelled from China after the revolution and from Burma in 1965, when the military strongman Ne Win began the "Burmese way to socialism."

Lisu in Thailand, roughly 50,000, are the least receptive to the Christian message and are more likely to convert to Buddhism or to integrate Buddhist aspects into their animistic practices. This is the case despite a long tolerance of foreign missionaries there.

In Thailand only a few thousand Lisu had converted to Christianity by 1985, and numbers there remain low today. Lisu skepticism in this overwhelmingly Buddhist country, where there is little economic or social incentive to become Christian, might have been fed by rivalry among many competing Christian missionaries and groups. The Morse family moved to the Thai Kingdom in the early 1970s after working in northern Burma's Putao region since 1949, when their six-year exodus to the territorially uncertain Hidden Valley ended in deportation.

Third-generation missionary Tommy Morse told me in 2014 that the Lisu church founded by his family has become the "go-to" place to drop off Lisu drug addicts and alcoholics, as they've had success curing them. Ill Lisu, including HIV-positive sex workers and others, often take refuge in the church. Morse, a fluent Lisu speaker, told me that many missionaries who come to Thailand today preach mostly in urban areas and do not attempt to learn Lisu or other minority languages. He singled out a group from Korea, which he said resorts to giving away motorbikes and other bribes to poach converts from rival churches. "After they crash their motorcycles, get in trouble with drugs, or begin missing their Lisu culture, many return to us and we take them back," he told me. He echoed Lisu in China and Burma who claim Christians are the main preservers of Lisu culture against the forces of assimilation—because groups such as his conduct services in Lisu, encourage Lisu to live in discrete villages or enclaves, and teach Lisu children to read and write in their own language.

Why and under what circumstances do Lisu convert or resist conversion to Christianity? There are numerous underlying Lisu affinities with the evangelical tradition followed by most Lisu. In addition to both groups' love of singing, Durrenberger noted something Calvinistic or puritanical about the Lisu. According to him, the first sign of depression or insanity in a Lisu individual is when he or she doesn't want to work. The Lisu habit of pairing opposites could be compared to the evangelical Christian preoccupation with the ongoing battle between good and evil; however, Lisu are more concerned with balance than with one side winning.

My own research and interviews confirmed that Lisu culture and even its spirits could be considered rather straight-laced. Unlike other groups with whom they are often compared, such as the Akha, Lahu, or Mien, most Lisu hold virginity before marriage in high esteem, and adultery is considered a crime. Although premarital sex has become more tolerated today, monogamy after marriage is still the norm. The elaborate system of sex avoidance in relationships is breaking down in some places, however.

Lisu spirits frown on men and women having sex in a rice field or other agricultural setting or even the forest. For this reason, a child born out of wedlock is referred to as a "forest child." When visiting a Lisu family over the New Year with my husband and young daughter in the 1990s, I was taken aside and discretely requested by our hostess not to engage in sexual activity in her house because it might offend Lisu spirits. Ceremonies to appease spirits offended by sexual misbehavior are not uncommon, however. Lisu don't always live up to their ideals.

These few examples are given to suggest that there are behavioral aspects and beliefs within Christianity, particularly the evangelical style, that resonate with traditional Lisu culture. Perhaps most significant, they share a philosophical egalitarianism. Lisu Christians in all three countries asserted to me that "we are all equal before God," often citing women's equality as an example. Eugene Morse identified another thing he said Lisu have in common with Christians: they've never worshipped idols. A last affinity worth mentioning is that the Lisu migrating spirit is in step with the American pioneer tradition and down-to-earth evangelical Christianity promulgated by missionaries who have dominated this region.

Christian Lisu speak the same language, dress the same, eat the same food, and use the same farming techniques as animist Lisu living nearby. They share an oral tradition of proverbs, stories, and songs. Yet they have made profound changes. Christians produce and drink far less alcohol than other Lisu and raise pigs for market instead of for reciprocal feasting. These adjustments have crucial economic implications. However, the tradition of sharing food remains strong among Christians. As for the complex pantheon of spirits that formerly concerned him, a Lisu Christian pastor in northern Thailand told me, "I know they are still there, but I don't talk to them, fear them, or bother about them anymore. I don't *do* anything about them now." Lisu Christians in all three countries expressed this sentiment to me in 2014 as well.

A group of Christian elders I interviewed in a village near Myitkyina, in northern Burma in the late 1990s, revealed a comfortable familiarity with spirits. Sitting in a stilt house with woven bamboo walls and split bamboo floors, these second- and third-generation Christians, some of them preachers, had clearly not lost touch with former beliefs. "The ne-pa (shaman) works very scientifically, very precisely, to find out exactly which spirit is offended and what it will take to appease him," a man named Julius commented as he described a complicated elimination process to identify which spirit is causing trouble.

Christians sing from hymnals in Myanmar, 1997. A similarity that resonates between the Lisu and the evangelical style of Christianity that most practice is a spirit of egalitarianism. Author photo.

"We have a saying: all ne-pas are liars," another, called Andrew, added. He expanded on this, explaining that the lying concerned the spirits' demands (but not their existence). "Maybe the ne-pa hasn't eaten pork for a week. Even if the offended spirit would be satisfied with an egg or a chicken, the ne-pa might say he wants a pig because then he can fill his belly better."

A general nodding of gray heads concurred: yes, ne-pas are known to lie about such things.

How is it then, I asked, that Christian Lisu can escape the wrath of easily offended residents of the ethereal world—whose existence they don't doubt—such as weretigers, vampires, and powerful landowner spirits, as well as lesser minions such as the bad-talk spirit or the spirit of the bitter-fleshed porcupine burrow?

I posed this question in every country, and the Lisu Christians' answer was always the same as that of the elders in Burma and likely learned from the missionaries who converted them: "Once we dedicate (or give) our lives to Christ, we no longer have to fear the sprits. They leave us alone because the spirit we worship, Wu-sa (God, formerly understood as the Lisu sky god and creator), is more powerful."

Because most research and writing on the Lisu has been academic and focuses on animistic Lisu, a sort of black hole exists around the culture of Christian Lisu. With notable exceptions, missionaries who know them well haven't written much either because documenting Lisu culture has not been their chief concern.

Anthropologists and missionaries have tended to be like oil and water; subsequently, little cultural sharing takes place between them. Anthropologists often consider missionaries destroyers of culture and Christian Lisu as somehow irrelevant (or "pathetic," as one commented to me after attending a Lisu Christian singing service). Missionaries keep busy with their own development activities, biases, and belief that anthropologists are self-serving. Such polarization has softened somewhat today, and there is a burgeoning literature on the continuities between converts and non-converts, exemplified by Deborah E. Tooker's work on the Akha. However, this doesn't change the fact that the default positions of the two groups for most of twentieth century could be described as mutual contempt.

While perhaps overly simplistic, anthropologists come to observe and analyze; missionaries are there to teach and help and change. Neither goal is intrinsically superior, but they do conflict. In addition to the philosophical divide, a class distinction illuminates their long-standing antipathy: anthropologists are intellectuals who consider the Bible college educations of most missionaries second-rate. This belief isn't universally true, and I have met anthropologists who admire the stick-to-it-iveness, linguistic skills, and cultural observations of missionaries, who spend years living in harsh conditions compared to the relatively short-term field study of most anthropologists. Missionaries today seldom exhibit the cultural insensitivity common to former generations, but they do have that reputation and history to live with.

While it's impossible to judge motives or missionary and anthropologist behavior generally or historically, I will add a few personal observations about the Lisu—as a non-Christian, non-missionary, non-anthropologist. The issue of changing religions and absorbing outside influences needs to be commented on in any investigation of a migrating minority such as the Lisu.

My research preparatory to this book consisted mainly of reading academic and non-academic sources and talking to anthropologists concerned with traditional Lisu culture. Generally, this material concerned Thai Lisu, by far the most studied. One exception was information I gathered from the multi-generational Morse family, who have been active in all three countries since the 1920s.

I initially focused on non-Christian Lisu in Thailand and China. My rationale was that in Burma I'd meet plenty of Christians, so I deferred study of them until I had a firmer knowledge base for comparison with traditional culture.

The biggest surprise of this project was how similar Christian (mainly in Burma) and non-Christian Lisu (in every country) are in their basic outlook. They are clearly the same people.

Having begun in Thailand, at the end of the Lisu migration trail, what impressed me was how much Lisu have borrowed from other religions and cultures without losing identity. They are considered a dominant culture despite being so few in number—dominant in this context refers to the universally noted fact that any outsider, man or woman, who marries a Lisu generally becomes Lisu rather than the other way around.

From ancestor worship, to clan rituals, to prayers that contain Buddhist elements such as the candle spirit, much of Lisu religious practice in Thailand has non-Lisu origins. Even Apa-mo, the grandfather village guardian considered the Lisu's oldest ancestor in Thailand, is unknown by Lisu I questioned in China, unless the "Old Friend" spirit propitiated there is related. Also, the placement of Apa-mo's shrine in Thailand (east-facing slope above and outside the village) corresponds with the placement of prominent gravesites and grave monuments in China. Could Apa-mo as propitiated in Thailand be an idea transferred from the site of buried ancestors in China? Or, perhaps memory of him was erased as an effect of Mao Zedong's campaigns against religion as one of the "four olds?" We don't know, but we do know that the Lisu have borrowed beliefs and practices in their migrations.

It did make me wonder why Christianity is viewed so differently from other borrowed religions and influences—including education and acquiring written language. All of these forces integrate minorities into the dominant culture and move them toward modernity. Seen through the lens of nostalgia, they may be viewed negatively. Yet since culture is always dynamic, a key question is how important the element of religion is in the overall shifting mosaic. If I pose this question and try to answer it in Lisu terms, I end up thinking something like "culture is bigger than religion."

Successful missionaries become absorbed in Lisu culture themselves. After living with Lisu, they develop or begin to articulate a belief in spirits that might shock the brethren back home. Several members of the Morse family confirm this: comments like "oh, the place was swarming with Shan spirits" or "don't think for a minute that spirits aren't real" popped up in casual conversations with them, and they have an impressive inventory of stories involving weretigers, familiar spirits, and other supernatural characters.

Bobby Morse (son of missionary/linguist Robert Morse), who accompanied me to Myanmar in 1997, said, "Missionaries who deny the reality and vibrancy of the spirit world don't have any business with Lisu, they have no common ground to meet. The Lisu think anyone who doesn't realize how alive everything is with the forces we call spirits must have impaired senses and live in a dead and boring world."

Who has converted whom?

Different holidays, altered behavior, and changes in professed belief are called for by Christian Lisu. But Christianity itself, as with all newer religions, overlays what came before it, including Judaism and Roman and Greek practices. The Lisu bring much that is their own to Christianity, as they do to Buddhism, Marxism, and free-market capitalism.

I noticed that Lisu Christians, for example, pray in a formal way more often than most of their Western counterparts. In fact, in every situation that called for a ceremony or sacrifice in the old religion, such as field clearing, tree felling, naming, beginning a significant journey, or in times of sickness, the Christian Lisu now says a prayer. "We pray before we have a cup of coffee," one old Christian Lisu man in Myitkyina quipped.

But instead of praying to a number of lesser land, ancestor, candle, or healing spirits, Lisu Christians now addresses all entreaties directly to Wu-sa, who in their former pantheon was considered remote and unapproachable. He was so remote a "clockmaker," in fact, that many traditional Lisu in China and Burma have forgotten about Wu-sa altogether—and now consider him a Christian god.

"Oh, the Lisu aren't stupid," Helen Morse commented to me about their deeply practical attitudes. "They don't stop appeasing their own spirits until they are convinced that Christianity offers them a better deal."

Many pre-conversion cultural practices persist: although the poorest Christians (particularly those in Myanmar) have abandoned the practice, most Lisu still pay bride price. Or (unlike the common Western practice), the "bride-taking" side at least pays to feast both families. Sometimes called a "gift" instead of bride wealth, the practice is very much alive in all three countries today and expresses the relatively higher status of Lisu women compared with cultures where dowry is the norm.

Agricultural techniques, child rearing, folk wisdom, folk medicine, proverbs, and a basic way of seeing the world continue pretty much unchanged after conversion to Christianity. In a practical sense, raising pigs for market instead of for rituals and reciprocal feasting, along with giving up alcohol, are probably the most impactful changes.

But though traditional and Christian Lisu sometimes share villages and even work together (as they do in Myanmar today in cultural preservation), there is a noticeable divide. There's more than a little competition, and they seem to enjoy misunderstanding each other. Both qualities—competitiveness and a certain skewed sense of humor—are signature Lisu characteristics.

"Christians are stingy. They don't *do* anything for their spirits, no sacrifices. Just prayers," a Lisu woman in northern Thailand remarked to me. "They close their eyes and look *down* before they eat instead of looking up toward where Wu-sa (the sky god) lives," another commented, as if the practice indicated daftness.

Abeno Leeja, a former Lisu headman of Doi Chang, echoed the common opinion to me that "Christians are just lazy. They don't want to go to the trouble of making sacrifices when they are ill or when they have offended Grandfather Spirit or one of their ancestors." The general feeling is that Christians have decreased their repute, myi-do, by giving up the old ways—and that they converted for material advantage because they weren't "making it" in their own society. In India and China, they might be called rice Christians. Yet while true that poor Lisu and those in so-called cursed clans convert to increase access to resources, if there is a pattern of conversion, it seems to run more along family than economic lines.

Christian Lisu have their own reasons for feeling superior to those who keep the old ways. There are many second- and even third-generation Christians in all three countries who retain strong cultural identity and who have enjoyed the benefits of conversion, including improved healthcare, education, and agricultural practices—in addition to spiritual instruction. Political and spiritual leaders have emerged, and they have become more organized than traditional Lisu—particularly in Myanmar, where this could be attributed to social and political adaptations necessary to survive brutal regimes. In both Myanmar and China today, Christian Lisu appear relatively prosperous compared to most animists, but again, this could be an effect of living in countries where they have citizenship and other rights, rather than of Christianity.

It cannot be ignored that Christian Lisu are likely to stay in school longer, to even attend college or university, and to assimilate economically into majority cultures more than animists. But hill tribe people, Christian or otherwise, are looked down upon by both lowland farmers and city people, particularly in Thailand. Those moving to urban areas often join an underclass living in poor sections of the northern Thai cities Chiang Mai and Chiang Rai. It isn't surprising that many people wish to blend in, deny ethnic heritage, and try to reap benefits available to majorities. This strategy has long been observed of minorities, from American Indians who blended into Mexican populations in the West, to assimilated Jews, to mixed-raced blacks who pass as white.

Missionaries have set up hostels where children as young as five or six stay in town while attending school for several years. They usually return to the village on longer holidays or over the summer. While some, such as the Hill Tribe Children's Hostel in Chiang Mai, accept children from all tribes and insist that they do not require children to convert, some pressure in that direction is understood as the quid pro quo for education. Allegations of sexual and other abuse have tainted a few such schools.

In the final analysis and regardless of how outsiders judge them, Lisu Christians claim Lisu cultural identity. "How can anyone say we aren't *real* Lisu?" a young man in Mogok, Myanmar, asked me. Dressed in the Wa State Lisu costume, which is black, to teach Sunday school, he rummaged through a clothes chest until he triumphantly pulled out a pair of traditional Lisu hemp sandals. These, he conceded, have become very rare indeed. He saves them for church.

At a crudely built chapel in northern Myanmar, listening to a Lisu hymn enthusiastically rising from the impoverished congregation at Wednesday evening services, I felt little inclination to judge or doubt these people's sincerity, Christianity, or Lisuness. Traditionally clad Lisu women, rag-tag gaggles of children, and a few tired-looking men had gathered after a hard day's work in the fields. Taking part in this favorite Lisu pastime of singing, they reaffirmed both their religion and their culture as they let the daily grind slip away and lost themselves singing a rousing hymn in four-part harmony.

12

Economy

If you want to live, if you want to eat,
Have a spade and a knife by your side . . . otherwise, you won't last long.

—*Lisu proverb*

To glimpse the Lisu economic worldview, imagine standing in a semi-forested, steeply graded, rocky field surrounded by steep mountains. Ask the basic questions: What to eat? How to coax crops from this extreme environment? What about shelter? Just as important: What ceremonies are necessary to ensure resident spirits will help, not hinder, making a living in this spot?

Although Lisu proverbs warn of its perils and insecurities, swidden agriculture, in which farmers clear and burn land to produce relatively short-term fertility, then let it fallow, sustained generations of highland farmers. Most Lisu are still farmers. They grew rice, maize, cash crops such as opium in the last few hundred years, and, more recently, fruit, tomatoes, flowers, and coffee, along with traditional crops. Labor is the main element as well as the main variable of the Lisu economy, and reciprocity is the dominating form of exchange with other Lisu. When outside labor is hired, it is paid for rather than exchanged.

In China, swidden agriculture has been curtailed since the mid- to late 1980s, except in remote areas such as in the Gaoligong range. In Thailand and

Steep, difficult terrain is the environment in which the Lisu economy developed over the past several hundred years—until recently. Swidden agriculturalists clear and burn land to create fertility. This has suited their migratory lifestyle, and when there was abundant land, it was sustainable. Photo: E. Paul Durrenberger.

Myanmar its use, although decreasing, persists against mounting pressure to stop from the land itself, as well as from governments.

In Thailand, Lisu grow un-irrigated mountain rice at elevations from 4,000 to 6,000 feet (1,200–1,800 meters), while in Yunnan and parts of Myanmar they raise both wet rice in paddies on tropical valley bottoms as low as 1,500 feet (450 meters) and buckwheat, mountain rice, barley, wheat, hemp, sorghum, sesame, and millet in swiddens at higher elevations. The Lisu co-plant seasonal vegetables such as beans and squash with other crops, which, along with irregularly shaped swiddens, give their fields a hodgepodge look.

Shifting agriculture and reciprocity of labor support core Lisu values of independence and egalitarianism. Traditionally, every Lisu was a self-determining farmer: knowledge, means of production, and land were equally available to all households. Fields were free to anyone who could clear them for as long as they used them—when they stopped or moved on, land reverted to public domain. There *are no rights other than use* to the Lisu way of thinking. Use is understood to include fallow periods of years for fields that have been initially cleared and planted. This form of agriculture is practical and ecologically

Clearing land by burning on steep hillside in Thailand. Photo: E. Paul Durrenberger.

sustainable in the steep mountain locations where Lisu have lived—as long as land was sufficient and recycled on a sufficiently long schedule.

Their economy has been based on swiddening and the rhythm of life predicated by its demands. Lisu live close to the land and know it well—indeed, Lisu farmers can taste the soil, tell whether it is fertile, and identify which crop is likely to do well in a given patch of dirt.

The environmental impact, however, has grown dire as less land becomes available to support more people who migrate less frequently. Effects can be seen in denuded mountains and erosion-gullied laterite around Lisu and other hill tribe villages. While hill farmers are not entirely blameless for the devastation that has stripped Thailand and, to a degree, Myanmar and China of forest cover in the past forty years, governments, corrupt officials, insurrections, clear-cut logging, and drug-trade interests have more agency in the destruction than they.

Numerous forces, some from far away, have contributed. Fallout from the Vietnam War (including CIA activities) along with the international drug trade and political upheaval in Burma-Myanmar, China, and Laos since the late 1960s pushed highland farmers into increasingly limited areas. Political and commercial forces in Thailand, combined with a lack of central planning, created pressures on highland terrains that would not otherwise have been as intense. Absence of national reforestation programs exacerbated loss of habitat where logging, often illegal, continues at a terrible environmental cost. Poor highland farmers usually follow at the bottom of the food chain in the wake of the initial destruction, burning off secondary forest in areas loggers have already decimated.

Yet minorities such as the Lisu, whose lifestyle is destroyed along with the trees, are often held responsible—rather than large commercial interests that profit enormously and flee the scene. Needless to say, having powerless subsistence farmers as scapegoats suits such interests. It is true, however, that highland farming methods do little to help reclaim the land when there is not enough of it.

The Lisu stand out as experts in land management and rotation among Thailand's highland farmers, and only a few other groups in Myanmar and China are known to practice similar land conservation. When they use their traditional methods, which are contingent not only on sufficient land but also on villages of only twenty to thirty houses, their system is sustainable. For every two or three fields a household clears and plants, another ten are left fallow. Land is used for a year or two and then allowed to "rest" for another five or six years before being burned and replanted. Lisu leave live trees in their fields, as well as stumps, to control erosion. In these practices they are unlike the Akha and Lahu, who clear every stump and plant over and over until fertility is spent.

In most places where Lisu farm today, however, severe land pressure doesn't allow the luxury of enough territory to practice this form of agriculture sustainably—and governments have phased it out or banned it. Without resources and training, it is difficult for Lisu and other highland farmers to change their ways. In Thailand, as soon as such farmers, who lack basic land rights, allow a field to go fallow, the government declares it abandoned and will not allow them to replant. This wouldn't be so unfair if the same government didn't then grant logging interests use contracts to clear-cut thousands of acres of forest in so-called preserved areas or provide lowland Thai farmers with tenure rights after kicking Lisu and other minorities off land they've farmed for generations.

Farming jungle-covered mountain slopes and valleys is labor-intensive. Methods the Lisu developed to eke out a living make use of the land to maximize profit with the technology, experience, and skills at hand. While the Lisu farm in many environments, including valley floors, steep hillsides, and secondary-growth forests, the following, condensed from Eugene Morse's book *Exodus to a Hidden Valley*, is a good description of the basic land-clearing method his family observed in China and Burma:

> Agriculture as practiced by the Lisu may seem crude to farmers elsewhere, but it requires considerable knowledge and expertise. Our own effort at clearing one small plot increased our admiration for the Lisu planters, not only for the amount of labor they were willing to perform but also for their technical know-how. First, the area to be burned must be judiciously chosen for quality of soil, exposure to sunlight, water supply, and accessibility. Then the jungle growth has to be carefully appraised and the burning skillfully executed.
>
> In clearing jungle terrain, the first step is to cut down all undergrowth, leaving only trees. Some of these are felled so that the wood in their crests can be used as tinder for the flames to consume the dense jungle underbrush [that has been cut], converting it all into wood-ash fertilizer to be evenly distributed. The trunks are usually too big to burn, and remain on the ground to serve as paths through the eventual crop area. The only tools available to the Lisu besides the fire itself are machetes and primitive axes. Hence the number, size, and position of the trees that need to be felled must be accurately taken into account. For a field about an acre in size, four or five trees between one and two feet in diameter are ideal. Trees too big or too numerous take too much time to cut down and trees too small or too few will not provide enough fuel.
>
> To fell the trees so that their trunks serve as pathways and their limbs provide proper fuel is a task that calls for a high degree of woodcraft and manual dexterity. Incisions in the trunks must be placed only after shrewd calculation of the angle of growth and weight distribution of each tree. Sometimes, in the case of trees with especially thick trunks, cutting platforms are built so that the incision can be made ten, twenty, or even thirty feet above ground.
>
> Most Westerners think that slash and burn causes danger of forest fire. In reality, this presents no problem at all. The main concern is how to coax the foliage to catch fire in the first place, and then how to keep it burning. Both

feats can be performed in the rain-forest jungle only towards the end of the six-month dry season. Felling the trees so that they fall in a favorable pattern and then setting the flames to work under advantageous wind conditions are both critically important—a heavy shower at any point in the procedure can be a serious setback or even a catastrophe. After the flames have consumed most of the foliage, the farmer is faced with much work in clearing away the remnants of vines, shrubs, and weed cover with ax and machete.

Planting follows clearing. There are two seasons for which farmers must prepare, with the first just before the rainy season. The Lisu often plant rice in man-woman pairs: the man walks ahead, poking two- to three-inch holes with his long dibble pole, and the woman follows with a basket of seed rice, dropping a few kernels into each hole. The sexual suggestiveness of planting this crop, significant in terms of fertility, is not lost on the Lisu. Interestingly, husband and wife never make up planting pairs, as this would cause acute "shyness." Lisu Christians in Myanmar and China use a different technique, in which planters work individually with a short dibble stick. Lisu are nimble workers; and laughing, teasing, and singing often accompany fieldwork. Spontaneous races among couples to get to the end of the row, along with other playfulness, relieve the tedium.

Each family works its own fields, but labor is also exchanged and carefully accounted for among the three to six families who cooperate in household affiliation groups. In addition, a form of cooperative labor, called a *wadi* in Thailand, might see a village-wide workforce of thirty or forty men and women planting a field or weeding. This is accomplished by separate groups of men and women working their way up the slope pulling weeds. The family that called the wadi pays the workers with a feast, and how many turn up is a sort of popularity contest. The meal is held at midday, typically in or around field huts—pork, rice wrapped in *lo-jee* leaves, fresh beans, and cucumbers are enjoyed along with home-brewed corn whiskey and roasted chilies. The hostess presides over the rustic luncheon while her daughters-in-law serve: first the men and then the women, who are seated in separate groups. Bamboo troughs serve as tables, and wisecracking groups of field diners seated on banana-leaf carpets gossip about the size of the pig and the quality of the liquor. Betel nut might finish up the meal and energize women for the last hours of work, while men indulge in tobacco hand-rolled in cornhusks. It is beginning to get dark before the workers trudge home to their village along mountain pathways, the hike often taking an hour or more.

Crop portfolios differ according to soil, elevation, and distance from markets and government control. Opium is no longer cultivated on a large scale in China and also far less than in the past in Thailand and Myanmar. Lisu grow corn everywhere, including popcorn, and at high elevations they co-plant it and other fast-growing grains to shelter tender mountain rice shoots from intense sun and rain. Beans are co-planted with opium for the same purpose, as well as to enrich the soil. In the Upper (Nu) Salween and parts of Burma, hemp was grown widely to produce homespun cloth, but it is grown far less commonly today, as most cloth and clothing is purchased. Early crops ripen in late June or July: often millet, corn, squash, and cucumbers. In China I saw corn drying on large racks in front of Lisu houses in late October, and it is a common sight through November. Corncobs are stuffed under the rafters and in every other available storage space for later consumption. As much as possible is hung above the hearth, where smoke deters bugs. Early rice is harvested from August to October, along with other crops such as sesame, which in Yunnan turns the fields a gorgeous purple hue in autumn. The main rice crop follows in November or December.

Most labor in the Lisu economy is expended in agriculture work, and the calendar is set by planting, weeding, and harvest times. Lisu farmers have a good idea whether soil and crop conditions make an additional weeding worthwhile, and if they judge not, they will use the time to accomplish other tasks. During agricultural slack times, they occupy themselves with other work.

ECONOMIC ACTIVITIES IN THE FOREST

Harvesting forest products for home use and cash is still common in Myanmar and China but not as much in Thailand. Remote areas of northern Myanmar are especially rich in plants with pharmaceutical uses, and there is a good market for them. Alpine lilies, or *peimu*, are the base of tonic for pulmonary ailments, and another root collected at very high elevations, *si-ge* is brewed as a tea and is an effective blood pressure–lowering medicine that also heals burns. A rock fern with the botanical name *Coptis teeta* is an antimalarial as well as a germicidal lotion, and there is a huge Chinese market for various aphrodisiacs. Many Lisu go on medicine-collecting trips every year. In Burma/Myanmar, most Lisu lacked access to modern healthcare until the twenty-first century; and malaria, dengue fever, and diarrhea were common killers. Herbal medicine was often the only kind available, and Lisu have long curing traditions using natural products.

Foraging for mushrooms and other forest foods such as edible vines and shoots (bamboo and rattan are the most popular) is a more routine activity. Done closer to home and mainly by women, it provides important supplementary food. Most Lisu in the Tengchong area of China are subsistence farmers. But in Myanmar, especially in areas without adequate land, some men regularly collect mushrooms for cash. The Lisu diet everywhere is enriched with home-raised chicken and pork or wild game when available. Traditionally, pork was raised for ritual purposes—widespread raising of pigs for market by Christians, who don't offer spirits pork or engage in reciprocal feasting, began in the mid-twentieth century.

In China around Tengchong, some Lisu have grown relatively prosperous from the timber trade—they cut planks from trees harvested from the forest by the Han Chinese. This is a traditional skill mentioned in the early accounts of Lisu in Burma and China. In 1937, horticulturist Francis Kingdon-Ward described what he saw of the trade during an expedition to northern Burma near the Chinese border:

> I had not yet found a mature coffin tree, but the coffin plank industry was
> in full swing. There were planks drying against the huts, and from time to
> time a Lisu would pick up one, balance it on his back, and set out over the
> mountains for China. It was a formidable journey via the Hpimaw pass or the
> Feng-shui-ling, with that immense load.
>
> The largest coffin planks are about nine feet long, 2½ feet wide at one
> end, tapering to 18 inches at the other, and from two to three inches thick.
> The heaviest weigh about 130 pounds. A man will carry a plank weighing 100
> pounds or more over the 10,000 foot Hpimaw pass, sometimes through snow,
> the journey taking him ten or twelve days—his pay is about four pence a day,
> with rice. We must have upset the local labor market for a time, as we paid
> one rupee a day, with rice.
>
> The Chinese rich man's coffin is a rather weighty oblong box, comprising
> two side pieces, two small but immensely thick end pieces, a large bottom

In the Tengchong area of Yunnan, China, the coffin plank trade has employed Lisu for generations. I met these plank carriers and saw many drying planks in the area in 1997. Author photo.

piece, and an enormous lid 9 feet long. The total weight is between 400 lb. and 500 pounds. It is also very costly, but the cost of dying has always been high for the rich and is ever rising as timber becomes scarcer.

While Lisu are keen hunters, they consider it sport rather than work; a steady Lisu man will always make sure his fields are taken care of before he takes to the hills with his long-barreled powder gun or crossbow in search of barking deer, guar, or smaller game. Because the area directly around Lisu villages is usually hunted out, such expeditions require several days. Men and women build two beaver-like dams and drain the water in between them so the fish can be easily scooped up in cooperative fishing. In 1997 I saw a lone hunter station himself in a tree above a still pond in Myanmar and shoot fish from this vantage, collecting his catch with a long-necked net. The environmentally damaging dynamite fishing is popular among some Lisu in the Putao area, where fish in markets are getting smaller and smaller and Lisu have the reputation of being despoilers of nature. (See more on Lisu hunting in Book II, Chapter 3.)

Wild honey is usually found on high overhanging cliffs; hunting it is dangerous and only sometimes profitable. Activities such as this and smoking out wasp nests for grubs are undertaken by adventuresome Lisu skilled in woodcraft—most often in Myanmar and China. There is also a Lisu tradition of mountain-men hunters who neglect fields in favor of forest and who might keep an entire small village supplied with game in exchange for rice and other sustenance for their families. Sometimes they hunt musk deer, which live around the snowline from Tibet down into northern Myanmar, for the abdominal gland used in perfume. In China, such men are said to have a special "animal-killing" spirit who guides their shots. When such a hunter returns to his village whistling, villagers prepare an offering to this spirit, called Hwa-shi-ne.

Sweat: The Lisu Capital

His or her own labor has always been the main element a Lisu man or woman can manipulate, according to Alain Dessaint, an American anthropologist who studied the group's economic organization in northern Thailand in the 1970s. In the Lisu world, land is equally available to everyone, technology's role is small (albeit increasing), and Lisu have little financial capital or credit. Unlike other groups such as the Karen, Lisu do not work community fields, and they live in smaller family groups—thus each individual's effort is of great importance. Households keep strict track of exchanges of labor among household affiliation groups to make sure they are equalized. Unlike many hill tribesmen, Lisu individuals rarely hire themselves out for agricultural work. In their value system, this is shameful; instead, they aspire both to hire labor (often Akha or Lahu addicts) and to profit from it. Also noteworthy is that Lisu seldom become full-time traders (whom they consider untrustworthy), although they do engage in liquor making, pig raising, and collecting and selling forest products as economic activities supplementary to farming. In Thailand, Lisu women frequently make handicrafts to sell to tourists.

However, the primary economic concerns are deciding what, where, how much, and with whom to plant crops. Mountain rice, the staff of life for many

Lisu who live in high mountains in China, Myanmar, and Thailand, is usually grown below the village. The search for good highland rice land, which becomes exhausted quickly, has triggered many migrations. Wet-rice cultivation at lower elevations is labor-intensive at the front end when terraces are built and water supplies developed. Wet-rice fields and terraces can be used for a long time, however, and they suit the lifestyles of Lisu in long-established villages such as those around Myitkyina and Putao in Myanmar's Kachin State and in China. In the Upper Nu Valley of Yunnan, vast stretches of steep terraces were reclaimed from sheer slopes and valleys in the 1980s, when the ban on slash-and-burn farming began to be strictly enforced. These terraces were generally un-irrigated and were used for newer crops such as orange or tung oil trees, but irrigation is being developed as electricity makes pumping possible.

Opium thrives on extreme slopes, as high as 5,000–7,000 feet (1,500–2,100 meters) in poor, black lumpy soil and maximum sunlight. Myanmar's remote Shan State and areas in Thailand and Laos are prime for growing opium. Since there is plenty of this kind of habitat and rice land is diminishing, opium as a crop has not disappeared, though it makes up a smaller portion of crop portfolios than in the past. (See opium sidebar in Book I, Chapter 5.) Maize, grown everywhere, is used to feed pigs, for popcorn, and to make liquor for offerings and feasts.

The Lisu weigh many factors in deciding the family's portfolio: having more daughters than sons in the allegiance group that cooperates economically, living closer to or further from markets, and whether new fields will be opened or old ones used. Decisions are based on knowledge and experience and in consultation. They are made rationally: comparative advantage, diminishing returns, and substitutability are familiar concepts. Lisu are highly conscious of price and have excellent memories for price information over time. The first question a Lisu will often ask when observing a new or unknown object is "how much did it cost" rather than the more basic "what is it." The Internet has made reliable price information easily available, and the Lisu have pounced on this advantage to free themselves from rapacious middlemen.

LISU WOMEN: EQUAL PARTNERS

Something more must be at play in the greater status and independence of Lisu women, something about cultural and economic value. Women are equally indispensable in regenerating all societies, yet they do not enjoy equal status in most. The metaphor likening men and women to chopsticks simply acknowledges the complementarity that exists and is shared by Lisu and other hill tribes, such as the Lahu. More hierarchical Thai folk wisdom calls women "the back legs of the elephant," which bespeaks complementarity but in a workhorse, following sort of way. The Lisu woman's father-in-law expends significant resources to transfer her labor from her father's family into his because she is deemed worth it. Her labor is highly valued, and marriage opens up new labor affiliations with her kinsmen. Although there is some freedom in choosing a marriage partner, marriages are as much about economic as social alliances. Gender equality among Lisu is by all accounts exceptional. Lisu in Thailand, Myanmar, and China—both sexes, animist and Christian—invariably expressed that men and women are equal when I asked them to tell me about sex roles and relationships.

Every marriage involves circulation of wealth—which might include silver rupees, jewelry, horses, and a period of service to the bride's father in addition to a cash payment and a feast. This custom has been a chief means of distributing resources and leveling wealth among the Lisu. Since labor is the main factor in their economy (as in most) that can be manipulated, it may be considered the key resource discussed in the marriage negotiation. New kinship roles, also the subject of protracted discussion in such talks in all three countries, generally have to do with potential labor alliances—every marriage deal has economic consequences that are far-reaching in this small society. As a Lisu proverb goes:

> When you shout, it echoes down the valley;
> When you pull one vine, the whole jungle shakes.

The high price of a Lisu bride compared to a Lahu, Akha, or Karen bride is an interesting point but one from which it is difficult to draw specific conclusions. Hmong, Mien, and Chinese brides are even more expensive. No one supplies more labor than the Akha woman, renowned as a workhorse—yet she is more subservient and enjoys lower status than the Lisu woman. In the modern money economy, the least expensive hill tribe brides are also the ones most likely to be forced into prostitution. Not unknown among the Lisu, until recently, working in the sex trade was relatively infrequent for them compared to other economically pressed groups.

THE LURE OF LAND

In addition to labor, another key to the Lisu economy has been the tendency to migrate with regularity and in small groups—the moving process itself is deeply entangled in economic decision-making (see Book I, Chapter 5). At the front or back of the Lisu mind was always the quandary: is it more advantageous to move now or later? Where will the family relocate? Usually to a place where they have kinsmen. How will the move be financed? With whom will they go?

The fact that free access to land is a prerequisite to this lifestyle has been mentioned; until the last thirty to forty years, this was a given in areas inhabited by Lisu. For them, the concept of land ownership by human beings is foreign. The land is already "owned"—by the spirits, with whom one negotiates over usage rights. The lure of fertile, yet-to-be-opened land exerted an irresistible force over the Lisu through the 1980s and into the 1990s. This is hard for lowland and other non-farming, city-dwelling people to empathize with or understand.

A passage in Eugene Morse's *Exodus to a Hidden Valley* illustrates how deeply land lust and will to independence affect Lisu economic decision-making. Morse was part of a sudden migration of 5,000 Lisu who left Putao in Burma's extreme north in 1965 to reach a "no-man's land" near the border with India. The Morses were complying with General Ne Win's order to leave the country, and many settled Lisu went with them into mountainous territory to avoid conscription into government or insurgent armies.

> At the top of the ridge, which must have been at least 9,000 feet high, we paused to look around us. Off to our right, range upon range of sparkling snow-capped mountains rose higher and higher until they reached a jagged horizon in the Tibetan highlands. Even at our altitude we were in what might be considered a pass, for the peaks around soared to 13,000 feet or more. The valleys on each side dropped away so sheerly that we seemed to be walking on the edge of a knife . . . It was here, balanced on this ridge, that I first sensed we were free at last. We seemed to be at the top of creation, with open land spreading in every direction as far as the eye could see. How could anyone but God stop us from taming this land to our needs? It is difficult now, back in civilization, to evoke the sense of freedom that comes upon a man when he stands on a mountain top and looks out over tens of thousands of acres

of fertile and unexplored land in the valleys below. It is only then that a man knows that, given the wit and will to survive, he need not bow his head to any government, to any ideology, to any small-minded men who feel that they control the essentials of his existence. I understood more fully than ever before why the Lisu had apparently given so little thought to abandoning their fields and their oxen and their other evidence of wealth in the Putao plains to move on . . . Freedom is a far more heady emotion than a sense of security.

With a people so ready to pick up and leave everything behind, it becomes clear why labor is the most important element in Lisu economic organization. It also explains why labor reallocated through marriage is of greater consequence to them than to others who migrate less frequently. According to Morse, the fact that Lisu migrate in smaller groups than others is yet another factor that weights the labor aspect of their economic equation. It supports their strong work ethic because every person's labor is important.

Farming, along with every other productive activity, is accompanied by ceremonies and offerings that have economic impacts of their own. These represent a sort of bargaining with territorial spirits, as well as with those of one's ancestors, to allow success. Swine and chicken, although they add protein to the diet, are raised primarily for offerings and to keep up the family's part in the reciprocal feasting required to maintain status as well as social and labor alliances.

As Durrenberger observes, it is not enough to have a large herd of pigs and some luxury consumer goods to be regarded as successful and honorable. To have and to increase myi-do, the Lisu must also distribute household resources back to the community. Liquor making is also strongly associated with ritual offerings and hospitality.

While drinking is woven into Lisu spiritual, social, and economic life and every village has alcoholics, the lion's share of drinking is concentrated around village feasts. Most Lisu work too hard and have too little money to drink or get drunk on a regular basis. In his survey of Lisu liquor production, Alain Dessaint found the amounts produced and consumed do not indicate that alcoholism is a bigger problem in Lisu communities than in others. The missionary saying "leeches for blood, Lisu for liquor" is an overstatement, but one that doesn't seem too far off the mark if one happens upon a Lisu bride price negotiation, feast associated with curing, or Lisu New Year or other festival. These are peak drinking times when trays full of small china or bamboo cups of liquor are constantly passed around. Hosts increase their myi-do by getting others drunk at such times; to refuse insults not only them but possibly the spirits as well.

The Lisu think propitiating spirits with alchohol and other offerings increases the spirits' myi-do, too. When offerings are made to ancestors, Apa-mo, or other spirits, they are thought to consume only part of the offering to renew their strength and then to sell the balance to other spirits, Dessaint reports. Thus spirits participate in markets, gain status, and help the Lisu in their endeavors, so that, in turn, the Lisu will continue to make offerings. This is in keeping with the goals of achieving happiness and *do* (power or news) in this world and the next. Do, as mentioned, refers to individual productive capacity or the ability to transmit influence to others for one's own benefit, not power in the sense of control or applying sanctions. When coupled with *myi* (name, fate, or potential), it creates the Lisu's most highly ranked value: myi-do.

The power achieved through the help of the spirits and one's own earthly efforts is further increased by hiring labor, extracting the maximum service from sons-in-law, and associating with a successful household allegiance group, according to Dessaint.

It is often said that Lisu people like to grow opium very much, but they don't like to smoke it. In this they differ from the Akha, Lahu, and non-Christian Karen, who like to smoke but not grow it, or the Hmong, who like both.

Dessaint and Durrenberger, working in two Thai Lisu villages in the late 1960s and early 1970s, arrived at different conclusions regarding the relative return on a day's work on subsistence crops such as rice, maize, and vegetables, compared with export crops like opium or fruit. At that time, all sixty Lisu villages in northern Thailand had economies based on the rotating cultivation of opium poppies, hill rice, and maize. Opium was also used to pay itinerant labor.

In the former's study village, the return on opium was better; in the latter's, rice. Their results disagree, but each makes keen observations about the Lisu and other highland farmers that clarify micro-economic differences among villages. Dessaint explains that the search for an efficient portfolio of crops varies over time and place and that vagaries of risk, cultural goals, climate, and markets make absolute profitability impossible to predict. In one area, missionaries or government officials might be influential; in another, opium traders hold greater sway.

Durrenberger notes that it has always been those who trade opium, seldom its growers, who become rich. In addition, opium is relatively more rewarding when there is a lack of good rice land, less so when rice-growing land is abundant. Opium can always be sold to buy rice. Although Lisu are hardworking and somewhat entrepreneurial, in the Golden Triangle where they cultivate opium, it was formerly the Haw Chinese and then the Wa who controlled its trade and became prosperous—and whose sons and daughters went to college to become doctors and lawyers.

The Lisu base status on accumulation of portable luxury goods such as silver, horses, and weapons, with which they finance their migrations, rather than on inherited land. "Getting ahead" has always depended on external markets and on producing a cash product or crop. On many counts opium, originally pushed on the Lisu by traders in China and later by Kuomintang (KMT) forces in Burma and Thailand, has simply been the crop that made the most economic sense to Lisu. It is easier to transport and holds up better than peaches, lynches, or swine—which also require nearby markets. Unlike rice, opium has no spiritual significance.

Road construction has done more to change the way the Lisu interact with markets and national authorities than anything else in the last quarter century. Roads facilitate getting produce to market, but they also rob villages of the inaccessibility that supported independence and provided cultural insulation. Particularly in Thailand and China, new crops such as coffee and fruit have been substituted for the opium that dominated as cash earner for a century. But because these crops require four or five times as much land to generate a similar proportion of income, they exert pressure on land and labor and contribute more to environmental degradation than did opium.

An ongoing switch from mountain rice to paddy, or wet, rice in both China and Myanmar has dramatically affected the Lisu economy and migratory way of life. Building terraced fields requires an investment in time and labor that makes farmers less keen to move on. The same is true as Lisu in Thailand become adept at orchardry. The issue of land title is also of increasing importance as highland farmers compete for dwindling supplies of arable land. If a Lisu has improved a piece of land by terracing it or making any

Road construction, mostly in Thailand and China, has impacted the Lisu dramatically. From making age-old tasks such as carrying wood down steep slopes in the rainy season less hazardous to connecting them to global markets, nothing has changed their lives more in the past twenty-five years. Author photo.

other improvement, he will ask for compensation to transfer use to another person. Today, only in Thailand are Lisu and other minority farmers unable to register and own land. Greater personal freedom and mobility there must be weighed against such drawbacks, yet I heard no reports of Thai Lisu returning to Myanmar or China.

While all the changes going on around the Lisu are having huge effects, their culture has not shattered, and their equilibrium has not been as unbalanced as might be expected. One reason for this, concluded by Dessaint in 1972, still has validity: the nexus, or point of contact, between Lisu and non-Lisu is mainly cash, while between Lisu and Lisu, labor and social relations remain paramount. Because credit and capital have been generally unavailable to them, the Lisu have not been drawn into *si-so* (patron-client) relations with traders or bankers or extensive enmeshment with lowland economies. Relations between traders and Lisu, in fact, remain as mistrustful as ever. Middlemen used to come with trucks to their villages to buy produce and squeeze them on price. Some things never change, but in this case, in Thailand today and coming soon in other countries, many Lisu have trucks. Access to price information on the Internet is universally available.

While Thailand is still probably the most globally integrated place in which Lisu live, because its economy is smaller and more exposed than China's and there is less political stability, life in the kingdom is more erratic. Income gaps between prosperous and poor Lisu there are growing.

In China, many Lisu have become city dwellers or at least urbanized, but this has happened in Yunnan Province—in both Nujiang Lisu Autonomous Prefecture and nearby Weixi Lisu Autonomous County within Diqing Prefecture (adjacent to Tibet), where they are in the majority and have as much political voice as anyone else in this centrally controlled nation.

In Myanmar, protracted insurgencies and military dictatorship have affected them the most negatively: Lisu there are materially the poorest of those in all three countries, paralleling the general population. Change and reform there, however, began accelerating rapidly after elections in 2010 and 2012. Many ceasefires have been signed with ethnic armies with which the central government has been in conflict for the last fifty years, although not with the Kachin Independence Army (KIA) in Lisu territory. The air is redolent with hope even there, following Aung San Suu Kyi's National League for Democracy's huge electoral victory in 2015. Amid so much flux, it is a fool's errand to predict the future's direction, other than to note that a turn away from recent improvements would trigger major upheaval.

The push-pull between Myanmar and Thailand regarding illegal immigration continues, and while Lisu and most undocumented border crossers into Thailand work in agriculture, they are increasingly subject to human trafficking. Thais are prone to look the other way, accentuating the fact that numbers of their own young women, girls, and boys from rural areas, formerly caught in the "Green Harvest" of sex trafficking, have dramatically decreased. The Thai sex trade has not shrunk, however—its sex workers are now simply being drawn from other countries, such as Myanmar and Bangladesh.

The search for the perfect mountainside to support life and livelihood continues to fire the Lisu imagination—even as the quest itself, as for all modernizing people, begins to shift from actual ground to more conceptual landscapes. The connection between the Lisu and the land remains strong with most, even as pioneers explore and push the limits of their world to establish beachheads in heretofore unknown economic territories. Lisu will continue to adapt their culture and economy, trying to maximize gains and minimize losses with the resources and technology at hand. An observable adaptation in all three countries is that Lisu are supporting sons' and daughters' educations longer, hedging their bets, and planting one foot in the rapidly modernizing world.

BOOK II

The Lisu by Country:
Contemporary Sketches

Ponies mean prestige. Thailand, 1997

A blacksmith in his hut in Northern Thailand. Photo: E. Paul Durrenberger

Lisu New Year group in northern Thailand

Lisu woman in northern Thailand with opium pod

The headman of Dton Loong, Alay Pa, 1997

Thai Lisu raised bamboo house.
Photo: E. Paul Durrenberger

Thai Lisu rest bench

Woman working at her matrilineal pillar in Doi Chang

The village rice pounder

*Modern Lisu coffee house
in Doi Chang*

*Mosquito extermination
in Dton Loong*

Son in front of his mother's coffin in Doi Laa

The village shaman
praying with incense.
Photo by E. Paul Durrenberger

Lisu girl at a New Year celebration in Shan State, Burma, 1987. Photo by Richard Diran

David Ngwa-za Fish, right, Lisu
scholar and collector of sayings, 1997

Gem market by a
temple in Mogok, 1997

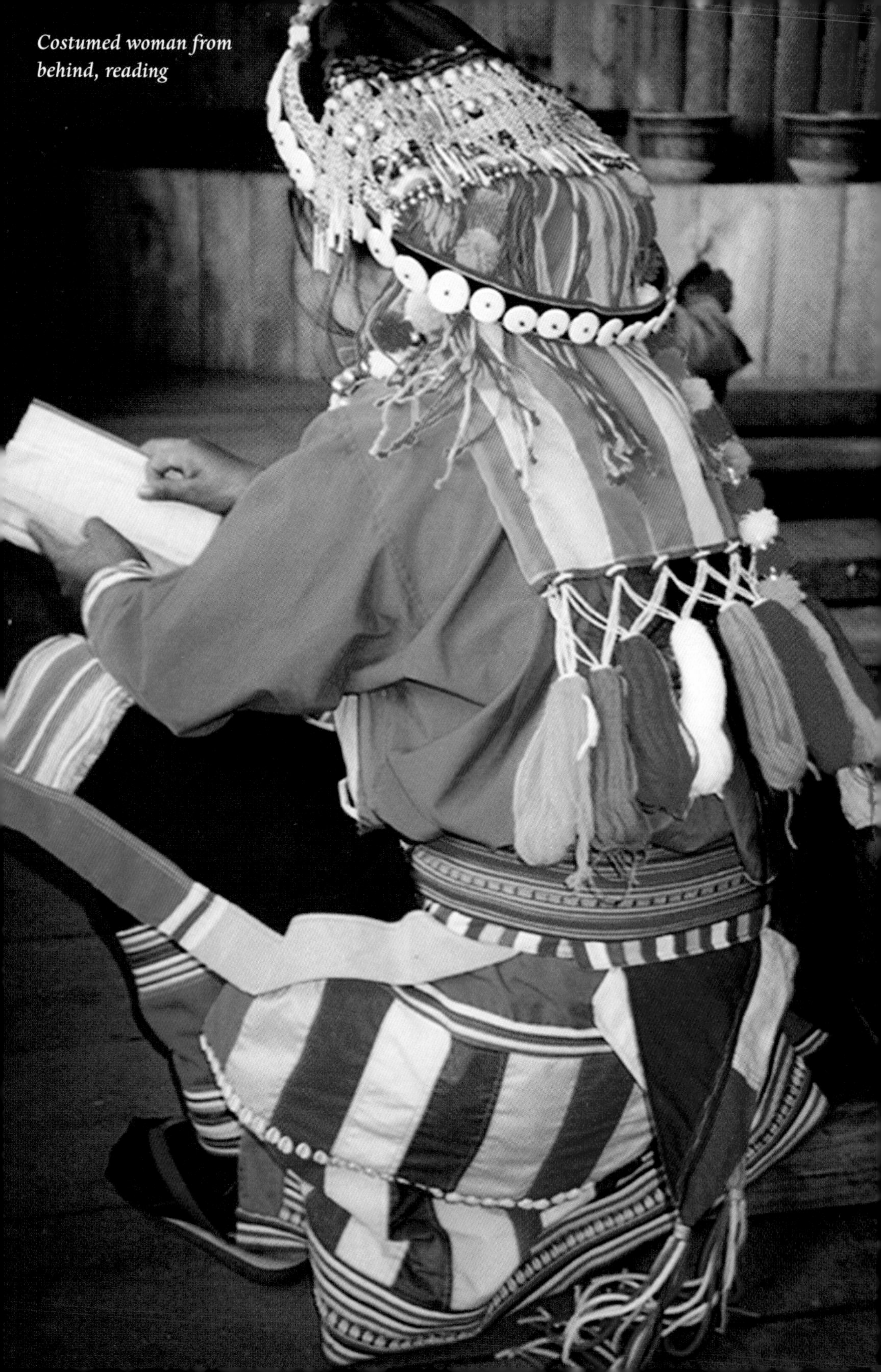

Putao Township in Kachin State, northernmost Myanmar, within sight of Tibet

Modern bridge in Putao Township

Girl fishing with a basket in flooded rice fields, Putao Valley

Man weaving basket, Putao Valley

Putao airport

Solar panels for sale in downtown Putao

Women in Putao kitchen

Another Putao kitchen

*J Pa-da, Citi-lo headman
and village tract chairman*

*Senator Jay Yawu at home in
Yangon with wife and sister-in-law*

Gassing up a tuk-tuk miniature truck

Putao Valley river landscape

The ruins of a cruciform church in Mulahdi, *2014*

Crossbow Party leaders
outside their headquarters
in Myitkyina, *2014*

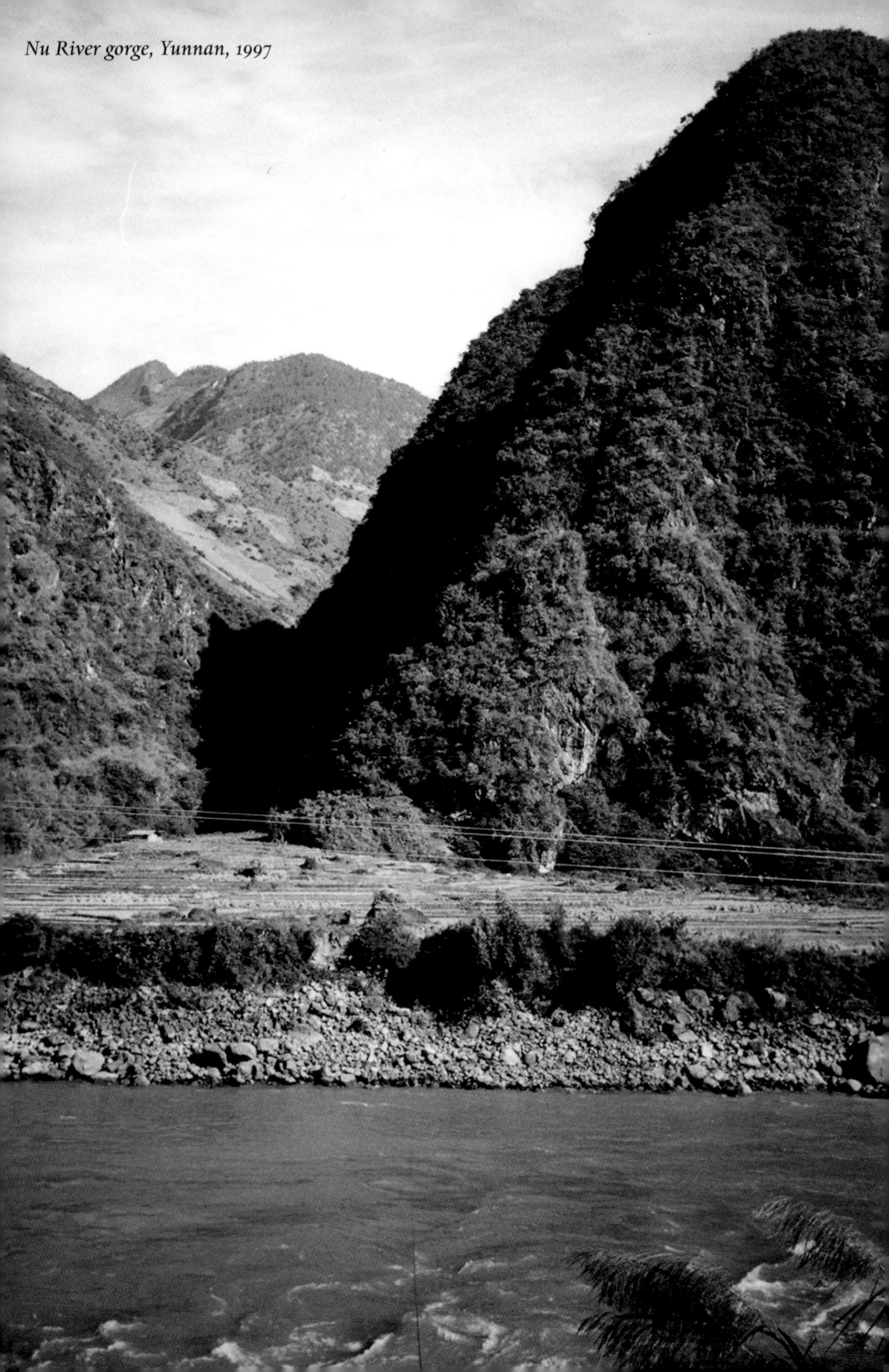

Nu River gorge, Yunnan, 1997

Looking across field to house in the Dansha area

Man carrying wood in basket on road near Liuku, 2014

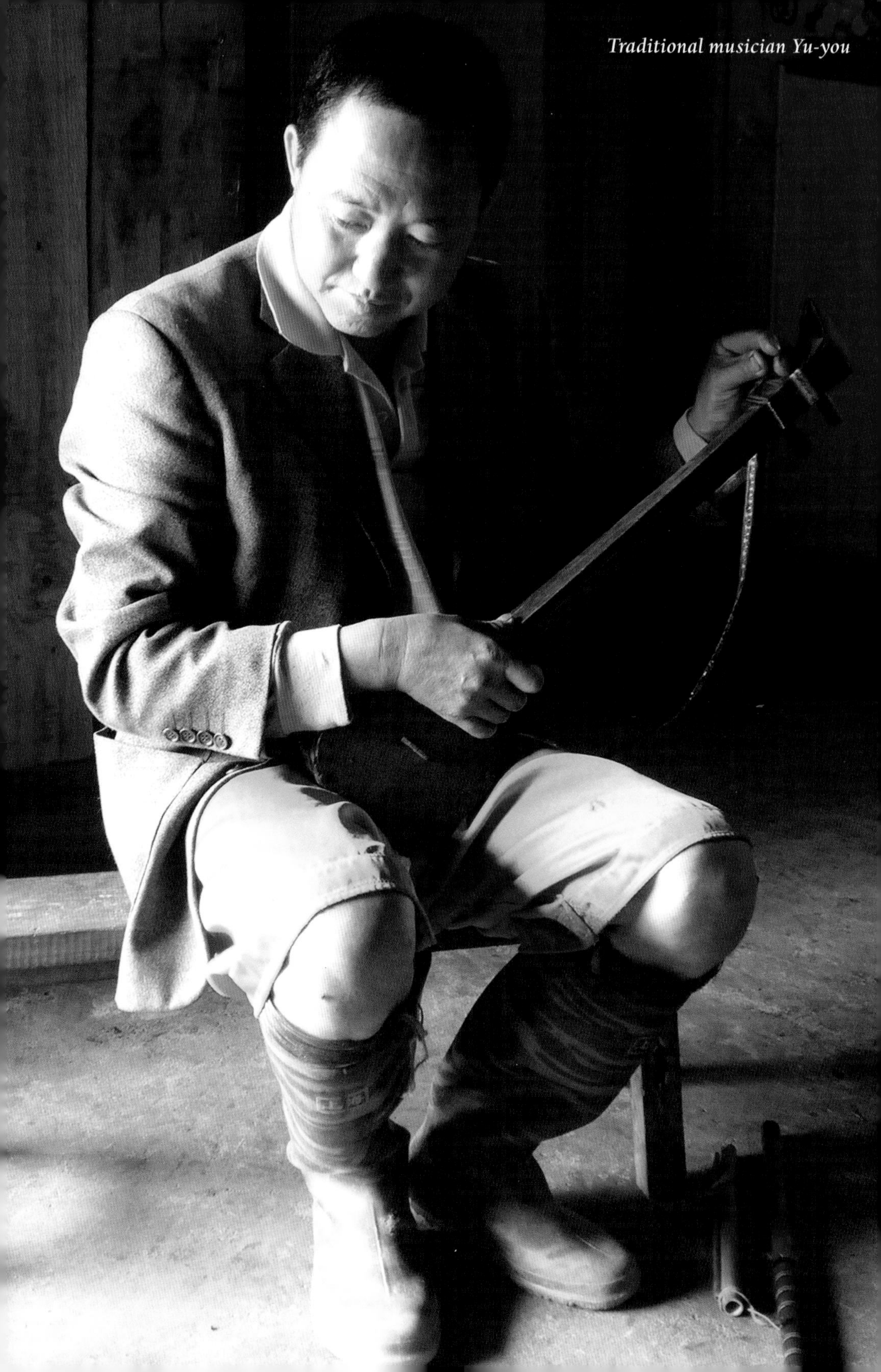

Traditional musician Yu-you

Suer-yẹ-tsa, a shaman, demonstrating a Woh clan healing ceremony

Shaman Aki Li-tu at home

Chos-o-pho with his wife outside their home

Modern Chinese Lisu woman at a Lishadi market, 2014

More traditional women at a Lishadi market

Construction on superhighway bridge through the mountains to Liuku

Street view in Liuku, the capital of Nujiang Lisu Autonomous Prefecture. Note crossbows for sale.

Lisu cultural show for Chinese
tourists in Tengchong, Yunnan

Prosperous Lisu woman in traditional
clothing in market town near Tengchong

Author with Nujiang Autonomous Lisu Region's foreign minister Molido and entourage, including Senator J Yawu of Myanmar

Author with Lisu drunks at a Lishadi market watering hole

1

Comparing Lisu National Scenes

FULL OF OPPORTUNITIES TO BE WRONG

Whatever comes, count on it.
—*Lisu proverb*

Near Mae Hong Son in northern Thailand, rainy season 1996

Forested mountains glisten green-black around the sunny valley; a few heavy-bottomed clouds lumber across the bright blue sky. They do not cool the air, and I wonder if they will dump rain on us before a bus comes along. The middle-aged man in knee-length blue pants and an old polo shirt, carrying a Lisu shoulder bag, chats away as we wait. I understand maybe half of what he is saying, but the gist is his enthusiasm for the country he walked to from Myanmar in 1993.

"What do you like best about Thailand?" I ask in Thai as crude as his, though I've been here a few years longer.

"Numba one (he extends his index finger to clarify): you get to ride here, you're not so tired from walking everywhere."

A truck rattles by, hauling a trio of water buffalo. He points and we laugh at its perfect timing—his case is proven. A few minutes later clouds open and we shelter under the umbrella he extracts from his bag.

Once forested mountains in northern Thailand are under extreme land pressure as low-land farmers move up the slopes, pushing Lisu and other highland farmers even further up. Government officials blame farmers rather than logging interests for despoiling the hills, despite contrary evidence, and reforestation efforts are creating new conflicts. Author photo.

Thailand was the most free, modern, economically developed, and globally integrated of the Lisu national environments when I began this book in the mid-1990s. Set aside political speech and opinions on the monarchy, and it remains so. Thailand is favored by millions of annual visitors for its beaches, fabulous food, friendly people, and a society in which *"sanuk-sabei"* (enjoy-relax) is a highly regarded value. There are other criteria to consider. In China all Lisu are citizens, and along with everyone else they've achieved prodigious material progress in the new millennium, subject to its centrally planned system. The 1990s are for them ancient history. Lisu there register land and have access to education and healthcare, but they still live in an authoritarian state.

Compared to both China and Myanmar, Thailand still *feels* open. A free-market breeze wafts over this land—which has had a dozen coups d'état since 1932, when it has been overseen, as it is in 2017, by a military government. It has had nineteen constitutions in that time, and the military recently voted down a twentieth, written by the committee it appointed for the job. The army has toppled two democratically elected governments since 2006, muzzled the press, and put off elections indefinitely. Minorities, including people who have lived here for generations, are particularly looked down upon in this hierarchical society—about half are still not citizens.

A free market is not the same as a free country. Instability and political repression over the last several years have eroded Thailand's charms, and its economy is suffering. In 2015 an independent watchdog organization, Freedom House, downgraded the country from "partly free" to "not free" and said the junta's rule has sent its "human rights situation into free fall." In the World Justice Project's overall rule-of-law ranking, Thailand slipped nine places in 2014 and dipped even further in the "fundamental rights" category. From being the most free country in the region, it ranks eleventh out of fifteen today.

When looking at a single ethnic minority in three different countries, how is it possible to weigh and balance access to healthcare and education, ability to register land and take title, or the likelihood of becoming a sex slave with concepts that have consequences such as economic and individual freedom and rule of law? Entrepreneurial talent in Thailand may still be highly rewarded, and free rein in this realm has allowed gifted, advantageously placed Lisu to prosper. But in Thailand authoritarianism is on the rise, and income disparity among Lisu is growing. In China income inequality is shrinking; however, authoritariansim is well established, with no sign of abating.

In Myanmar things have improved astonishingly, but the starting point was so low that comparisons are problematic. The country has failed repeatedly and often horribly since independence in 1948 to square its multi-ethnic reality of a 40 percent non-Burman population with the chauvenistic ambitions of Burman elites to create a single-nationality state. From the 1960s until after the turn of the twenty-first century, it suffered under a brutal "socialist" military dictatorship engaged in intermittent wars with fifty or more ethnic armed groups representing minority groups and sometimes drug, mining, and logging interests. A shift toward market capitalism around 1990, along with several ceasefires, started the country on an uneven road toward reform that did not begin to look credible until 2010. Before then, security and living conditions for many ordinary people, including ethnic minorities, were so appalling that Myanmar was a clear "worst" in terms of national milieu. In 1997 several Lisu reported that in 1995 the government in Rangoon declined to respond to a malaria epidemic in the Putao Valley. International aid organizations were not allowed in to help, and thousands of Lisu were unable to get treatment and died. I met a doctor who claimed to have treated 30,000 cases; a Lisu man told me that in his village of 300 families, 98 people died.

The off-and-on war in Kachin State where most Lisu live resumed in 2014 after a seventeen-year ceasefire. In addition to conflicts over autonomy and control of natural resources with the central government, today the conflict is increasingly over Chinese business interests overrunning the state.

Life is changing and improving in Myanmar, however; Lisu I spoke to in 2014 and 2015 are upbeat about the future. Any reform is met with joy, and just since 2010 opposition political parties became legal along with foreign investment, the press was freed, healthcare became available, and land ownership became possible. There is reason to celebrate.

However, it is too early to predict the effects of Aung San Suu Kyi's National League for Democracy's November 2015 landslide victory because her party's ability to share power with the military, which still controls key ministries and at least a quarter of Parliament, is unknown. Also unknown is whether reforms have already reached the outer limits of "disciplined democracy." Disciplined is code for authoritarian and has always been the more heavily weighted of the two concepts in this country ruled by military strongmen under the influence of astrologers.

Comparing countries and conditions is inexact but not irrelevant. Drawing useful conclusions in rapidly evolving circumstances is full of opportunities to be wrong. I originally intended to take the first global view of the Lisu, looking at country variations to compare Lisu adaptation strategies. I believe this approach has value. Looking back in time is one thing—but by 2015, future outlooks in Thailand, Myanmar, and China had changed so extremely that many of my original conclusions became moot.

This does not decrease the importance of where you are born or live as a fateful force—being controlled by a nation-state is not something Lisu can opt out of, as they did in the past.

China is the country where most Lisu still live and where they all come from, including those now living in Myanmar, Thailand, India, and

Roughly half the world's Lisu population of 1.5 million lives in Yunnan, China. Most are in the Nujiang Valley in Nujiang Lisu Autonomous Prefecture or in nearby Weixi Lisu Autonomous County. Although Chinese Lisu inhabit villages longer settled than in other countries, the government continues to shift Lisu from the most remote areas to newly constructed villates, such as this one along the Nu that did not appear to be inhabited in 2014. Author photo.

Laos. They brought a language, worldview, and oral tradition to these other countries beginning around the turn of the twentieth century, and Western anthropologists began documenting them from the 1950s. Thai Lisu (about 50,000) constitute less than 5 percent of the worldwide Lisu population but are by far the most studied. By the mid-1960s, as anthropology's influence was growing and interest in the field exploding, Thailand was the only country accessible to Western scholars. Thai Lisu are the least Christianized, which also made them the most interesting to anthropologists. This must be acknowledged because so much remains unknown about the other 95 percent of Lisu living elsewhere, a large plurality of whom (if not an outright majority) are Christian.

China does not represent the Lisu past, however, or Thailand their future. Over 700,000 Lisu live in China today—but groups there are many, varied, and scattered. What is true about one isn't necessarily true of another. China is the second-largest economy in the world, and Lisu there have moved up economically along with everyone else. Political stability and strong economic growth are obvious advantages. Although China is well-known for its lack of commitment to individual or human rights, the majority of Lisu there enjoy benefits still lacking in Thailand and Myanmar. China's judicial system cannot be counted upon to uphold everything that belongs to them and other citizens "on paper," but the economy has uplifted its masses on a scale that is difficult to conceive of in the West. Like Myanmar's recent reforms, this creates popular support. Without question, China's policies toward minorities (with many exceptions, including Tibetans, Uyghurs, and political dissenters) are strategically enlightened compared with both Thailand and Burma.

Thailand's formerly open society is today becoming more like China or Singapore: authoritarian, but with economic freedom sufficient to stimulate material progress and investment. "Business-friendly" policies tend to favor large commercial operators everywhere in the world, but minority farmers such as Thai Lisu are especially vulnerable to land grabs because most do not hold property title—and logging, agricultural, and other real estate interests, often in cahoots with government officials, take advantage of their vulnerability. Ronnachit Mahattanapreut, senior vice president of the giant hotel and food conglomerate Central Plaza Hotel PCL, is typical in his attitude toward Thailand's military takeover. In May 2015, a year after the last democratically elected government was ousted, he opined that while this precipitated negative "short-term" economic and other impacts, "We want political stability so that businessmen can project long-term investment plans. Countries like China, Vietnam, and Myanmar, their governments can implement key economic policies to keep investments going."

The Thai press is now constrained when it comes to politics and the monarchy; otherwise, reporting still feels candid compared with China's. But now that Thailand's long-standing lese-majeste law is commonly wielded to imprison human rights activists and dissidents, a bone-deep chill has beset civil society. Minorities, including the Lisu, live with great instability and have the weakest legal protections of Lisu in the three countries. On the surface, though, Thai smiles and sunny beaches prevail; if one does not tangle in politics or its corrupt judiciary, Thailand remains free of government intrusion into personal things such as sex, books, the World Wide Web, and individual travel. Tourists are not likely to notice the clampdown unless they look for it, and travel sections of newspapers around the world are still full of features about paradise destinations in the kingdom.

The following chapters provide country-specific background and updated snapshots of Lisu lives and circumstances in Thailand, Myanmar, and China based on my personal observations. They are not comprehensive or necessarily representative of the majority of Lisu, who continue to live as the highland farmers who are the main focus of this book.

Whereas Book I emphasizes Lisu overall cultural patterns and history, Book II focuses on differences today in Thailand, Myanmar, and China. My goal is to provide glimpses of possible futures and directions, as well as cultural adaptations. Some Lisu have left their villages; many have one foot there and the other in contemporary urban life; most still farm—increasingly at lower elevations cultivating wet rice. Going back to all three countries, meeting Lisu eighteen years after first writing about them, was shocking. While some surprises appear in previous pages, Book I is based largely on research conducted in the 1990s.

I wanted to retain the flavor and mood of that time to document the dramatic changes since wrought by modernization and globalization on a single generation of preliterate minority people. My admiration for Lisu agility has only increased as they continue to survive and sometimes prosper against the odds.

Their story teaches us about ourselves and the adaptive genius of culture. Is humanity headed toward the dreary monoculture and mass civilization Claude Lévi-Strauss predicted at the mid-point of the twentieth century? The Lisu face cultural assimilation every place they live; their experience helps clarify not only ways to think about loss of ethnic identity but also what we, further along the globalization path in more developed countries, might choose to *do* about it.

2

Thailand

When a rich man looks for new land he depletes his riches,
When a poor man looks for new land, he's asking to die.

—*Lisu proverb*

September 2014

Extra spirits and protectors joined the Lisu on their long, dangerous migrations. Groups leaving the isolated Upper Salween (Nu) Valley heartland with a simple coterie of animistic spirits are not the same ones who began arriving in Thailand after the turn of the twentieth century.

Actually, none from the Upper Salween came here directly. Thailand's Lisu population has been traced to more southern, Chinese-influenced groups, who settled in the Thai Kingdom after spending a generation or more in Burma. In China they are called Lushui, or flowery Lisu, because the women's clothes are so colorful compared with those of northern Lisu. Their religious practices include Tao, Buddhist, Confucianist, and other elements picked up as they moved south. Their dress also evolved; it is as colorful, but not exactly the same, as what they wore in China.

The first Lisu group arrived in Thailand at Mai Sai from Burma right after the turn of the twentieth century, followed closely by Lahu and Akha. The

Karen came earlier, and most of the Hmong, Pa-O, Padong, and Kayaw arrived later, from the 1950s to the 1990s.

Lisu pioneers settled in Mai Ei and Fang. The oldest continuously inhabited village is Doi Chang, a Lisu/Akha mixed community about 60 kilometers from Chiang Rai. Population and ethnic mix have fluctuated here since 1915, from 10 families up to the 2014 census of 320 families, 210 of whom are Akha. In the past it was an opium-growing area, but today Doi Chang is known for coffee. Around 1950 the offshoot village Doi Laan established itself on a mountaintop 7 kilometers away after a dispute over opium fields. Only since 2010 has the ultimately scenic, scarily precipitous road between the two villages been fully paved.

Before, it was not unusual to spend hours stuck in the mud getting from Doi Laan to Doi Chang. I gave up once in the 1990s, went back to Doi Laan, and waited a few days for the road to become passable. In 2014's rainy season, this journey took fifteen minutes.

What such improvements mean to the people here who live, farm, go to school, and transport produce to market cannot be overstated. Lisu and other highland farmers have adopted modern farming techniques over the last twenty years, and the number of pickup trucks in villages like Doi Chang and Doi Laan indicates that many have been successful. But roads also increase exposure: to illness from chemical pesticides and fertilizers, access to drugs, land grabs from loggers, and harassment by government officials.

On a recent trip with an extended Lisu family of twenty men, women, children, and babies filling two small Toyota pickups (cabs and beds), we stopped on the village outskirts at Doi Chaang Coffee House, a large handsome structure of teak that was "up-cycled" from an older building. A huge parking lot separates the coffee house from the coffee-processing plant. The air was warm between downpours, and we sipped organic "beyond Fair Trade" iced lattes and gazed over hills reforested in the past ten to twenty years.

Coffee was introduced as a substitute crop for opium with help from the King's Projects and Germany's Development Aid Agency (GTZ); today, Akha coffee growers partner with Canadian marketers and a nonprofit to produce Doi Chaang Coffee and distribute it around the world. You can buy it at Costco and read about the partnership's community development projects, such as a new health clinic, on its website. All of Doi Chang is wired for Wi-Fi. Lisu farmers, with whom the Akha have long shared Doi Chang, have

Coffee, introduced as a substitute crop for opium in the 1980s, has brought investment and change to hill farming communities such as Doi Chang, the longest occupied Lisu village in Thailand. Author photo, 2014.

gradually became the minority over the past twenty years and don't find the terms offered by the biggest operation in town agreeable. There is talk of splitting the village in two so Lisu would have their own headman to lobby for them. They are behind but striving.

Cho-me Orn-anong personifies the dash of Doi Chang's Lisu "catch-up" efforts. The daughter of its former Lisu headman, she is married to a Hmong technical college *ajarn* (professor) and has a home in Chiang Mai. She divides her time between there and her family's Abeno Coffee Cooperative of fifteen growers, a store, and an eco-resort in Doi Chang. She thinks nothing of the 200-kilometer commute.

"If you sell to the big coffee company, they set the price and it isn't high enough," she told me. Plump and cheerful, she is both a generator and an implementer of plans, such as the cooperative she organized for older women to make hand-sewn Lisu garments and handicrafts to sell in her store.

She is most intent on developing a model for the coffee co-op that pays growers more. A month after I met her in Doi Chang, she was off to America to learn how to do this in the Economic Empowerment Fellows Program of the Mansfield Center at the University of Montana in Missoula. At age forty-five, she gained the scholarship opportunity through her involvement with the Women's Studies Program at Chiang Mai University. She returned there in her late thirties to earn a masters degree after having studied business when she was younger.

Her Hmong husband is more conservative and wishes she would narrow her focus to simply improving family finances. Her own broader aspirations, however, tumble out: "I want empowerment, knowledge about business, how to market, how to network, I am very interested in learning, I don't want to stay home. I like to go out." She wants to apply what she is learning about culture, the economy, and politics to help Lisu people develop their potential, not just her own. She said that while she is in America her husband is okay with staying home in Chiang Mai, teaching and minding their teenage sons and a nephew from Doi Chang who lives with them while attending a decent high school. "My husband already visited [the United States], now it is my turn," she told me, a glint in her eye.

Cho-me, clearly on the move as a member of the Thai middle class, still embodies Lisu values: her entrepreneurial spirit and status are growing with age; she has a strong, if not dominant, say in family finances; and her equality with her husband as decision-maker appears secure. She told me that Hmong women are not as assertive as Lisu but that her husband has adjusted. I'd expected him to possess a quiet temperament, willing to take a back seat to his energetic wife. When we met, however, it was clear that he, too, is a person of muscular opinion—a professor used to commanding respect and a lively conversationalist. He had visited his pharmacist sister in the Bay area and more recently in Minneapolis, where she moved to be closer to the Hmong community. As an educated, two-minority husband-wife team in freewheeling Thailand, they are an example of moving forward and changing while retaining village and cultural connections.

Lisu villages in Thailand often lacked headmen until the 1960s, when Thai officials began enlisting them as administrative links to the central government. They worried that Lisu and other poor highland minorities, as non-citizens receiving little beyond disrespect and bribe taking from the state, would come under the influence of Thai communist insurgents hiding out in mountain areas during the Vietnam War. A man from each village was chosen and given leadership training that included anti-communist indoctrination. With the Lisu, there was little to fear—they are among the least communally oriented of the ethnic groups in Southeast Asia. Lisu do not take well to authoritarian rule; leadership roles are viewed with suspicion because traditionally they came with more trouble, even danger, than benefits. However, Lisu are rational and do their best to exploit any advantage life hands them.

In 2014 I returned to Dton Loong, an hour's drive north of Chiang Mai in rising countryside and perhaps Thailand's most accessible Lisu village. I was looking for Alay-pa, the headman I'd interviewed in 1997. The village had changed, with old bamboo and wood houses replaced by concrete ones and former mud lanes paved. But it retained the familiar deserted feel of a village at midday; people were at work—some in fields, some at jobs as far away as Chiang Mai. Many come home only on weekends, leaving behind barking guard dogs. The day I visited, two minimally protected young men roved the village section by section, enveloping it in swirling thick clouds of pesticide.

Lisu Lodge, established in 1992 adjacent to Dton Loong, was still in business, still operated by its original owner. Among Thailand's first ethnic eco-resorts, it had upscaled a bit and joined a network of hostelries offering "hill tribe packages" to entertain education-minded tourists. Lisu Lodge provides service employment to locals as hotel workers and as singers, dancers, and musicians who perform cultural shows. Workers dress traditionally, and they and villagers make handicrafts to sell guests.

I was disappointed not to find Alay-pa, but in my search I was directed to the homes of other former headmen. An older, energetic woman in Lisu dress beckons me to take a seat on the veranda of her sturdy cement house. She sits at a tabletop sewing machine overlooking the lane surrounded by four or five giant multicolored plastic bags and stacks of cloth. She is Ali-ma Loy-yee-pa, a member of the Sin-lee clan. She was married to a former headman, she told me, but he'd taken up with another woman and moved away. She delivered this information with a "what are you going do" shrug. She

A cloud of poisonous vapor indicates mosquito extermination in Dton Loong. This curbs diseases such as dengue fever but comes with its own health concerns. Author photo.

was born here and has four daughters but doesn't read or speak standard Thai well. She uses Lisu for most needs and gets by in the northern Thai dialect at the market in nearby Mae Malai.

Ali-ma told me that things are much better today than they were fifteen or twenty years ago. She feels her Lisu identity is stronger, her culture more protected. I asked for specifics. Number one, she says, is that Thai citizenship problems have been solved for most people in her village. Now, only recent immigrants from Myanmar struggle to gain identity cards. She describes herself as prosperous, as a Thai citizen who is also proud to be Lisu. In the past, this wasn't possible. She has a smartphone and holds it up to show the village's strong signal. Next, she opens up one of the large bags, revealing it to be full of Lisu purses and bags that she makes. "I do it to keep busy, I don't need the money," she states. They are well-made, small to big, with tiny colorful folded cloth triangles and squares stitched between multiple borders—a motif adapted from Lisu baby caps.

My eye falls next on a glass cabinet on the veranda overfilled with household objects, topped with a framed dusty photograph of a young woman and an older Western man.

"Oh, that is my eldest daughter, she lives in California," Ali-ma explains, adding with an almost-chuckle that *all* her daughters married foreigners. One is in New York, another in Osaka. Her youngest moved back to Chiang Mai a couple of years ago from Studio City, a Los Angeles suburb. She shows me the telephone number of that daughter, Mayura, in her cell phone so I can jot it down. While she's at it, she points out her absent husband's number in case I want to talk headman business with him. She is pleasant and matter of fact. I, however, am nonplussed—smartphones with four bars, daughters in America, husband with *mia noi* (second wife, Thai/northern Thai). This was my first day back in the field since 1998, and I'd forgotten how unabashed and friendly the Lisu are. That has not changed, and neither had Lisu humor. Saying good bye, Ali-ma quips that she's thinking of taking up with a *falang* (foreigner) herself: did I know a good one who'd like an old woman who had become just a little bit fat?

When I returned to Chiang Mai, I called her daughter, Mayura Sinlee Seagrave. She responded with "cool," "yeah," "okay" in a brief conversation in which she agreed to have dinner with me the following night.

She picked me up at my guesthouse in an SUV, back seat strewn with the detritus of schoolage children: orange peels, soccer jerseys, empty cups. Mayura doesn't sound as much like a Valley Girl in person as on the phone. Slim and attractive, with a cascade of shiny black hair, she wears a turquoise tunic over leggings and looks to be in her mid-twenties rather than like a thirty-five-year-old soccer mom. She chooses a hip vegetarian restaurant for dinner and tells me her story:

> I grew up in Dton Loong but was sent to Suksasongkra boarding school in
> Chiang Mai when I was seven . . . the village school was no good. All the
> kids in my family got decent educations because we lived so close to Chiang
> Mai. The school was fun. I liked living in the dormitory and meeting other
> hill tribe kids, just coming home on weekends. My father was a successful
> headman and farmer, also a silversmith. He attended ag school and took
> classes in things like composting, planting rice between fruit trees, and raising
> pigs efficiently. Because he was headman, he got involved in economic devel-

opment. Some Lisu didn't understand the importance of Thai citizenship. He "got it" earlier than many and moved ahead. For older, poorer people it was hard—too much work. You had to walk a whole day to renew your ID. You had to pay money, be insulted, and many just didn't do it. And it was actually not so bad in our village; we live closer to government offices than most. Even before Lisu Lodge, foreigners came there and we were exposed to modern things.

My Dad tried to steer me to ag, but I wasn't into it. Chose not to go to university, I took a vocational course in sewing instead. Later, I realized it was important and did a distance learning course through Sukhothai Open University. They send you books, you study anywhere, just turn up to take tests. I got a bachelor's degree in English. Now I'm trying to get a biz degree, but it is hard with two kids and working in the family business.

I met my husband, Sean, fifteen years ago in Chiang Mai, when I worked at an Internet café. His background is Burmese-American, and his family has lived in Asia for five generations. His parents are both writers. My husband and I have a graphic photography and retouching company, Ultrafina, and do advertising for cosmetics, movie posters, and so on. It's US-based, and first we lived in New York. It was too cold there, though. Then we moved to Studio City in LA for a few years. But after the second kid [her children are now eight and fourteen] it was easier to come back to Chiang Mai. We moved here in 2009 to be closer to my mother, for good schools, and because household help is better here. Because we live here, my kids can understand, and one even speaks some Lisu. At home we use English and Thai.

I ask Mayura if she feels Lisu. "It's me, of course. I feel kind of happy to be Lisu but also northern Thai, Buddhist, animist, and some American. I also feel good about the opportunities I've had to learn and to travel—not just stay in the village like my mother." She said all her sisters had married foreigners much older than they and also left the village. As a young girl she thought she would follow their examples: "Marry an older guy, have a peaceful life."

This was a practical matter: she didn't judge her parents wrong in allowing her eldest sister, at sixteen, to marry a man near sixty. Their age difference isn't important. Unlike her parents, whose marriage led to divorce and was hard on the family, her sister is still happily married (today, she in her forties, her husband in his eighties). Mayura said her father had picked up "Thai ideas"

Mayura Sinlee Seagrave (right) works with an employee in her company's Chiang Mai office. Photo: Sean Seagrave.

from involvement with government officials—especially the idea that men have more power than women. In the standard Thai way of showing success, he took a younger second wife, which her mother, as a Lisu, would not accept. This caused terrible fights. He divorced her mother but still supports her financially. Today, Mayura, as the only daughter living close by, sees her mother regularly and encourages her to branch out in the things she makes, to "move into backpacks and other useful things people need and like."

I ask if her father received bride price for her. "Father took 50,000 baht for each of us daughters [then worth about $1,300] to keep everyone equal," she said. "But I think he turned around and spent it all on our wedding feasts." Mayura's husband is eleven years older than she, not a significant difference, she said. Cultural conflict has not been a big issue for them: "Marriage is hard for all couples sometimes, but we are together, we work together at our company. Our kids are happy, our family is good."

Mayura, whose mother is illiterate (but who clearly has held on to her myi-do) and whose father used the advantages of being a headman to advance, has used her own agency in moving from village girl to international business-woman in one generation.

———————— ■–■ ————————

Thais and their government have an ambivalent relationship toward the Lisu and other minorities in northern areas bordering China, Myanmar, and Laos. Overwhelmingly, they look down on them and consider them backward. But there are economic benefits from having such exotic people in their midst, flowing from both tourism and agriculture. Opium's importance has waned (methamphetamine is today's largest illegal trade item outside of human trafficking), but tourism's hasn't: in Thailand this sector accounts for about 15 percent of GDP (agriculture is under 9 percent), and almost 30 million visitors arrived in 2015. Arrivals dipped to under 25 million in 2014 because of the military coup, which in turn hurt millions of people relying on tourism to make a living. That year, cab drivers, people working in hotels and restaurants, sex workers, vendors, travel agents, English and Thai language teachers, and gem traders are just a sampling of those who told me some version of "business is down."

I was in my thirties in 1985 and a "budget adventure tourist" when I first encountered Lisu in Thailand. My boyfriend and I joined a trek from Fang in the northwest. After hours of being jostled on bad roads in a pickup bed with backpacks and fellow trekkers, eight of us followed our Thai-Chinese leader on a long, hilly walk at the beginning of the rainy season. For five days we visited villages belonging to Akha, Karen, Lisu, and Hmong. We were the only Americans; our group of Swedes, British, a Canadian, and his Thai girl-friend spent nights in smoky and mostly raised bamboo houses—from funky to exquisite. The scenery was stunning; we met very friendly subsistence farmers dressed in amazing clothes living far from roads. The chance to see and briefly share their lives, technology, art, culture, and food was a great gift. The fact that we couldn't communicate with them except through gesture and minor gifts of medicine did not make the experience *unmeaningful*. In my case, it sparked a lifelong interest. What the villagers got out of the exchange is less knowable. Were we exploiting them? Not intentionally. I did note a parallel between Thai attitudes (and some of my fellow European trekkers') toward minorities and those of pioneer Americans toward indigenous peoples whose land they coveted.

Data on tourists arriving in Thailand were not kept until 1960, when 81,000 visitors arrived in the kingdom. While the majority then and now hang at southern beaches and spend most of their money there and in Bangkok (the best-known sex and medical-tourism destination in the world), many visit Chiang Mai. The ancient capital of the Kingdom of Lanna, it is the cultural capital of the north; hill tribe treks are arranged from here. Chiang Mai University has been a research hub for Southeast Asian studies since the 1960s. Because of its proximity to Burma/Myanmar, Cambodia, Vietnam, and other war-torn, refugee-generating states, it is a center for political groups in exile, nongovernment organizations (NGOs), and writers and academics engaged in "Peace and Conflict" studies and reporting.

While anthropologists began combing the still-remote hills for doctoral theses in the 1950s and 1960s, "hill tribe tourism" didn't begin until the early 1980s, according to Del Phaywong Guat, former vice president of the Chiang Mai Tourism Federation. An urbane middle-aged Lisu man who lives in Chiang Mai, like most new members of the middle class, Del darts through the city's traffic on a motor scooter. We met in the city, and he agreed to scooter down to Hang Dong, 10 kilometers south, where I was staying and writing up two months of field notes in September 2014.

He told me he adopted a Thai name in his twenties and became Buddhist to avoid the discrimination he suffered growing up. He said the animistic form of Buddhism practiced in Thailand is not so different from Lisu religion. He is observant in such things as giving up meat for two months during "Buddhist Lent"—fairly unusual for easy-going, carnivorous Thais and Lisu.

Like Mayura, Del left his village to attend a boarding school for hill tribe children (the same school, but he attended a different campus further away in Tak) and speaks Thai and English fluently. He was eleven when he left home and did not return often after that. As a teenager he transferred to a different boarding school in Chiang Mai.

> The problem with hill tribe treks is they are unregulated and run by private
> tour companies that "sell" the people without giving them anything in
> return. Maybe certain villagers get 20 baht (less than a dollar) per head to
> host in their homes or sell a few handicrafts, but the village has no voice, no

part in organizing. And tour guides give little information on culture, either because they don't know or they know but don't speak English well enough to be educators.

Guides are busy once the group arrives in the village with cooking and setting up for meals and sleeping. They are not paid well; they get commission on sales to tourists so they concentrate on that. The better tour companies have a "no shopping in [the] village" rule, an improvement of sorts, but which cuts out villages even more—so is not a solution.

Del says it doesn't have to be that way; better models exist that value the cultures of touristed villages and create positive exchanges. But first, the villagers themselves have to understand and recognize the beauty and value of bamboo houses, mud floors, well-made traditional handicrafts, and smoky meals served fireside. Appreciation of natural beauty and simple rural existence usually follows industrialization and takes time to develop; the urge toward modernity is universal, he patiently explains. He mentions an Akha resort, Baan Loasha, near Chiang Rai, managed by the village in consultation with an NGO, as a positive example. He worked for a year at Lisu Lodge in Dton Loong when he was younger and says "the owner's proposal is good, but on-site managers vary; some are better than others. I think they should consult the elders and pay more respect to the village itself."

Del explodes with an emphatic "nothing!" when I ask what the Tourism Authority of Thailand (TAT) does to develop a better model of tribal-village–based tourism—unless you count taking pictures of stunningly beautiful minority women and children to "sell Thailand" to tourists. Typical, he says, is the fund TAT established to help villages develop as tourist destinations. It didn't come with workshops on writing proposals or any support to show minorities how to access the money. A few villages have been assisted by NGOs, but this is erratic and the government has no plan.

Thailand has weak public-sector development, and fewer resources are directed to farmers and minorities in the hinterlands than to urban dwellers and commercial/industrial centers. Hill people are particularly overlooked in terms of education and other benefits. Rural schools are mediocre at best. More often private, church, or temple-funded boarding schools have been where Lisu turn to better educate children. Many such institutions make conversion to Christianity or Buddhism an unspoken quid pro quo.

Del took the experience he gained working with a credit union for the Tourist Federation to establish the Lisu Conservative Credit Union Group. He also started a funeral fund for people under age fifty-nine. "Lack of credit and financial services are big obstacles for Lisu," he told me. "Farmers can't register land or hold titles, so they have no collateral. They also go bankrupt paying for funerals." Absence of government support and education makes establishing or growing businesses difficult. He mentioned one of the (many) reasons the elected government of Thai prime minister Thaksin Shinawatra was ousted by military coup in 2006 was his popular "One Village, One Million Baht" (about $25,000) initiative, meant to help rural people learn money management. "It was not a gift, villages were expected to pay it back and grow the money," he explained, saying that many amassed 10 million baht or more, gained credit experience, and began administering small loans to students and village businesses. Del claims entrenched banking interests *hated* this initiative because it was in direct conflict with their business.

His credit union and funeral fund are tiny steps to educate people on how cooperatives work, along with the concept of mutual benefits. While micro-lending is a proven idea, minorities in Thailand, many still not citizens or fluent in Thai, don't understand it. "They are conservative and suspicious because of past experiences. It is hard for poor Lisu to see how they are able to help others without causing loss to themselves," he says of his programs, which have minimum monthly contributions of just 50 baht (less than $2 per family.)

Lisu distrust of *si-so* (patron-client) relations with traders, bankers, and middlemen continues to keep many out of debt today as in the 1970s, when Dessaint wrote about this habit of thinking. Many Lisu are still wary of all forms of credit.

------- ■ ■ -------

On the subject of citizenship, government policy is strict. Thais can't be said to single out minorities for discrimination. People such as the Lisu, however, who may lack written language or not speak Thai well and who reside at the bottom in this hierarchical society, are at the mercy of petty bureaucrats. Being born here or residing in the country for decades does not offer guarantees in this regard. It is under such circumstances that having an effective Thai-speaking headman, such as Mayura's father apparently was, pays dividends for the average Lisu. For each favor, though, for each trip to a Thai office or department, the headman must be paid his expenses plus a small gift. A trip to Chiang Mai from a highland village is costly and can be dangerous for undocumented people. Most Lisu in Thailand today claim they want to be citizens, yet even parents with children born here find obtaining birth certificates difficult if they gave birth at home—still more common than hospital births. Older people who arrived here from Burma or China have often haggled with Thai bureaucrats for decades to "become legal." Dozens of pieces of paper must be duly submitted, stamped, and taken on to the next office.

A woman's response to my question in the mid-1990s was typical: "Trouble, trouble," she said, closing her eyes and shaking her head when I asked about getting a house registration so her child could attend a Thai school or obtaining other slips of ephemeral pink and yellow paper demanded by bureaucrats.

In 2014 I met with Sakda Saenmi, a pleasant, sophisticated Lisu bee clan member who is the founding director of IMPECT (Inter Mountain Peoples Education and Culture Thailand), a non-government organization established in 1991 to advance minority village development and give political voice to indigenous people. IMPECT has expanded from representing five ethnic groups in northern Thailand to thirty-five all around the country today. It moved from small offices I visited seventeen years ago into a large compound on the outskirts of Chiang Mai. Several overseas NGOs help fund it, and it was abuzz with workshops and people wandering around in traditional dress the day I visited. A few weeks later Sakda agreed to meet me at a highway-side fish restaurant. We retreated to the "VIP" room inside to get away from end-of-rainy-season mosquitoes and diners cheering a televised soccer match.

"Citizenship issues continue, but things are not quite as dire as in the past," he said. For years the government stance was that unless you could prove you arrived in Thailand before 1985, there was no path to legal residence. As recently as 2005, families that had been in the country for twenty years but lacked acceptable evidence were simply out of luck. He said the law changed four or five years ago, allowing more flexible criteria so that anyone who can document that he or she has lived in Thailand for ten years or more can gain permanent residence and then apply for citizenship. IMPECT and other NGOs are pushing to expand acceptable evidence beyond hospital-issued birth certificates. As more Lisu attend school, families gain advocates to assist older non-Thai speakers in navigating through the bureaucratic thicket.

The new rules providing greater flexibility, however, haven't reached all civil servants, and in 2015, still only about half of all minorities living in Thailand had citizenship papers. A young man born in Thailand interviewed by anthropologist Amanda Flaim in 2011 reported: "Everyone in my family is a citizen. My mother, my father, my grandparents, my brothers, my sisters . . . The officials do not believe me. I gave them pictures. I showed them my household registration. I took a DNA test with my father, and it shows that I am his son. But still I am not a citizen. [The district official] asked me, 'If you are a child of citizens, where is your proof?'"

Sakda admitted that IMPECT's expansion to include thirty-five minority groups at different development levels all around the country has added greatly to its challenges. In northern Thailand alone, this agency has grown from representing five to fifteen minorities today, including the tiny group of the Mlabri who are nomadic hunter-gatherers who did not even begin to live in villages until the 1990s. The approach has been to divide IMPECT's work into two segments: one Sakda calls "a learning space," where minority people network and learn from each other's experiences, and the second is a more policy-oriented Council of Indigenous People in Thailand that deals with government officials. Well-intentioned and wired-in as they are, IMPECT's resources seem stretched beyond the capacity to deliver help to and represent Thailand's underserved minorities.

―――――――――――■-■―――――――――――

Wiwat Tamee, a contemporary of Sakda's from Doi Laan (the two are among the first Lisu to gain advanced university degrees in Thailand), were together at Chiang Mai University in the 1990s when they founded complementary organizations. I locate Wiwat's cul-de-sac headquarters with some difficulty, finally tipped off by a tiny van parked outside with a Highland Peoples Taskforce logo stenciled on its door. His office occupies a shop house at the end of an overgrown lane in a semi-rural backwater of the city. This NGO focuses on human and land rights, and Wiwat represents Thai minorities on national bodies such as the Human Rights Sub-Committee and the Health Committee for Stateless People. Funding is tenuous and comes from the United Nations, foreign NGOs, and Thai government sources.

Wiwat's porcupine shock of black hair flecked with white, his bright eyes and sweet manner suggest a *Wind in the Willows* character. He leads off our conversation with the news that land rights for minorities are at an all-time low in Thailand: "Last month [August 2014] land worked by an entire Lisu village, Laowu, in Chiang Dao District, was confiscated by the government. Some of the men were thrown in jail. This in a village that has been there almost 100 years!" He said the government justifies its actions with strong forest protection laws that it applies or ignores selectively. Because Lisu tend to site villages and farms near tops of mountains, on the steepest, most difficult land, they are disproportionately affected. The law declares land at greater than 60 percent grade unsuitable for farming. In fact, land pressure has turned even less steep areas, just fifteen years ago not considered for cultivation by lowlanders, into contested space. Lisu and other highland farmers are now squeezed from both below and above.

"The rules of the forest are strict and haven't changed for years; they were written to sound good to environmentalist ears," Wiwat says, explaining that the Thai government has a long record of allowing deforestation and using minority hill tribes as scapegoats.

This story line is easily debunked, he demonstrates, by superimposing a tissue map of today's forest cover over one showing Thailand's forests forty years ago. Wiwat says it is provable that hill tribe areas have retained more forest than other areas—and that loss as a result of their farming pales in comparison to that eaten up by logging interests and lowlanders allowed to buy "use contracts" at lower altitudes within national forests.

"Hill farmers, especially Lisu, have land management skills," he said echoing what Eugene Morse wrote forty years ago and told me in the mid-1990s. Wiwat said a protest is planned in mid-October, when hill farmers who've had land confiscated will travel to Bangkok. He said the main question they want to ask the new military junta is, why can rich people buy land or "use contracts" while poor ones are not allowed to stay on land they have worked for more than fifty years?

A huge obstacle to land reform is that Thailand has yet to comprehensively survey its own land or create a database identifying who has been where and for how long. Wiwat hopes completion of the government master plan he is working on (thus the maps all over his office) with NGOs, the army, and the forestry department will provide a new legal basis to decide cases. They are making a map that includes all this information, and the new government has committed to "check if it is true or not."

The other obstacle to reform is old-fashioned corruption. Many court cases have already adjudicated specific areas, in which the monied side generally prevails. Even the rare judgments won by minorities are often vacated over new claims that a farmer encroached into the forest "a little more" (Wiwat holds up almost-touching thumb and forefinger to show how much) than allowed. Then the entire case is thrown out and the farmer is left with nothing, he says. He confirmed my impression that minority land rights today in Thailand, especially for the poor, are weaker than those in China and Myanmar: "Yes. It is true these other countries have been getting much better as Thailand gets worse."

In mid-October, a month after I visited Wiwat and returned to California, I read on *Prachatai* independent web news a short item about a convoy of Lahu villagers making their way to Bangkok to protest land confiscations. Twenty vans were turned back by the army. In February 2015 the president of the Southern Peasants' Federation of Thailand, an activist for land rights at the other end of the country, was detained for work he does that is no different from Wiwat's. The news report stated that he was undergoing "attitude adjustment."

Mimi Saeju, thirty-three, is returning to her Lisu home village of Doi Laan to do something like "induct" her boyfriend, Jo, into her family. Jo is a cheerful-looking member of the Rakhine minority with shiny black hair down to his waist. He is also a political activist who recently spent time in prison in his native Myanmar. The couple has known each other for nine years, and it was during his imprisonment that they became more serious: "No, it's not like we've set a date to get married or become engaged in *your* sense, but we decided to be together," she explained. "It is time to show respect to my parents by including him my family. This is tradition."

Unsure I understand, I ask if there will be a ceremony. "Oh yes, there will be something, but nothing really . . ." she trails off. "You'll see."

Mimi received her masters degree in ethnicity and development in 2015 from Chiang Mai University. In 1994, at age eleven, she was sent to a boarding school in Angthong Province, central Thailand. Until she went to college, she was allowed to return to Doi Laan one week a year, two days of which were spent in travel. She is the only one of four siblings who went away for school and the only one who today lives far from her village.

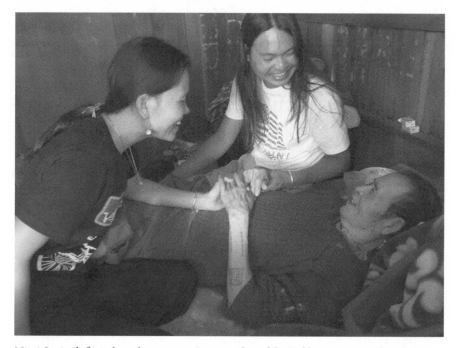

*Mimi Saeju (left) inducts her partner Jo, a member of the Rakhine minority from Burma,
to her family, including her bedridden grandfather, in Doi Laan. Author photo.*

"My parents tried to send the others, but they hated it, they cried, they
didn't last long," she told me. Long absences from family and village, her
education, and exposure to Thai, Western, and other influences combined
to create a situation in which Mimi says "I now negotiate with myself
about what it means to 'be Lisu.' I question why being Lisu has to be like
this and not like that, if it even exists, or if it is necessary." In particular,
easy-to-spot cultural markings are less important to her than are internalized values and behavior: she equates "being conscientious" much more
with being Lisu than wearing traditional dress or with being Thai. Living
in Chiang Mai, she says, makes her feel Lisu, and she is always aware of her
difference from others.

Mimi continues to "do" many Lisu things: she remains close to her parents, returns to the village at the New Year and other occasions, and appre-
ciates that her mother, A-wu, conducts "soul-calling" ceremonies for her

when she feels unwell or has a bad dream. Her father and brother built a Lisu-style bamboo hut in the garden of the Chiang Mai home she shares with anthropologist Otome Klein Hutheesing, with whom she has lived since her late teens and now cares for along with Otome's partner, the Cambodian scholar Michael Vickery (died 2017). The hut, she says, is to make Otome less lonely for Doi Laan. She herself does not long for the village but enjoys the hut. Without a car and since she works and studies, it is difficult to make the six-hour return journey there more often than every few months.

Their home on a quiet Chiang Mai lane is a gathering spot for minority friends who live in the city. Mimi often posts photos on Facebook of parties, children's classes, and other educational events in the hut and garden. She devotes a room inside to displaying Lisu clothing and artifacts. This was unplanned, it "just happened," according to Mimi, "because of my two mothers." A-wu, her biological mother, had no room to continue storing the stuff in her village house and was about to deal with it the Lisu way—which is to "burn old things you don't need." Otome, who had collected the items over the years, proposed the "closet-thinning" approach: she would give or throw away only things she no longer wore or that didn't fit. Mimi realized that "all these things are Lisu arts and mean a lot, especially gathered together," and so at some point they "became" the labeled collection she now displays. "Maybe one day it will become a small museum," Mimi says, with the "how should I know" shrug favored by Lisu.

———————————■-■———————————

We stop in the last market town on the main road before the turnoff to Doi Laan. It is latish afternoon, and we need to pick up food and liquor for the appointed weekend when Jo will "join the family." Good cell phone reception reaches almost every corner of Thailand, and normal checking back and forth about needed supplies ensues, along with an admonition from Mimi's mother, A-wu, to "hurry up, the food is ready and we're starving while we wait for you."

This visit is not traditional but an adaptation; Lisu custom is for the girl to join the boy's family, and living together before marriage was uncommon until recently. The fact that Jo is not Lisu but a foreigner and a member of Myanmar's Rakhine minority who spent two years in prison for political crimes adds to its novelty. Recent political reform in Myanmar makes it possible for him to return home for work and visits now, but he lives in Thailand on a temporary visa as he attempts to gain legal residence.

Nonetheless, as our rented SUV pulls up to the family compound of thatched and cement buildings at the top of a steep, windy lane, the sense of occasion is not unlike what I remember when I arrived at this same household at the New Year in 1997: trays with little ceramic cups holding shots of rice liquor await us and are immediately passed around, the women are in full Lisu dress (synthetic velveteen sleeves in deep blues and purples paired with chiffon prints for the body of the garment are now in fashion), the men slightly less so, and the kids run in a gang of cousins and neighbors—climbing trees, shooting marbles, and keeping their own society. The smallest girl eventually defects to take refuge in her mother's arms.

Food is served, and liquor flows. Mimi's two sisters and their kids are there without their husbands (her youngest sister is separated), and her brother won't come until the next day because he is at college studying to become a tourist guide. Friends and neighbors drop in and everyone eats and drinks—with the host family encouraging everyone to eat and drink more. Daylight fades. Jo bonds with Mimi's father, uncles, and others—the two smallest girls, including one in his lap, hang with the men when their mothers are busy. The kitchen is a hub and some people sit on mats around its fire, but there is no real center; it is a shifting feast with tables and lounging platforms outside as well. People come and go, eating bananas and rambutans in between substantial courses. Adults get quietly drunk.

I have to explain more than once that is not my custom to drink while working; I must take notes. An intoxicated brother-in-law or cousin with a deeply lined, soulful face nods with understanding: "I cannot work my fields when drunk, either," he says. "I will drink tonight and maybe tomorrow [Sunday] as well . . . but Monday"—here, he makes a muscular chopping gesture to indicate his projected return to sobriety.

Mimi's middle sister, Ale-ma Ee-su, is thirty years old, has two older boys, a little daughter, and an air of bemused resignation. She lives in nearby Hwe-San village and married at age eighteen. I ask what she sees as the biggest change of the past ten years. "I don't think anything's changed much. I follow my mother and have the same life. Once you have kids, life is mostly work, and money is always running out."

Her response is a surprise; she is the first one of many whom I've asked this question who doesn't immediately begin listing changes affecting daily life. Because I've heard it from so many other Lisu women, I feel compelled to point out that on top of working the fields, her mother, Awu, used to also make the family's clothes when *she* had kids at home. A few minutes earlier I'd asked Ale-ma if she'd made the adorable Lisu dress with tiny velveteen sleeves her three-year-old daughter was wearing. She replied with mock exasperation, making her eyes big: "Two hundred baht" (about six dollars).

"Isn't that a change, that you don't have to make clothes?"

Unwilling to cede her point, she answered, "Well, now we have to work harder to *get* money instead of working to make clothes. It's a wash." Her cash-versus-subsistence economy comparison is sharp, and I wonder how different her life would have been if she'd stayed in school like Mimi. She and her husband grow corn and coffee for cash and rice to eat. They have a vegetable garden, too: "At least we don't need money for food. But I have school expenses Mother didn't have," Ale-ma said, adding that she takes care of her husband's elderly parents as well as her own children.

When I bring up expectations for them, she focuses first on her daughter: "I want her to have a chance for higher education; I don't want her to be in my position." She adds that she hopes all her children will go to university and earn good salaries instead of farming so they are able to take care of her and her husband when they are old.

I praise her sons: not only are they handsome, but they take care of their little sister, are polite and helpful to elders, and seem natural leaders. She admits, "They are very good boys now . . . but who knows how they will behave in the future?" She has seen many good boys in her village turn into troubled young men with drug and alcohol addictions; some are now in jail. Unlike in the 1990s, when Lisu girls were the least likely of the minorities to join Thailand's sex trade, today they more equally fall prey to it. Ale-ma fears for her children's futures and, at thirty, doesn't exude much confidence about her own.

She, her family, and her mother and father are more representative of the majority of Thai Lisu, who live in villages and lack higher education, than are urban counterparts such as her sister Mimi, Cho-me, and others. But everyone has a connection to the city, and it is likely that, as Cho-me has, in the future Mimi will take one or more of Ale-ma's kids to live with her in

Chiang Mai to access a better school. Similar to American immigrants who serially emigrated from Russia or Italy, minority families in Thailand depopulate villages one member at a time—a son or daughter goes to the city and gains a foothold, then others follow. Most urban Thais and ethnic minorities alike keep strong ties to home villages; they return for holidays and help hold on to family land so they can retreat to the countryside as necessary, where they know they will always have something to eat.

Mimi and Ale-ma's mother, A-wu, is fifty-five years old, the mother of four. Her family came to Doi Chang from Padang Luang and before that from China in the early 1950s, after the revolution. They soon moved to Doi Laan. She answers decisively when I ask about the biggest changes she's seen the past twenty years: "Well, people are consuming more alcohol—not just on feast days. The drug trade is more popular than ever. Also, people are not singing as much. We used to gather at full moon and sing through the night until morning . . . actually, that began changing thirty years ago—but I miss it still. Now I sing only for my son, who asks for songs to sing while working his fields."

I ask her to sing one for me, and she obliges with "The Orphan Song":

Mother has died, Father is still there.
If Mother were here, we wouldn't suffer as much
It would be wonderful if Father and Mother could still be together.

Awu believes both father and mother are needed to raise a family; the two are equally important in upholding traditions and rituals. She is worried about her youngest daughter, who has a three-year old daughter and recently split with her second husband.

"At least we are not Hmong, we can take her back without too much trouble," she says, raising her eyes to the night sky in thanks for that. She is referring to the fact that Hmong clan spirits are more strict than Lisu ones. Hill women usually join their husbands' clans upon marriage, but reintegrating them back into birth families when marriages don't work out poses bigger problems for some groups than others—Hmong spirits in particular do not allow non-clan members to live under their roofs; some families won't take daughters back, and others build them separate houses at great expense. "We Lisu are more lenient with daughters," Awu notes, a trifle smug. This attitude is further testament to the high comparative status of

Lisu women. Just then her husband, Ale Baba (who might have been listening in), joins the conversation, adding that he is also greatly relieved not to be Akha, who think twins are unlucky; traditionally, they had to kill one. "Imagine that?" he asks, eyes widening, the thought as horrible to him as it is to me.

A-wu is generally an upbeat person, but when I ask about the future, she looks me directly in the eyes and says: "Five years from now, I wonder if I will be this tired . . . or more tired? I am getting old, child labor is not allowed anymore, who will take care of my fields? My son's wife is away working; my son can work only on weekends because he is studying."

I ask if she gets satisfaction from having two of her four children educated or from owning a big truck to get the rice, coffee, corn, and kidney beans she grows to market. Her family has added new rooms and a couple of buildings to their compound since I visited at New Year in the late 1990s—do these things give her happiness?

"I guess my worries are short term; long term, I feel more positive. We have a saying 'Al-ee du LA, al-le SWA.'" "It means 'what will be, will be,'" translator Mimi explains, adding that a more literal Lisu translation is "whatever comes, count on it."

News is exchanged; more food and drink follow as the evening winds down. Surely, I am the last person to hear that a woman in the village died in the early hours of this very day. I wonder if her death precipitated Awu's mood and choice of song and Ale-ma's claim that nothing has really changed. The deceased was between thirty-five and forty, the mother of a one-month-old daughter and three older children. She was ill during her pregnancy and gave her baby her last strength. The doctor sent her home from the hospital to die a few days earlier. The cause of her death is unknown; something to do with her stomach and cancer was mentioned. Highland and other farmers suffer from many pesticide-related illnesses in Thailand, and this was suspected even though no diagnosis was given, according to A-wu. The reality that commonly available products present long- and short-term health hazards is understood. Here and in other developing countries, rat poison and other agricultural agents are what poor people use to commit suicide.

Jo's introduction to the family is an important occasion, but the family decides to dispense with the small ceremony planned because it is not custom the day of a death or the next, when the woman's funeral takes place. So

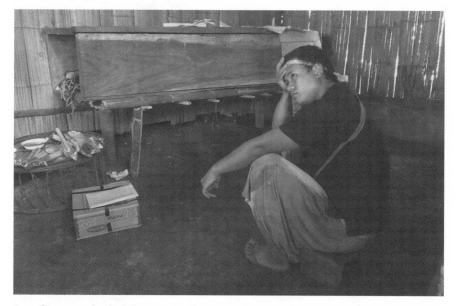

*Son of woman who died the previous day in Doi Laan, in front of her coffin at her funeral.
Author photo.*

the following morning the couple sits down with Mimi's father, who advises
them on living harmoniously. Her mother joins them to proffer tips, including the Lisu insight, "When two cups are placed together, they will rattle."
This saying speaks to living together: married or not, close relationships are
bound to include conflict.

The funeral the same day is a few sharp turns and perhaps three minutes
by car from the Saeju family compound. A mellow, resigned, and casual atmosphere prevails. Thirty or so people sit at plastic tables outside, eating and
drinking under blue shade tarps. Inside the traditional, earthen-floor house,
more people mill around or wait to pay respects to the family. Many offer 50
baht and 100 baht notes to the son to help with death expenses; he looks to
be in shock but carefully notes the gifts in a small notebook. A closed coffin
made of thick planks of wood is raised on blocks in a corner, perpendicular to
the tabiya, or house altar, with nine cups. Another son is performing a ritual
there; this is interrupted by the squeals of the baby pig about to be sacrificed.

Acceptance of death and the pulling together of community to embrace
the grieving family is comforting and learned from experience. Here, as in

much of the world, lives of poor people are often difficult and short. In villages, life is experienced directly, not represented, abstracted, or conceptualized. For Lisu, what you *do* is more important than what you believe or what you say that might mean. Knowing what to do when someone dies is no exception: those who die of sickness are buried, those who die in an accident are cremated and then buried, and deaths of babies or the very young are not ceremonialized because their souls are weak and unformed—it is easy for spirits to take them away. The size of the pig sacrificed is a calculus of the age, social standing, and cause of death of the deceased person.

Two hundred kilometers away in Chiang Mai, even these small comforts of "doing" offered in the village are absent for poor urban Lisu. A shantytown I encounter there houses about twenty women whose families have scattered and whose husbands are dead or addicted. They live by making crafts to sell at the night market. Some have children and grandchildren with them who are not attending school. The twenty-year-old son of one woman recently died from AIDS contracted from sharing needles.

These are Lisu who have lost their myi-do, yet even in these circumstances they exhibit remarkable spunk. They don't leave their cardboard and plywood hovels without donning Lisu dress, and they manage to keep themselves and their children fairly clean. In Lisu fashion, they crack jokes about their plight. You can meet them in Chiang Mai's Night Bazaar, sewing clothes and bags to sell to tourists, gossiping together, and planning how to get back to their mountain.

3

Burma/Myanmar

If you want to go broke slowly, smoke opium;
If you want to go broke fast, play cards!
    —*saying among Christian Lisu in Putao*

Military dictators backed by a strong army (Tatmadaw) ruled here absolutely from the 1960s until recently. Business cronies and a rubber-stamp legislature completed the picture. In this time period, over fifty bloody insurgencies have disrupted the lives of millions of people, particularly members of Myanmar's 135 ethnic groups living in frontier areas—who comprise close to 40 percent of the country's total population. Because of these hardships and because most Lisu in Myanmar are Christians, I thought the culture might be less intact here than in Thailand and China. But to the contrary, it felt like those who have adapted in the most difficult environment of all led me to the pith of Lisu cultural values and style.

Most, but not all, Lisu migrants to Burma from China arrived after the revolution and were already Christians. This is the best place to look at little-studied Lisu forms of Christianity.

The first documented Lisu converts, in 1910, are claimed by the British-based China Inland Mission. Within ten to twenty years, several Protestant groups discovered that Lisu and other preliterate animists were more receptive

Women are generally the drivers of bullock carts, still the main way of moving goods in rural Myanmar—especially in the rainy season. Author photo.

to their message than were Buddhists, with their written canons and institutions. An early focus on converting Tibetans, for example, yielded meager results. By the 1920s and 1930s, two dominant Protestant missionary families in Yunnan, the Canadian Morrisons and the Bible-Belt American Morses, were concentrating efforts on Lisu and Rawang (the latter an even smaller minority) in the Mekong and Nujiang Valley regions of Southwest China–adjacent Burma. Soon, they and indigenous preachers they trained were making proselytizing trips across unmarked frontiers to gain converts and establish tiny congregations in Burma's far north. The Morrisons established a mission there in the 1920s that included a Lisu and Rawang branch by the early 1930s. Both the Morrisons and the Morses shifted operations to Burma's Putao Valley after the revolution, when foreign missionaries, advisers, and anthropologists were expelled from China.

Some Lisu settled further south in the state, around its capital, Myitkyina. Another American dynasty of missionaries, the Tegenfeldts, dominated the missionary scene there with a Baptist church established in the nineteenth century, which attracted Lisu converts as they began arriving. Catholicism also found Lisu converts but far fewer because their missionaries arrived later, after Protestants had divided up the regions and claimed territories.

In waves of migration from the late 1940s through the early 1970s, thousands of Lisu migrated to Burma from China. Those arriving immediately after World War II in Northern Kachin State found a dozen small churches, according to Gertrude Morse, who wrote in *The Dogs May Bark: But the Caravan Moves On* that in 1945 the first Burmese Lisu Christian convention consisted of twelve church leaders. Morse claims many migrants were turned back to China by Burmese officials, including a group of several hundred starving Christians, in 1954. Most who made it settled in Kachin's Putao Valley; many had previous connections to the Morses, Morrisons, and other evangelical missions. The forced collectivization of agriculture and industry during China's Great Leap Forward (1958–62), in which 18 million to 60 million people starved to death, and the excesses of the Cultural Revolution (1966–76) continued to drive Lisu migration into Burma.

A vast majority of Lisu in Myanmar today practice a form of Protestant evangelical Christianity that proscribes drinking alcohol, smoking, and gambling. It is a results-oriented "old-time religion" reminiscent of pioneer camp revivals and American westward expansion. It also resonates with Lisu history and culture, especially when compared with more hierarchical or mystical Southeast Asian religious systems. A key to fundamentalist Christianity's success with the Lisu is that the missionaries delivering it, such as the Morses, from the southern and midwestern regions of America known as the Bible Belt, were pioneers, explorers, and risk takers themselves—and independent from church hierarchy.

When I asked Helen Morse what denomination of Christianity her family practiced, expecting to hear Baptist, Pentecostal, or perhaps Methodist, she answered tartly: "We're Christian Christians." Spirits, possession, and the devil, are not unknown in this brand of Christianity, however, so Lisu didn't have to change their belief system as much as their spirit allegiances. With conversion, Lisu raise pigs for market instead of reciprocal feasting—an economic adjustment the larger world was already pressuring them to make. The hardest and perhaps the most significant change was probably giving up alcohol—which most have done as far as I could determine. I did meet Lisu Christians who claimed to be "social drinkers," but this is a far cry from the communal drunkenness that accompanies reciprocal feasting, bride price negotiations, and every holiday bash among animists. The alcohol proscription, however, does fit with the Lisu emphasis on *what you do* being paramount over what you say you believe.

My first trip to Myanmar caused me to reconsider religion and to rethink ideas about organized religion. Adapting or changing religion is personal; yet when conversion occurs en mass, it must affect culture. Is it more significant than other adaptations people make: dramatically, to survive, or prosaically, because we live in a world in which jockeying for resources and power is basic to our condition? I began questioning if or how adapting one's religion incrementally by adding local spirits or Buddha or borrowing ancestor worship from the Chinese was ultimately that different from converting somewhat more dramatically to Christianity. The Lisu have done all of the above since leaving the Upper Salween. They've made other big changes—such as moving from subsistence to market economies, going to school, and moving to urban areas—that seem equally significant. As a practical matter, market capitalism and land ownership, realities Lisu now must adapt to, align more with Christian than animist belief systems—in which spirits, not people or governments, own the land. Religious conversion could be just another step, part of the unstoppable process of joining a globalizing world.

Burma-Myanmar's civil wars, poverty, and isolation from the 1960s through the end of the twentieth century appear to have acted as a crucible to hone and intensify the distinct Lisu recipe of fatalism, practicality, and resilience that unifies their culture—and is "bigger" (as the Lisu would say) than the particulars of religious practice.

I considered whether converting to Christianity, with its institutionalized social structures, had been another practical decision made (consciously or not) to survive. Must Christianity, as more than one anthropologist has asserted, take away from "Lisuness?" How different is it to say a prayer to Jesus Christ before clearing a field than to a local land spirit? Leadership and hierarchy are not the same thing, and it could be argued that the base of Lisu leadership in Burma, developed through the church and in some cases going back a generation or two to China, provided survival advantages.

The church has grown enormously under its own, consensus-driven Lisu leadership; General Ne Win ejected Western missionaries in 1965. Westerners and their financial support have been absent for fifty years. Lisu and other minority Christians should be credited with resourcefulness and agency in maintaining and supporting their own institutions, including a professional clergy, under difficult conditions. It is likely they wouldn't have succeeded without the writing system missionaries provided, a potent unifying force. Literacy enabled churches and Bible-based schools and colleges to keep attracting new converts and developing ways of governance acceptable to this people known not to tolerate authoritarian leaders as wars posed existential threats all around. Myanmar's government broke up an existing large association of ethic minority Christians in the 1980s; this had the effect of emphasizing Lisu and other ethnic identities while diffusing a potentially strong coalition of tribes and churches.

In 2015, according to most estimates, 400,000 to 450,000 Lisu were living in Myanmar; they were the thirteenth largest of 135 recognized minority groups, and 75 percent to 80 percent were Christian. The government has not published data on ethnic/religious breakdowns of minority populations in years, however, so the numbers aren't verifiable. A respected Lisu party organizer told me that in 2006 the government counted 550,000 Lisu, a number he estimates has grown to 700,000 today. Academics and researchers I questioned all cite some version of "nobody knows." Accurate minority counting is impossible: the issue of whether to include sub-groups with larger groups or count them separately hasn't been resolved. Numbers are political in Myanmar, especially numbers of minorities seeking political representation.

Everyone agrees, however, that the Lisu birthrate here, unlike the ones in Thailand or China, is extremely high. In the 1990s and in 2015, most Lisu women I met had eight to ten children; more are surviving today as medical care improves and food supplies increase. The push for greater political representation coincides with Lisu's professed love of having many children. Land pressure, however, already severe in places such as around Myitkyina in Central Kachin State, will drive poverty—even in more prosperous areas such as Putao. If Lisu continue to multiply at current rates as they strive to improve economically and increasingly educate their broods, large families must give way as they have everyplace else.

How or if conversion to evangelical Christianity relates to earlier adaptations the first Lisu arriving in Burma made to survive is hard to know; facts are sketchy, and political borders were not very important then. Unlike today's majority of northern Lisu stock, who came just before, during, or after the Chinese Revolution, Lisu migrating to Burma in the mid- to late nineteenth century belonged to southern, Chinese-influenced Baumee and Cho-me groups, some of whom continued on into Thailand. Upheavals in China, as well as the Lisu habit of migrating as an internal pressure valve, triggered their movement, consisting mostly of small groups. What is known is that at least a few thousand Lisu settled into vertiginous border regions between China and Burma—some in mountains around Putao Valley in Kachin State but more further south in the Shan and Wa States bordering China and Thailand. British Army Handbooks of the 1920s and 1930s (Burma was then part of India and the British Empire) note that Lisu here neither grew nor smoked opium. They were joined by subsequent diasporas of southern Lisu who arrived around the turn of the twentieth century. British government sources estimated between 1,000 and 2,000 Lisu in Burma around this time; it is possible they under-counted because of the remoteness of Lisu villages. Today, the Lisu in Shan and Wa States are still mostly animists.

By the mid-1930s Handbook for the India Army for Burma estimated that there were 35,000 Lisu in the country. This number begins the better-documented story—that of a trickle of northern Lisu migrating down the Salween Valley from the 1930s through World War II, with numbers swelling after the Chinese Revolution through the early 1970s. Most settled in Kachin State, where women wear the distinct northern Lisu long, flowing skirts and shirts of blue and white with sleeveless black velvet tunics over long-sleeved blouses.

Members of the nationalist Chinese Kuomintang (KMT) army of Chiang Kai-shek migrated to Burma at the same time, after Mao's army defeated them. They traveled further south and expanded the opium trade into Shan and Wa States where Lisu were already long-established. The KMT filled the vacuum created when post-revolution China purged itself of its narcotics trade. Shan and Wa State Lisu are far fewer in number and less homogeneous than those in Kachin State: they include members of roughly ten distinct Lisu groups living in Burma. Travel restrictions make it all but impossible to visit them today.

The majority of Lisu in Myanmar are from the Nujiang Valley in Yunnan, China, or are their descendants. A high birth rate since they came here grew their numbers sufficiently to qualify them as a minority with guaranteed political representation under reforms instituted in 2011—the smallest ethnic group to achieve this status.

Because most Lisu live in Kachin State, the government combines Lisu with the Jingpo (the largest minority in the state) and four other groups, including all within the Kachin ethnic designation. Analogous to everyone living in California being a Californian, this designation is based more on geographical proximity than on close cultures and language (Jingpo is Sino-Tibetan and Lisu, Tibeto-Burman). The Kachin Hills include border areas of Raunchily Pradesh in India, as well as of Tibet and Yunnan, China, where Lisu are not considered ethnic Kachins.

The Jingpo, today mostly Baptists, arrived a generation or more before the Lisu and dominate state politics. It is they who support and fight in the Kachin Independence Army (KIA) that has waged civil war for many of the past sixty years: first seeking autonomy, then income from Kachin's natural resources, and today control of Chinese cross-border commerce. The KIA is one of the last and largest armed ethnic groups (AEGs), and since 2015 it has been fighting again after a seventeen-year ceasefire with the government starting in the mid-1990s. This renewal of hostilities has caused more than 100,000 to flee homes and farms in Kachin State, creating a new, internal refugee crisis and camps for displaced people along the Chinese border and around Myitkyina. Twenty years ago there were fifty to sixty such insurgencies and even more internal displacement of minority populations. Current Lisu involvement in this struggle is negligible, limited to being conscripted by the KIA or caught in its crossfire. This was not always true. Lisu identified with the political goal of greater autonomy during earlier years of the war; they gradually withdrew as a result of internal rifts, power struggles, and religious differences with the Jingpo.

To finance the long-running, on-and-off conflict, both KIA and government forces rely on jade, a key element of Myanmar's mineral wealth whose industry is linked to the heroin and methamphetamine trades. China's rising middle class drives Myanmar's jade market—estimated at $31 billion in 2014 alone by Global Witness, a UK-based research organization. Kachin State has the largest, most valuable deposits in the world, and Myitkyina, its capital, is the gateway to the mining center of Hpakant. The area is restricted to outsiders not only because of the active war zone nearby but also because the government does not want eyes on drug and jade smuggling accompanied by environmental disaster here.

Lisu and other groups have been caught up, vulnerable to widespread heroin addiction in the mines as well as to HIV infection, as they labor in often horrific conditions rife with debilitating or fatal accidents. There are full-time miners, but most are farmers moonlighting after harvest to support their families and earn cash for extras such as sending a child to high school (public support of school ends in the eighth grade). The nexus of jade, corruption, war, drugs, HIV, and environmental destruction creates an ongoing disaster recent reforms have not begun to resolve. Wealth that might improve the lives of Myanmar's people instead flows to Chinese jade merchants and corrupt officials and to fund an endless war.

Further south and east, Lisu who arrived 50 to 100 years before those from the Nujiang Gorge live in the vast Shan State, which covers a quarter of Burma's landmass. The state shares a 500 kilometer border with China and a shorter one with Thailand and includes an autonomous zone now designated as "Wa Special Region 2" (often still called Wa State), where several thousand Lisu live. Formerly, the Wa were called the "Wild Wa" because of purported headhunting until the 1970s, and less is known about the Lisu who share this high mountain region outside national control. Trade here is mainly with China but also with Thailand and includes billions of dollars of legitimate goods as well as traffic of people, drugs, arms, timber, and counterfeit merchandise. It's estimated that armed conflict in Shan State since 2015 has caused as many as 30,000 ethnic Kokang to flee across the border into China, causing new tensions between Myanmar and China.

––––––––––– ■-■ –––––––––––

The tangled issues arising from Myanmar's highly diverse minority populations are beyond the scope of this work to cover. My focus is the Lisu, but the preceding context is offered to hint at the enormity of complications in the two main states they inhabit. Readers may extrapolate to the entire country to begin to understand why pejoratives such as "basket-case country" and "failed narco-state" have been often applied until very recently—"military dictatorship" simply doesn't cover it.

Overwhelmingly, the country is unknown in the West except for one famous political prisoner. Nobel Peace Laureate Aung San Suu Kyi was freed in 2010 after spending fifteen of the previous twenty-one years under house arrest. In November 2015 the National League for Democracy (NLD) party she leads won a stunning landslide victory against the military party, the Union Solidarity Development Party (USDP), which Myanmar's latest "reform" constitution favors by granting it an unelected 25 percent of Parliament's seats. Constitutionally, the military also legally controls three key ministries (Defense, Home, and Border Areas). How effectively the new NLD-led government will be able to share power is unknown. A further complication is that while Suu Kyi controls the NLD, the new constitution was written explicitly to bar her, a widow and mother of foreigners, from holding the highest office of president.

--------------------◼◼--------------------

Before returning to Myanmar in 2014, I met with Tom Parks to attempt to get a handle on changes in the country since the 1990s. Parks is boyish and intent, a longtime American ex-pat married to a Thai, who until recently served as the Asia Foundation's director of conflict and governance. We met in Bangkok at the serene, high-design Sukhothai Hotel set back from Sathorn Road. He's spent years studying and writing about impoverished countries with "weak state capacity and legitimacy," focusing on sub-national conflicts. These are deadly and enduring not only in Myanmar but all across Asia, where the average such conflict drags on for forty-three years. One of Parks's more surprising conclusions is that expansion of the state and economic development have not made resolving conflicts easier.

In the Wa State (where many Lisu live), he explained, peace was achieved by separating completely from central authority: "In Myanmar's current peace process, armed groups in peripheral areas are the de facto power, and they always negotiate for more autonomy and control over [the] resources of their region. The Wa made a deal with the military government early compared to other insurgent groups, in 1989. Wa State is not like the rest of Burma; they rule their own small world as a 'self-administered zone.'" For most practical purposes, the Wa war with Burma's central government ended long ago, "when the Wa agreed to stop fighting in exchange for keeping the [insurgent Burmese] Communist Party out of their territory."

Although by all accounts the Wa now concentrate on trade, including narcotics, rather than fighting the Tatmadaw, Wa political representatives do not admit to illicit trafficking. Parks noted they still have the largest ethnic army in Myanmar with 20,000 soldiers, who, while no longer fighting the regular army, come into frequent conflict with smaller AEGs over trade and territory. The Lisu's relationship to the Wa or involvement in their army is unknown.

Over the past twenty years Myanmar's peace process has consisted chiefly of ceasefires negotiated one by one between each AEG and the central government, which is its divide-and-conquer strategy. This is probably because under current law, Myanmar's central government owns or controls all natural resources, and generally what every group wants is a federalist system allowing more wealth to stay in and be controlled by states, where it is generated at the peripheries. Multilateral peace negotiations have been secondary until recently, supported by the National Ceasefire Coordination Team. Significant for the Lisu, the Kachin Independence Army has not signed the current multilateral peace agreement on offer as this book goes to press.

Anyplace else, fifteen lingering civil wars would be a catastrophe. But for Myanmar's government, even before the November 2015 election increased the NLD's power, three factors mitigate. First, negotiations and ceasefires with dozens of AEGs coincided for the first time with elections in 2010 that, while flawed, were viewed as an improvement; second, opposition political parties have become legal for the first time since the 1960s; and third, real reforms since 2011, including freedom of speech and the press, signal that Myanmar is heading in a direction the international community wants to encourage. President Thein Sein, who headed the ruling USDP, has been reform-minded and an improvement over SLORC (State Law and Order Restoration Committee) leader Than Shwe, in power from 1992 to 2011. He has so far honored 2015 election results, in which his party was basically routed, and committed to a peaceful transfer of power. This is unlike the behavior of the former military party that nullified Suu Kyi's NLD election victory in 1990 and placed her under house arrest.

Among Myanmar watchers, however, hope remains diluted with skepticism. The faith expressed in the positive trajectory of political, legal, and economic reform—by the NLD, ruling generals, and outsiders alike—could be self-serving and premature. Rather than reflecting just reality on the ground in Myanmar, it is equally a reaction to counter China's domination in the region. Foreign investment and actions, such as President Barack Obama's surprising visit in 2014, however, speak loudly. (It was the first in a flurry of engagements with "pariah" regimes, followed by reopening a US embassy in Cuba and multilateral negotiations with Iran to deter its nuclear weapons capability.)

Myanmar's global reengagement is occurring simultaneously with its increasing persecution and forced migration of the Rohingya minority and the rise of so-called Buddhist nationalism. Official involvement in narcotics, logging, wildlife, human, and precious mineral trafficking is ongoing, driven by voracious international markets—mainly China's. Clearly, the Tatmadaw's influence has not ended, and the degree to which the institution will allow atrophy of its constitutionally guaranteed powers is arguable.

The country's extraordinary wealth in natural resources owned/controlled by the central government creates incentives to paper over corruption and dysfunction, raising all the usual engagement-versus-isolation arguments. Without ironclad legal protections, Lisu and other minorities are likely to suffer land and resource rip-offs as newcomers enter Myanmar's emerging markets, encouraged by government promoters on aggressive foreign investment fishing trips.

"The door is now wide open. It's a gold rush," Myanmar's foreign minister, Wunna Maung Lwin, told an eager audience at a March 2015 investment forum in New York. The Gap, Coca Cola, Visa, and numerous property development companies are among thousands of multinationals with major new investments in Myanmar today.

———————————■-■———————————

The neologism "Zomia" is a geographic name the Dutch historian Willem van Schendel coined in 2002 to refer to the mountainous Europe-sized peripheral zone in Southeast Asia that has historically been beyond government control. Its territory falls within nine separate nations today, including five with Lisu populations. Preceding van Schendel in 1997, anthropologist Jean Michaud identified roughly the same area as "the Southeast Asian Massif." Regardless of what it is called, the concept provides a less present-minded framework in which to place the history and politics of the region and to view its ethnic mosaic of a hundred million minority peoples.

Taking the long view, the rise of endless war in Myanmar has coincided with the rise of state capacity and economic globalization. Preceding this were centuries of more or less borderless autonomy in which minority peoples used migration as the "state evasion" tool of choice. Groups also integrated, cross-pollinated, and fought to resolve conflicts that were far shorter and less lethal than those of the past sixty years.

One of Zomia's enthusiastic advocates is Yale University anthropologist and political scientist James Scott, who styles himself a "foot soldier in the Zomia Army (psychological warfare branch)." Scott uses a non-state lens to write alternative political and historical narratives of minority groups such as the Lisu, whom, he argues, made rational choices when fleeing the oppression of the "state-making project" both in the deep past and within the last few hundred years of dramatic state expansion. Rational because it helped them avoid *for a time* the slavery, conscription, over-taxation, corvée labor, epidemics, and wars suffered by those who join state hierarchies on the bottom rung.

Scott argues that Lisu and other egalitarian minority groups should be credited with agency in creating non-hierarchical societies. It is a mistake to assume it never occurred to them to create—or that they were simply incapable of creating—state-like structures. His interpretation requires stepping out of the nationalist perspective that automatically labels people beyond control as underdeveloped. Such a default view assumes superiority of the state, ignores the fact that all states are not created equal, and is blind to the possibility that some cultures *choose* to create non-hierarchical social and civic structures. *Illi Lisu* (Lisu custom) is an excellent example of such agency—it is an oral tradition that provides an alternate road map to living together cooperatively that clearly privileges egalitarian and individualistic values over hierarchical ones.

Without idealizing anarchic aspects of "Zomia's" past, it is important to acknowledge that this past comprised most of human history. Often, "statelessness" has offered the best option available to those desiring autonomy—and was not the existential tragedy today's state-minded people have been conditioned to view it as. Refugees pouring out of war-torn areas of the world in 2015 remind us that individuals have the choice to act, that action involves risk, and that the lucky ones do better than those who hand over their fates to whichever state (Lisu would say "ruler") claims them.

Google "Zomia" and you will find it has developed into a cyber home where democracy's current troubled status is discussed by people living in developed states far from this conceptual territory.

———————■-■———————

A July 2014 rainy season walkabout in Putao Valley was not only sublimely, drenchingly beautiful, it was overdue. Not getting a permit to go there in 1997 was a disappointment because seeing this place is crucial both to understand recent Lisu history and to look at the effects of Christianization. This has been little studied despite the fact that many, if not most, Lisu today practice Christianity in some form. Putao is a fertile valley just 450 meters (1,500 feet) above sea level, 30 miles long, and 15 miles wide—the only place outside China where Christian Lisu (about a hundred thousand) make up the majority, live in isolation, and cultivate wet rice. Because of the abundance of arable land and the fact that most of those who settled here were either already Christian or converted in the 1950s and 1960s, Putao offers a unique case study in cultural and economic adaptation.

Gaining permission to go to Putao requires deep engagement with the formidable bureaucracy that keeps it isolated. A permit to travel there comes at a high cost—you must be part of a government-approved group tour, and most of the few hundred foreigners a year who visit arrive by air in small groups during the dry season. Many stay at the Malikha Lodge just outside Putao ($10,000 per couple for a four-night guided stay). Some are part of elite mountaineering, wildlife preservation, or academic expeditions.

In addition to Lisu and small numbers of Rawang and Shan people, Northeast Kachin State is home to Myanmar's corner of the Himalaya, including the 19,296-foot-high Hkakabo Razi peak (also called Ice Mountain), an almost-extinct pygmy race, and a spectacular, remote national park. Rare botanicals, orchids, and exotic wildlife abound. A confluence of a "high-value, low-impact" tourism policy and political/military concerns combine to isolate and conserve the Edenic valley within sight of Tibet.

Putao town is about 350 kilometers (218 miles) north of the state capital Myitkyina and is reachable by air, by motorcycle, or on foot. High-end chartered bicycle tours occasionally peddle there in a week. Insurgents intermittently dynamite bridges to obstruct most vehicular traffic, so there is no reliable road through this marvelously forested, mostly uninhabited area. You can't buy a plane ticket to Putao without a government permit—13 copies of which, along with 13 copies of passport name and visa pages, must be taken into the restricted zone. Our party of three traveled with 120 pages. Only visitors with government-approved guides can set foot outside of Putao's four-square-block "downtown."

Putao Township in Kachin State, northernmost Myanmar, within sight of Tibet. Lisu are the majority population here. Author photo.

In 1997, permission for me to visit Putao was dangled and retracted, predicted and withdrawn, until my Myanmar visa ran out and I had to leave. I spent time instead with Lisu living in marginal circumstances around Myitkyina, Mandalay, and Mogok. Many were recently urbanized or else seasonal miners who farmed the balance of the year. I didn't meet anyone who hadn't lost immediate family members, usually young children, to malaria, dengue fever, or diarrhea. In the market, many people were disfigured with permanent purple-black bruises up and down their necks, the result of scraping blood supply routes to the brain to break high fevers—a Chinese remedy of questionable merit that was often the only available therapy.

While most Lisu around Myitkyina are Christian, I also met animists. My then-guide, Bobby Morse, is a third-generation member of the Morse family of missionaries, a native Lisu speaker born in Kachin State who is also fluent in Burmese. I never discovered whether having him as my intermediary helped or hurt my chances of getting to Putao, but he knew the territory and had superb language skills. Although his family had been ejected from the country thirty years before, hearing its name was enough to evoke emotional responses and invitations to stay with just about everyone we met.

Putao airport is the main entry point to the region and the only access during rainy season. Flight schedules are erratic and depend on demand; each flight usually has fewer than ten passengers. Author photo.

Witnessing Lisu resilience on that trip affected me deeply; their particular against-all-odds zest for life was shared by Christians and animists, although traditional Lisu humor is noticeably darker. Perhaps more than anything else, the people I met in Myanmar in 1997 kept this project alive because they elicited in me a moral obligation to help tell their story.

An ancient Lisu Christian couple living in a stick hovel across the Ayrewaddy River from Myitkyina were two such people—they owned little yet possessed huge determination to provide hospitality and share their lives. Brandishing a crudely wrought spade, the old wife beetled out to her riverside field and returned a few minutes later with a few clay-caked roots: "They look ugly, but wait until you taste them!" As she prepared this simple meal, her husband, Eligah, recounted being pushed out of a Royal Air Force plane and parachuted in with fellow Lisu recruits just across the river in World War II as part of the successful British campaign to retake Myitkyina from the Japanese over the spring and summer of 1944.

Putao Township is crisscrossed by numerous streams and rivers but has only a few modern bridges. Most are for pedestrians and are not as sturdy as this major infrastructure. Author photo.

Downtown Putao today is a rural, semi-paved crossroads of rusty corrugated roofed buildings with electricity about four hours a day. Two uninspiring Chinese restaurants, dry goods shops full of Chinese merchandise, and a crusty warren of a market line its main street. In the distance, sparkling

Downtown Putao has limited electricity, and in surrounding agricultural areas solar panels are the sole source of power. These, along with other Chinese goods, are typical fare offered in most shops. Author photo.

golden spires from a few Shan temples rise from fields of neon chartreuse. A couple thousand people live in this alternately dusty or muddy village carved out of Northern Kachin State's great greenness. Traffic is mostly on foot or bicycle, but motorcycles are becoming common. Cars are rare; the workhorse vehicles are the oxcart and an elongated three-wheeled tuk-tuk, with a miniature truck bed welded on its motorcycle front end.

Putao town is within a couple of kilometers of the former military outpost Fort Hertz, which remained in British hands during the Japanese invasion of Burma in 1942. Although completely cut off from military authorities in India, it became a refuge for retreating British and Indian soldiers. After being re-supplied by the 153rd (Gurkha) Parachute Battalion and having its airstrip repaired, Fort Hertz became an emergency landing spot for planes flying "the Hump" and for British and American forces engaged in intelligence gathering during the Burma Campaign.

What distinguishes Putao is the beauty of its low-lying valley, framed by mountains of shocking altitude. In 2014's monsoon visit, the mountains popped in and out of sight behind scrims of scudding tropical clouds. The

In addition to oxcarts, motorcycles and tuk-tuks are Putao's workhorse vehicles. Author photo.

tallest Himalayan peaks are in Tibet, seventy-five miles to the north. When dynamic cloud play aligns in rare moments, revealing summits of 20,000 feet and more, your heart almost stops beating. Here, rivers and streams crossed by extremely flimsy pedestrian bridges charge down forested mountain slopes before broadening and slowing down in the valley.

Many Lisu in Burma have come down from the highlands. Over the last sixty years, the relative peace of settled valleys in and around Mogok, Mandalay, Myitkyina, and Putao, plus the relative ease of wet-rice farming, drew them from vertiginous villages near battlegrounds and along drug trade routes.

I met eighty-year-old Timothy at a dark Chinese café in Putao—lack of electricity in daytime hours makes most places feel dingy, not to mention difficult to clean. The former headmaster of the town school, he attended both elementary and Bible school here, graduating in the 1940s. Converted at age twelve, he was given his Christian name by LaVern Morse. His birth name

Putao Valley scene along one of many rivers. Author photo.

is Ko-boo-day and he is an Anung, a Lisu-speaking sub-group from China's Upper Nu gorge. His family migrated from there to the mountains around Putao when he was very young. Following the typical sequence, first he and siblings attending school converted to Christianity, then his parents and finally his grandparents did so. The Morse family was the catalyst; based in Yunnan from the late 1930s, they traveled down valleys and across unmarked borders into Burma to preach, teach, and set up tiny churches and schools with Lisu pastors trained in China. They moved their mission to Putao Valley in 1949. Where Timothy grew up, as in most remote areas of Burma at the time, there were no government schools. Missionaries like the Morses and a few monasteries offered the only formal literacy or education options.

Timothy told me about an event that precipitated a huge exodus from the mountains and a mass conversion:

> I was in Putao on August 15, 1950, when there was a big earthquake. It was horrible! Enormous landslides, houses on hillsides disappeared, rivers rose 100 feet, even the fish died. The water was not clear but full of mud and trees and

In the rainy season, people rely on makeshift bridges such as this one. Author photo.

debris, dead animals, and people. The smell from the death was very bad; you couldn't go near the rivers.

Chapter 24 of the Bible tells of End Times, and since the Morses had been predicting all along that this would happen, many non-Christians converted. This created a pastor shortage—everyone wanted a pastor to come to their village. The Christians thought it was a miracle to get so many new Christians. People were very happy about that part of the tragedy.

The Morses, who from their China mission had done crucial work for the Allied forces during the war, after it received permission from the Burmese government to settle the Lisu in Putao Valley. The valley was malaria-infested, sparsely populated, and hardly a prize. "Putao was crawling with Shan spirits when we first arrived," Helen Morse told me in 1996. Much of its western land around Muladi (Ahkang Valley) was covered with 10- to 12-foot-tall elephant grass whose wiry underground roots made clearing with hand tools impossible.

This cruciform church built in the early 1960s by the Morse family in Mulahdi, just outside Putao town, held a thousand worshippers. The land was confiscated by the government after missionaries were expelled in 1965; along with the Morse family compounds, it lies in eerie ruins today. Author photo.

Prior to 1950, Lisu avoided lower altitudes, trying never to spend the night in malarial areas. They lived highland lives, hacking out and burning swiddens on steep mountainsides, using skills brought from China. The Morses' malaria eradication campaign (spraying DDT and providing medicine, mosquito nets, and public education) began as soon as they moved to Putao Valley; following the earthquake and influx of new settlers, they stepped up their efforts. In 1952 Russell Morse rejoined his family in Burma after being released by the Chinese, who had imprisoned and tortured him for eighteen months during the Korean War. He resumed his role as patriarch, fruit tree expert, and chief medical officer at their new mission. Arable land was soon insufficient to accommodate everyone who wanted to move down from the mountains to live and farm in villages with access to schools, medicine, and churches.

Village scene, Putao Valley. Solar panel tucked under eaves of house in center offers a clue that the year is 2014. Author photo.

Russell's son, Eugene Morse, had cultivated a relationship with an American agricultural adviser to Kachin State, Don Carter, whom he met in Rangoon in 1950. Carter was thinking about the possibility of agricultural development in Putao Valley; Eugene encouraged the idea and invited him to visit the mission, take soil samples, and see his family's success in improving nutrition by expanding Lisu crop portfolios. Russell traveled back to the United States in 1953 on an evangelizing, fundraising tour to tell of the horrors of his eighteen-month incarceration in China. He also spoke of the joys of building the new mission in Burma, then considered a bulwark against the "domino theory" of communist takeover of Asia. A donor in Oregon offered $5,000 on the spot to purchase and transport a Massey-Ferguson 25-horsepower tractor with plows and harrows to Putao. This was the beginning, in 1954, of a huge land-clearing effort that ultimately cleared about 6,000 acres of prime bottomland for agriculture, creating what the Morses describe as a "Lisu paradise." Thousands more came down from the mountains as land became available. Migration to Putao Valley accelerated again in the late 1950s, when Chinese Lisu, fleeing massive starvation precipitated by Mao Zedong's Great Leap Forward farm collectivization, began pouring down the Nu Valley and into Burma. Most who were not already Christians converted around this time.

I asked Timothy if Lisu stopped believing in bad spirits after conversion.

Oh no. Christians have the Holy Spirit, the most senior spirit. If we follow God's word, it protects us. Evil spirits exist, and if we don't believe in God that much, they easily come into you and infect your life. The Bible says, never leave a *seat free* for evil spirits, or they will become like a king and make you go wrong, wrong, wrong, mistake, mistake—they will take over your life!

In animist times we believed in two kinds of spirits, good and bad. If you make an offering to good spirits to call back a lost soul or some other favor, they will do it. But it's never enough. Today it's a chicken, tomorrow a pig, next week a cow. Unlike God and Jesus and the Holy Spirit, the little spirits are very greedy.

The majority of Putao Valley's residents today are Lisu farmers, living in small villages without electricity, paved roads, or plumbing. They are poor by worldwide standards, but they live in lovely traditional homes amid fertile land and stunning scenery. Most have enough to eat, schools are open, and medical care has dramatically improved in the last several years. There is a feeling of bounty because unlike other areas in Kachin State (and the rest of Myanmar), there is sufficient land and little population pressure from in-migration. Isolation has created a certain autonomy—the economy is no longer subsistence, but it is different from remote places in Thailand and China that are integrated by modern infrastructure into the national fabric.

Walking among several isolated Lisu villages, I was told by farmers, and pastors, women and young people that the biggest difference of the past fifteen to twenty years is that "Lisu now have open eyes." We heard this phrase again and again.

To a sixty-year-old pastor in Bahmadi village on the Tulong River, it means that while Lisu always worked hard—both in fields and off-season as hunters, miners, medicinal herb collectors—only recently have they embraced new ideas, such as "venture economy" and representational politics. Lisu began tuning in to the outside world: "Now we listen to radio, look at the news. Our children go to school and become educated, and we become curious about how people make revenue in other places."

The outside world comes to Putao Valley through electronic devices hooked up to solar-powered motorcycle batteries ubiquitous even in remote corners. You have to look closely to spot the 2-by-3-foot solar panels mounted atop stilted woven bamboo thatched houses.

The panels, along with most consumer items, come from China. The pastor said that since 2000, "Big trade started: construction machines and other heavy goods, fertilizers, clothing, medicine, and motorcycles." This last item costs around $600 and is a first step toward upward mobility. Often purchased after a post-crop season of work in amber or ruby mines and made largely of plastic, motorcycles provide crucial rainy season mobility. What they lack in strength and safety, they make up for with speed and agility. They can traverse flimsy pedestrian bridges and are so light they can be carried across swollen streams.

China has developed huge domestic markets over the last twenty years in which Lisu participate. Post-harvest, more and more have taken to mining: rubies, jade, and now amber, primarily sold in China. I realized how huge an economic impact this is having from a conversation with an exceptionally large, gentle man whose name translates as "Mr. Mouse." He has four acres and nine children, two of whom live with his mother and grandmother in Putao town to attend high school. I wondered how a farmer can afford this (education beyond middle school is private); he calculated it costs him thirteen lakhs, or 1.3 million kyat, a year. A thousand dollars.

"I work very hard. You can't imagine how hard," he tells me. In addition to farming, he sells cows and pigs and sometimes amber and gold. Post-harvest, from November to April, he and his friends pool money and become self-employed amber miners in Tanai, the center of the amber industry. He called the arrangement they make with the mine owner a "half-half contract" and said it's better than being employed because you rely on your friends to keep you alive. Conditions are harsh: the mines are 4-by-4-foot shafts that can reach depths of 100 or more feet. Amber is mined by hand, miners must often use oxygen, and every year men are injured and killed in collapses. In his best year, Mr. Mouse cleared $4,000; in his worst, he barely covered expenses: "We are in an amber rush now; everyone is going to the mines, which are mostly controlled and worked by Lisu. We used to go to the gold mines, but with amber we have the chance to make many lakhs."

Another way Lisu in Myanmar supplement income is by hunting wild animals and forest products, both to eat and to sell to make traditional Chinese and ethnic medicines. Plant-based medicine hunting is not generally illegal, but the size of the Chinese market has put pressure on resources, as well as on high-stakes animal-based medicines. Over-hunting in fragile areas has a negative environmental impact, but the pull of lucrative Chinese markets makes it irresistible. Lisu men are renowned for their hunting skills, long practiced to feed themselves and to build individual repute (myi-do). In Myanmar this is still the case, and Lisu have reputations as environmental wreckers and "cash hunters." Stories of individual poachers abound for feats such as hunting endangered species in natural preserves and across borders into northeast India and Tibet. Many die or are killed, such as one infamous Lisu shot by a suspicious park ranger a few years ago in India. He was camouflaged as a bear at the time of his death and found to have 148 bear gall bladders, several already dried, strapped to his body. A single gall bladder can fetch as much as $30,000 in Shanghai or Beijing.

While a few individuals and families have prospered with the venture economy, the pastor told me, most are still simple farmers and don't have much money: "They live subsistence-style, on rice, vegetables, bananas, chickens, ducks, and pigs they raise. Maybe sell a few bananas by the road, not for market far away." Income inequality is growing: today, one house costs less than 10 lakhs to build, another more than 50 lakhs (a lakh is 100,000 kyat—pronounced *chat*—worth about $100). The pastor said when he was young, villages had little income range. People still pitch in to help each other build houses, but if the family is prosperous and the house fancy, its owner must hire labor for masonry and other modern skills.

A man in another village estimated that "maybe a third" of its inhabitants are still "very poor," mainly because their land is bad or they lack good irrigation. He said the church sometimes lends rice to people in need, but it has limited resources. A government loan program exists, but it has high interest rates; debt service fees collected pay for scant village improvements. This means the poor support building a teacher's house or rice storage more than do wealthier

Sunday evening services attract a large crowd, many of whom already attended a service earlier in the day. The sermon is short; music and singing are the main attractions. Author photo.

people. He didn't consider this fair. When I mentioned that some American towns disproportionately raise revenue from traffic tickets and late penalties levied on the disadvantaged, he shrugged and said, "It's the same everywhere."

At Nyi Salidi, people were eager to talk once word got around that a visitor was writing a book about the Lisu. Here and in five other villages, I asked what "being Lisu" means to several of them.

"I was born in a Lisu family, I have Lisu blood, so I must be Lisu," one woman patiently explained. The usual telling of folk stories (often involving dogs) and sayings ensued ("if you want to become poor slowly, smoke opium; if you want to become poor fast, play cards"). People literally translated Lisu as meaning anything from "wraparound people," referring both to turbans and long belts wound around their midsections to make them strong and to stand tall as well as to a kind of fence tied together with twisted and knotted straw. Wandering ways made more permanent structures impractical.

"But what does Lisu mean *today*, since most of you no longer wear turbans, you live in settled villages, and you now are Christian?" I ask. "Is myi-do as important as in the past?"

Lisu women are equal partners and radiate strength. A woman sits in her kitchen, the center of the household that like every Lisu residence has a temporary, empty quality—table and chairs are stacked and pulled out when needed. Author photo.

Eyebrows shoot up and surprised looks circulate. A group question arises: "How do *you* know about myi-do?" They are taken aback to hear this internalized value spoken out loud by a foreigner. One woman responded passionately: "The one who is able to *do*, to say, to work, to speak well, has myi-do."

A middle-aged man explained that Lisu today must be braver than others, but simple bravery or riches don't automatically confer myi-do: "We hunt tigers, even though we understand they might kill us. The same with elephant, we might die trying to kill them. We always did these things, but now it is because of big money, and the Lisu *really* want to prosper. One tiger can bring 40 lakhs. Lisu die every year in gold mine, amber mine, ruby mine. But we go because we have ambition and don't care about the risks." He said in addition to being brave and ambitious, the one with myi-do must have good judgment, good ideas, and must see the future: "One example: as soon as the law changed, our best leaders encouraged everyone to register their land immediately and *never* sell it, no matter what. A few lakhs [of kyat] from land or amber will make you rich for a few years—but when money is gone and you have no land, you have nothing."

A woman said that unlike other groups, Lisu women control the money, and this makes them special. I asked the twenty people gathered if this were true, and nods all around confirmed it. No dissent from men, the majority in the room, on this point.

The woman explained that because husbands go away to make money, women are left in charge of pigs and poultry and sometimes fields. "We know the value of money and hold the purse! [She extracted a purse from deep within her bodice and pulled its drawstrings tight, to make her meaning clear.] We never splurge, and [we] control the men so they don't splurge, either." Others add that Lisu women have always been equal to men, even before they became Christians, and that there is little division between them, though custom generally divides up work: "When we need to, we plow, we dive in the river, put on the new roof, and sometimes hunt. We share the work." Lisu women, such as a mother-daughter team from another village, have even joined the amber rush to become successful miners. Another one, who climbs a mile or more through caves to collect swift-bird nests, valued for an expensive Chinese soup, was mentioned. The location is a family secret, but everyone knows she has a big business.

Flat-land wet-rice farming is far less labor-intensive than mountain swiddening, and several older Lisu identified this change, along with the move down from the mountains, as the biggest of their lifetimes. This is a new part of being Lisu. One woman commented, "Now we have time to do *other* things to make money." Her husband added that while farmers had experimented with high-yield "research rice" for several years, it didn't keep as long or taste as good as indigenous rice; almost everyone has switched back. "We plant local varieties because even if you grow it to sell, not eat, the new rice doesn't fetch as much," his wife, clearly a partner in the venture, said.

When I asked an older pastor if women could become church leaders, without hesitation he answered, "The Bible teaches that men and women are equal—God grants equal gifts to women. Men do not have power to forbid woman this or that." When I ask why I hadn't met female pastors, he answered with raised shoulders and a question: "Maybe custom?"

The high status of Lisu women has clearly survived religious conversion; it is even possible that the teetotalist style of evangelical Christianity practiced in Myanmar has strengthened it. When working among animist Lisu in Thailand in the 1960s, anthropologist E. Paul Durrenberger commented that Lisu ambition resonates with the Protestant work ethic he grew up with in Texas and that Lisu also reminded him of American evangelicals in their sexual prudishness. When separated from alcohol and the reciprocal feasting obligations of traditional culture, Christians, including women, appear to focus on the Lisu "desire for primacy" (identified by missionary ethnographers Paul and Elaine Lewis in the 1960s, among others) even more individualistically. To find out if Lisu women have the "enforcer" role associated with women in the nineteenth-century Temperance Movement in America would require more study. Several women pointed out the connection between prosperity and abstinence from alcohol, but so did some men. A Catholic enclave within one village, Whan Key #1, which couldn't afford to support a priest, was raised as a practical example: "Catholics drink, that's why they are poor," one woman explained to me, a trifle smug.

Lisu provide a converse, egalitarian example of what anthropologist Wednesday Martin wrote in a 2015 *New York Times* op-ed about the *disempowerment* of rich women in the city's Upper East Side: "Worldwide ethnographic data is clear: The more stratified and hierarchical the society, and the more sex-segregated, the lower the status of women."

Lisu are organizing politically and are involved in party politics more in Myanmar than in China or Thailand because the country is advancing in that

Girls often pursue entrepreneurial activities, such as these two fishing with baskets in flooded wet-rice fields. Author photo.

direction today. Registering land and voting in national elections are novel and exciting to them—and possible only since 2011. Yet everywhere I also heard versions of "big politicians are unreachable, they don't do anything, only local officials and elections affect us." People in several villages also opined that NGOs, particularly the Seattle-based World Concern—not the government—helps with real things like sanitation, medicine, mosquito nets, and agricultural assistance. Some complained that they even had to build their own roads and bridges, cooperating with and contributing corvée labor to area work gangs. Nevertheless, each village I visit has Lisu reps from two or more national parties who hang gaudy political banners from their bamboo houses. Arguing national politics is a new Lisu pastime.

They don't vote as a block, but the most popular are Aung San Suu Kyi's National League for Democracy and its twenty-two "brother" parties forming Myanmar's opposition block. The NLD gained the most new seats in the 2011 elections, but the government USDP had backers because it is in power, has a strong organization, and gets credit for recent reforms. Lisu are pragmatic, not ideological, but they know who was in charge during Burma's long years of oppression. Lisu in Northern Kachin State have the distinction of being represented in Myanmar's Upper House by the only Lisu in that body, Senator J Yawu, a Catholic. (He was reelected, and the Lisu gained a second senator, in the NLD's landslide national victory in 2015—fifteen months after my visit to Putao.)

I tried to detect any "Kachin State Lisu strategy" emerging during my 2014 visit to this area. I met Lisu Cultural Committee leaders who uniformly declared willingness to work with the government within the new multiparty system. In Myitkyina and Putao, Lisu take care to distinguish themselves from the Kachin/Jingpo majority, factions of which are still at war with the government. They offer that they do not have an army but are victims of KIA conscription as proof of their amiability. "We are Kachin, but we are not Jingpo" was a constant refrain, one meant to underline their nontroublemaker minority position.

That doesn't mean they lack grievances. Aki Dawoo, vice chair of the new Lisu Crossbow, or Doolay, Party and a member of the Gwa (Sesame) clan, enumerated a few of these on a warm, drizzly morning in a private interview during a meeting of Putao's Cultural Committee. Exceptionally tall for a Lisu, soft-spoken, and charismatic, Dawoo is in his mid-forties and has been involved with NGOs and Lisu development issues for years.

"First, we will advocate for poor people, whom the government does little for. Next, we will fight discrimination against all non-Buddhists because it keeps us from advancing in the most powerful institution [the army] and also the civil service. We need a law that bases acceptance to army officer school on merit and test results. The army has the best schools, housing, medical care, everything—until it is democratized, the country can't be," he said.

At present, people from ethnic and religious minorities serve only as soldiers or low-level civil servants, though there is no law, only a glass ceiling, suppressing advancement. Otherwise, farming or going into business or getting a job in the church are the Lisu's career options. Several people mentioned Myanmar's first female Lisu pop star, although her breakthrough hardly creates openings for others. Small numbers are gaining higher education; access to mid-level civil service and military careers would open jobs in engineering, math, medicine, science, forestry, and other disciplines in which a first generation of Lisu graduates is earning diplomas.

Aki Dawoo (left) with other Crossbow Party leaders outside their headquarters in Myitkyina. Author photo.

"Our party's purpose is to grow Lisu involvement in development at the national level," Dawoo said of its goals. The Crossbows are active in five townships in Shan, Kachin, and Kayah States where Lisu have a chance of getting elected:

> When I campaign around the country, I find people are still afraid even of the *word* "party." Fear is greater in villages than in urban centers, where people can see evidence of reform. In cities they read newspapers that contain criticism of the government and divergent opinions—and no one is being hauled off to jail. For so long, there was only one legal party and it represented the army and authoritarian government. There is history to overcome, and country people are cagey survivors who don't trust that anything has changed. Even among my friends there are people, including some on this Cultural Committee, who say now [that] I'm in politics I should resign. I say NO! Being involved in both politics and culture is not a conflict.

We are just beginning, and there are many difficulties. We are Lisu, we don't agree on everything, but we keep talking.

———————■-■———————

A story an older man from Nyi Saladi told indicates that Christian Lisu haven't given up wandering and that they still cooperate within economic affinity groups: "Six months ago 50 families picked up and moved when better land opened up somewhere else. Now our village has only 120 families." He explained that they left because even though some had been there for twenty years, other families had better land with superior access to the river for irrigation: "Families can share, but [they] cannot share if there is not enough. [He estimated that five acres will feed a family of ten, leaving half their rice harvest to sell for cash.] Only in the last five years can we register land; now people *really* want good land they can hold paper for in their own names. Since the government lifted restrictions on how much each family can have, this finished the commune system. Before, it was only four or five acres; now you can have much more, hundreds of acres, if you can pay for it."

The reality of having 30 percent of a long-settled village pick up and leave must have rent its social fabric in the extreme. Yet group migration—to a nearby hilltop or across borders—is the oldest Lisu story of all. Neither national circumstance nor Christianity has altered the dynamic of Lisu cooperating for economic advantage and migrating to seek opportunities.

Several hundred young, educated Lisu in Myanmar have taken migration's function in a new direction. Instead of moving to seek new farmland, they've joined those fleeing Myanmar's civil wars to claim international refugee status. Violent insurgencies have created thousands of political refugees; many young and educated, but not specifically imperiled, Lisu and Rawang have exercised this option for the chance for a life free of political and religious persecution. Blending in with the diaspora, small groups set out for a United Nations–sponsored refugee center in Malaysia where they languish for an unspecified time (usually two to five years) before being resettled in the United States, Australia, or New Zealand. The window on this possibility fluctuates with waxing and waning civil insurgency in Kachin State. (War has broken out again as of 2015.)

I first heard about the "fake refugees" (direct Lisu translation) during a house-shaking downpour at Mulahdee Bible Training Center, about 10

Fu-he-ma insisted we visit Mulahdee's Bible college. Author photo.

kilometers outside of Putao. Fu-he-ma, an outspoken mother of twelve who warned against the current slippery slope of liberal Christianity, took us there. We'd met her in a discussion struck up with a group of Lisu under a dry goods store awning in this small agricultural community. She insisted we visit her husband's college. Fu-he-ma led us through the village in about a minute and over a narrow suspension bridge to get to the bamboo and wood-stilted campus, where we were greeted warmly—the first foreign guests in the college's twenty-five-year history. The skies by then had opened in a midday deluge, and we were invited for lunch. Lisu dishes of kombucha soup, rattan shoots, cooked greens, mild fish curry, and indigenous rice provided the context for our second impromptu discussion of the day, this time with a dozen Bible college teachers and administrators.

The center offers a three-year bachelors program in theology for conservative Church of Christ (CoC) pastors who serve Putao Valley's fifty churches and thirty other CoC congregations around the county. It is an example of indigenous church-led education—the institution was established long after Western missionaries left. Its focus is religious, but the curriculum includes math, geography, and English. The faculty of 30 serves 120 mostly Lisu students but also a few Rawang, Naga, and Burmese. Practically speaking, Bible-based colleges offer the only higher education option for people without a lot of money. Teachers are earnest; quality varies.

An older, longtime pastor/instructor expressed mixed feelings when he mentioned that two of his eight sons now live in America. He hasn't seen them in years; they fled with a few cousins to the Malaysian Refugee Center around 2006. Consensus among college staff, and indeed most I asked, is that this is tragic but not surprising. Young people with educations abandon family and country because they see no future here. While there is understanding, Lisu I spoke with voiced shame along with hope that this brain drain will cease as reform takes hold in Myanmar.

However, every prosperous and even semi-educated Lisu I asked thereafter had at least one fake refugee in his or her family or social circle. The most impoverished Lisu living around Myitkyina had heard of this practice but didn't know anyone who had actually done it. Selina, an English teacher working at a Christian seminary in the area, was my Lisu translator and explained why: "You have to be willing to lie, to forge documents, and [to] keep your story straight for years. It isn't easy; simple people can't do it unless they are really refugees." She appeared ashamed but felt obliged to add that "even young pastors with jobs or who are abroad for training just tear up their passports and turn up at the UN center." When I asked if she, twenty-seven, unmarried, and the best translator I'd had, would consider this route herself, I think I insulted her: "Oh no! I come from a religious family; my first duty is to follow the word of God. I would like to go to America one day but will do it without lying—like my brother who is now in Minnesota, studying theology."

The Myanmar government allows freedom of worship, although Buddhism is the official state religion. Religious organizations may not operate K–12 schools, and until very recently non-Buddhists could only conduct summer programs a week or two in length and some equivalent of Sunday school. Buddhist clergy, after the army and the government, constitute the country's third-most-powerful institution. The clergy includes violently anti-Muslim factions that focus on the Rohingya minority of Rakhine State. Muslims are hated and persecuted while Christians are merely looked down upon. Their persecution is generally more subtle, although churches have been burned and had land confiscated.

In Myanmar, animist Lisu are far more likely to become absorbed into Buddhism and majority Burman culture than are Christians; perhaps that's why it is they who lead the Lisu cultural revival and unity movements. This movement is stronger in Myanmar than in Thailand or China. Only in remote areas or on special occasions do Lisu wear native dress, which most say is too expensive for everyday wear and too hot for lowland areas. Other than at New Year celebrations, one is most likely to see traditional dress at Sunday and Wednesday night church services.

The revival movement includes traditional Lisu, however, and is active in Mandalay, Putao, Mogok, Myitkyina, and Rangoon. Every Christian leader I spoke with mentioned some version of the proverb "Lisu two, Lisu not have," meaning there is only one Lisu culture, though Lisu religious practice varies. Starting in 2010, permission to form cultural organizations was granted, which spawned a building boomlet of cultural centers such as one I visited in Putao town. Lisu language, dress, music, literature, and even dance (the latter formerly all but wiped out among evangelistic Christians) are now encouraged through a committee structure akin to traditional village counsels. Even more recently, cultural committees have received permission to organize Lisu literacy after-school classes, several Lisu living in the United States told me in 2016.

In the 1990s David Ngwa-za (Fish), a Christian Lisu scholar living near Mogok, was the single Lisu I met who was engaged in documenting culture. By 2014 an active network, easy to tap into wherever Lisu live, was evident. Ngwa-za continues to compile the traditional songs and proverbs that

J Pa-da, Citi-lo headman and village tract chairman. Author photo.

begin each chapter of this book; his work has become encyclopedic over the past twenty years. He records and publishes in Fraser's script, which has the advantage of being understood by Lisu everywhere literate in their own language. Mainly Christian, often urban or semi-urban Lisu fall into this group.

In a discussion in Village Tract chairman J Pa-da's house in the village of Citi-lo 1 in Putao Valley, I asked if people worry that Lisu culture is disappearing or if political parties and secular education imperil it. J Pa-da is the most prosperous of our Lisu hosts so far, a rising leader trained in theology before he turned to politics. In his tract of eleven mostly Lisu villages, he organizes bridge and road building, administration, and public health projects. He was upbeat but pragmatic on this question.

> Our kids learn Burmese in school, but they grow up speaking Lisu and most
> learn to write it, too, in church summer school. We have five political parties
> in our village of 56 households and 350 people. We never agree; that makes

Author (with white hair, seated in foreground) meets with the Cultural Committee of Putao in the Da-goo Sheetza village home of its chair, Ngwa Pi-too (red lapels on jacket). Small new outhouse in the background is a project of World Concern, an NGO that has installed advanced, low-tech toilets in villages all over Putao Valley. Photo: Mark Goldschmidt.

us Lisu. But having democratic elections and the chance to choose this leader, to vote against that one, reinforces our culture even as we become modern. According to your philosophy, you can choose the party and leaders you think will help us most. The important thing is for a leader to be trusted, to have strong faith, and to have good speech. Those who only have good speech will never be elected by Lisu because we watch what you do, not just what you say.

But then a woman spoke up, saying "everybody tells us to keep our culture, but in fact we don't see as much singing, dancing, and musical instruments as before. When you think about it, it *could* disappear. Older people do consider that because not that many young people really know about *illi Lisu* today. They learn about culture from the Cultural Committee, not their parents."

She waited a beat and then with a "how should I know?" shrug added, "Maybe the committees and their new buildings will outlast our culture!"

The room bursts into laughter; this is a quintessential Lisu-style joke—equal parts dark observation and wry comment.

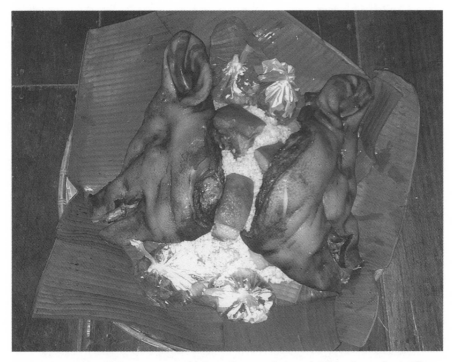

Putao's Lisu Cultural Committee made this offering to honor and bless the author's effort to write and publish the first book on the Lisu living in several countries. Photo: Mark Goldschmidt.

So much happens in the kitchen; it is a universal center. Da-goo Sheetza village, about 10 kilometers from Putao town, is the last in our walkabout. We're staying with Ngwa Pi-too, chair of Putao's Lisu Cultural Committee and a National League for Democracy leader, in another traditional stilted home. I've asked the committee to arrange a kitchen meeting for me with village women that excludes men. Women are more direct than men and invariably teach me something new. What might they share if their husband or pastor isn't there?

But before we gather with the women, a meeting has been scheduled with twenty-five local political and religious leaders under the raised house in its dryish open patio. Rain falls; glowing green paddy fields and thundercloud skies surround us. Lightning, downpours, and dancing sunbeams provide special effects. Ngwa Pi-too is handsome, with a deeply lined face and the

Most Lisu kitchens in raised homes are boxes of light filtered through split bamboo flooring and woven walls. Author photo.

carriage of a Navajo chief; he presides decisively over introductions and discussion but becomes really animated only when telling a Lisu dog story, of which there are hundreds.

Men gamely answered questions about the changes in their lives over the past fifteen–twenty years, bandying Lisu sayings with hilarious attempts at translation. When I bring up the role of religion in civic life, the pastor who speaks echoes what everyone tells me: "Christians live in a different world; the way we keep away from evil spirits is to pay attention to the Holy Spirit instead. We don't doubt evil spirits can harm us, you can see their effects in the world. But we don't like to talk about them because it gives them power."

Lunch was preceded by a ceremonial pig head offered on a giant banana leaf to honor my efforts to bring the Lisu story to the larger world. A troupe of old and young men and women in Upper Salween–style Lisu dress perform music, song, and dance.

Kitchen in Ngwa Pi-too's house is made of wood and is darker than the kitchen in the previous figure but is still a pleasant place to meet with Lisu women to discuss issues such as bride price. Photo: Mark Goldschmidt.

In the muddy lane outside, a respectful crowd of neighbors fortified with umbrellas, as well as a couple of curious oxen hitched to big-wheeled carts, peer in at the unexpected show.

After lunch it was time to retire upstairs to the kitchen with a dozen neighborhood women of various ages. A raised Lisu kitchen is a space of great beauty, a masterpiece of bamboo and light with one or two large open sandbox hearths fed by three or four tree limbs. These are pushed toward the hearth's center as they burn, precluding the need to chop wood into smaller pieces. Smoke wafts through the thatched roof, giving the room an aromatic pungency as it dries, preserves, and keeps bugs away from the corncobs stored above. Light filters in through bamboo lattice windows, split bamboo floors, and woven bamboo walls. We settle onto tiny stools or rest on our haunches as our hostess pours tea.

Lisu women hold strong economic positions and are outspoken, but each sex has roles; in formal situations such as this morning's, the few women present are quiet and let the men make speeches.

Rain continues, the hearth crackles—now it is their turn. An old woman sporting a snazzy T-shirt with "Vision Trip" emblazoned across the chest was the first to launch into my query about changes they've seen: "Life is much better now since we don't have to make clothes. Before, we had to gather material from the forest and step by step make thread from hemp, weave it into cloth, and then sew clothes. It was really bad if there were only one or two women in the household and four or five men plus children. Everyone needed a new suit of clothes every year. Sewing for the New Year celebration would take months, and we still had everything else to do."

"It's more convenient to just buy clothes and have variety," a younger woman noted. Nods and a couple "thumbs up" gestures around the room confirmed it.

One who looked to be in her forties piped up: "We had no containers except bamboo and leaves. We had to carry the children *and* the water from the stream. Now we have water next to our houses, we don't have far to walk, and we have plastic buckets. When I was young, I never saw modern plates; we had only bowls we made ourselves from wood. We had to gather food from [the] forest, and sometimes, some families ate rice only once a month."

Heads nodded; no one was nostalgic for the old days. The younger women, a couple holding babies, listen with bemusement. They'd heard it before. "Thank God we're not old-fashioned any more," their faces say.

"And another thing," Vision Trip added, "parents used to insist on picking husbands for us; now girls get to choose." This elicited laughter and prompted the oldest woman in the room to speak up for the first time: "But even when I was young, Father couldn't force me. I turned down the first three, and he was really worried. After I said no to the first suitor, no one asked me again for year. Then *finally* someone I liked showed interest, and we got married."

This pivot in the conversation provided an opening for a delicate question. Most Lisu in Myanmar, including all the women in this kitchen, had converted to Christianity a generation or more before. The practice of paying bride price or dowry is not animistic, Buddhist, Christian, or un-Christian— but a tradition most Christian Lisu men I've met claim to have given up.

I plowed ahead, hoping not to offend: "So, how much did your father get when you finally agreed to marry?" Amid twitters she said with pride, "One cow . . . that was a lot then."

Bride price is sometimes confused with dowry but follows a different logic—one that emphasizes the value of individual labor. The rationale is that since the bride moves in with the groom's family and henceforth provides his family with the benefit of her labor, her family must be compensated for its loss.

There is no equivalent abuse, such as India's bride burning or genital mutilation as practiced in parts of Africa, focused on females in Lisu and other "bride-giver and bride-taker" Southeast Asian cultures. Problems can and do arise if any part of the agreement between families before marriage goes unfulfilled, but it is not the bride who usually bears the brunt. It might be her husband or his family if they don't complete the promised payment of cash or labor or her father if she runs away from the marriage.

While today romance and perhaps what each party brings to the marriage are stressed, across time the linking of two families or lineages has been uppermost. Bride price and dowry are forms of wealth transference or early inheritance—their various customs reflect the values of the societies that created them.

In the West we might wonder where the tradition of the bride's father paying for the wedding comes from or how "dowry mind-set" behavior (hope chests, bottom drawers, trousseaux, and the like) contrasts with the thinking behind bride price. Is one more sexist than the other? At some point, do customs un-tether from social values as those values change over time?

Answers are beyond the scope of this work, but I have always found it fascinating that every Lisu woman, no matter how old, remembers the exact amount her father received for her hand. This amount is almost always predictable as it reflects an established market, but it still appears to be a source of pride because it shows she is as good as anyone else. If she fetched a higher-than-usual price, it adds to her and especially to her father's myi-do because it means she particularly embodies Lisu feminine virtues of hard work, skill, and modesty. Lisu are competitive.

Back to the Kachin kitchen, where I'm about to test this theory on a group of Lisu Christian women from farming families. I'm a bit nervous because I do not wish to offend my host, Chairman Ngwa Pi-too. Lisu Christians often overtly eschew payment of bride price (also called bride wealth) to outsiders or deny that it is still practiced. The New Testament, the focus of their religious practice, is silent on the subject. When the Old Testament refers to dowry, it describes what today is defined as bride price. As far as I can tell, the Lisu feeling against the practice is more a cultural borrowing from the missionaries who delivered Christianity to them than a religious prohibition.

"So," I ask a beautiful young woman with babe in arms, "how much did your father get?" Shyly and with clear satisfaction she said "four lakhs," meaning 400,000 Burmese kyats, about $400. Presumably, no big secret was being revealed, but murmurs of interested approval circulated the room in a country with annual per capita earnings of less than half that amount.

A middle-aged woman remarked that she had fetched 20,000 kyats, but that was a long time ago when the kyat was more valuable; still another, when asked, reported that her father received 120,000 kyats and a cow. One, married in 1976, seemed perfectly proud that her marriage had enriched her father and family by 600 kyat. It became clear that each woman was just waiting to be asked. By the time we got around to the chairman's wife, women were perched on the edges of their tiny stools. Married in 1977, her bride price included five cows, one buffalo, three pigs, and 90,000 kyat.

I, along with everyone else in the room, was really excited by this conversation—but just then the chairman popped his noble brow through the kitchen door. Uh-oh, I thought, I hope no one's in trouble.

Apparently, he'd been eavesdropping and could no longer bear to be excluded.

"Don't forget," he teased his wife, "about the two cows I gave your father *before* we were engaged, as a sort of 'advertisement.' So it was seven cows all together!" His reminder elicited merriment—and on my part, relief.

A question that needs further investigation is: how prevalent today is bride price among Lisu Christians? Only the poorest women I met (around Myitkyina) in 2014 reported that no bride price was paid for their hands. Indeed, until this conversation, I'd been told the practice had been abandoned by all Lisu Christians in Myanmar. Again, women had taught me something that underlined how very little has been documented on this group. My own efforts feel small and disorganized, unequal to filling yawning gaps of knowledge. Again, it is key to acknowledge that more is known about Thailand's 5 percent of the world's Lisu than about the other 95 percent.

Senator J Yawu, his Jingpo wife, Jacinta, and her sister in the couple's one-room Yangon apartment where the family of seven lives during the school term. (Note "Toilet" and "Showeroom" hand labeling on the doors behind them.) Author photo.

That rainy afternoon near Putao, only one woman related a story about her daughter's marriage taking place without "the sliver being paid." Taking my lead from old accounts of situations in which this anomaly occurred, I asked, "So, she must have been crazy in love with him?"

Yes, the woman nodded, no one could talk her out of marrying him, though neither family approved and it caused a lot of trouble at the time. "But in this case, it worked out," she said, gesturing with a nod of her head toward the young woman next to her with a toddler in her lap, "they are still together, still happy."

Said daughter smiled broadly; feminine sighs circled the Kachin kitchen.

——————■-■——————

August 2014, Yangon

The question I really want to ask Senator J Yawu, age forty-five, the first Lisu member of Myanmar's upper house of Parliament, is, how did *you* ever get elected? We are to meet at his family flat on Saya San Road above a convenience store in congested central Yangon. Streets have turned into rivers as the result of a monsoon downpour—I'm mortified to be running late.

J Yawu's breaking into the elite upper house as a socialist National Union Party (NUP) member is remarkable considering his backstory as a defrocked Lisu Roman Catholic priest who married his pregnant Jingpo girlfriend. Only 2 percent of Myanmar's Lisu Christians are Catholic, and J Yawu lacked the usual prerequisite for senate election—family wealth. Also unusual for Lisu in Myanmar in this overwhelmingly Buddhist country, he grew up as an animist. His father had been converted by and lived with the Morrison dynasty of Protestant Christian missionaries in Putao in the 1950s but fell back into old ways after being excommunicated for marrying outside the church. J Yawu grew up with traditional practices and was steeped in Lisu plant and medicine lore before converting to Catholicism at age fifteen while attending St. Anthony's boarding school. His father's death had left his mother in poverty with eight children to raise; the head of his school, the Reverend Father Peter Kareng Gam Awng, began acting as his guardian. He eventually sent J Yawu to the Philippines to study. J Yawu attended seminary in May-myo in the Shan highlands, taught school in the Kachin Independence Organization (KIO)–controlled Golden Triangle zone, and was ordained in 1998 after four more years of study in Yangon. Prior to his excommunication, he served parishes in Myitkyina, Putao, and the Philippines.

We've spoken by phone, so I know the senator's command of English is good. The Lisu bush telegraph has done its job in transmitting messages from contacts in Thailand, China, and Myanmar telling me I should meet him. But *really*, climbing a murky flight of stairs with my husband, I have little idea what to expect from his surprising invitation: "Come to dinner! Meet my family." I knock at one of two doors on the landing, the wrong one. Six women peer up in unison from sewing machines behind the one who opens, momentarily, to shoo us toward the other door.

The senator from the National Union Party greets us with a radiant smile, welcoming us into a single room, perhaps twenty feet long, with a kitchen at the far end. Four children from five to nine in age amuse themselves reading and playing on floor mats. His wife, Jacinta, with her sister and mother, are busy preparing dinner and have set a low round table surrounded by ten tiny stools. Two more doors, neatly labeled "Shower Room" and "Toilet" in script, complete the flat's amenities.

J Yawu's personal affect at the center of this domestic scene is dazzling. Of average height and stocky, his gaze is direct and he glows with health and jolliness. Four walls and modest circumstances cannot contain him.

The family's main home is in Myitkyina, he explained, but they stay in Rangoon during academic terms because all the kids go to school here. He lives in the new capital of Naypyidaw when Parliament is in session, often assisted by his "sweetheart" (wife) who joins him on yearly constituent walk-abouts. These are time-consuming and calorie-burning because his Northern Kachin senate district is the largest, most remote, and most sparsely populated in Myanmar. It has few roads but "lots of rivers and leeches," according to its senator. Mother and sister-in-law pick up the slack on childcare year-round.

We settle down into this harmonious family hive to talk. I relate our experiences walking around Putao and in Myitkyina, passing on the Lisu comment that "big politicians [such as J Yawu] do nothing but talk, talk, talk." I ask what he thinks he has accomplished for constituents at the local level:

> National leaders impact both state and local levels. Example: I am on the Rights Committee, one of those "distant" federal committees of fifty-two people from around the country that investigates human rights violations, crimes, wars, and land acquisition questions. Recently, a former military commander confiscated farmland. His company already owns 2 million acres and stole a few thousand more. We investigated, and he had to give it back. You can't solve *that* at the local or state level. The case is important because it sends the message throughout the country that land confiscation is now illegal. Compared to the past, it has almost stopped.
>
> In another case, [former president] Than Shwe's best friend wanted to confiscate 45 acres in Rangoon. He is a construction king and boss of Myanmar's legislature, notorious for showing that the military is still powerful. Even he was made to give the land back. He is appealing the decision, so we wait and see, but recent reforms have drastically reduced land theft in both urban and rural areas. We [have] had an anti-confiscation law since 1982, but only after a new law was passed a couple [of] years ago and our committee formed has it been enforced.
>
> I also fought with others against the huge Chinese dam project that had already started construction by the confluence of the Irrawaddy [in Central

Kachin State, 100 kilometers north of Myitkyina]; it would have destroyed thousands of acres of farmland. I consulted with leaders from around the country: bishops, priest, pastors, monks; they all gave me ideas for a paper I wrote opposing the project. I presented it to President Thein Sein, who congratulated me privately but asked that I not say anything to the media for ten days. After six days, he suspended construction. I'm not claiming I stopped it—but I was part of stopping it, and this directly benefits my constituents. Local and state government cannot solve our biggest problems; we can tackle these only at the national level.

What about ending the civil war in his own Kachin State? Does he support the KIA or the government?

"This conflict could be over in one week . . . but then what?" J Yawu asks dramatically, lifting his palms heavenward.

This is news to me; I'd never heard anyone say that before. On the edge of my seat, I bite: "What would happen?"

The government needs these conflicts to justify the Tatmadaw's [army's] outsized power and influence. Wars provide distractions. When a conflict gets hot in one place, you can bet they are up to something sneaky somewhere else . . . maybe Chinese pipeline construction or an oil deal, maybe a land grab, could be anything. There's so much the army controls all around the country, so many projects [through the ruling majority USDP] they have their fingers in. So conflicts serve their purpose—to cover kleptocracy and shady business deals.

Remember, Parliament is 80 percent military, active or retired. Our opposition coalition is no match for the USDP. Myanmar needs reform, the present government actually *wants* reform, but there are too many who think "I just need to get a little bit richer first." [Former junta leader] Than Shwe still controls the army; the conflict will end when he wants it to. This is out of our hands.

So if I support the KIA or the government really makes no difference. I should love the Tatmadaw: my father was a policeman, I am the grandson of a colonel in the British Burma Army, and my uncle is a USDP member in Parliament's Lower House. But I know the army is too powerful and too corrupt to reform. I saw their true colors as a student in 1988 when they fired on me and other innocents. It hasn't changed; blind obedience is the basic requirement to rise—and incompatible with democracy. I know about blind obedience because I was raised with it at seminary, but my church at least elects its leaders. The Tatmadaw is also more involved with logging and narcotics than the KIA, so they are the bigger evil. Adding everything up, using "the enemy of my enemy is my friend" logic, strategically, I should support the KIA.

But J Yawu can't quite bring himself to do it. An uncle and a "cous-in-brother" served as high-ranking intelligence officers in the KIA, and both were assassinated in internal purges over ethnic and religious differences—by spikes driven through their heads—in 1999 and 2006.

In the earlier years of the struggle, he said, many Lisu shared the KIA's aspiration for independence. Their solidarity was religious as well as political, as the KIA leadership and rank and file were mostly Jingpo Baptists from around Myitkyina—where most Lisu are also Baptist. However, when the Kachin Baptist Convention was divided into Lisu and Jingpo branches, the coalition unraveled and the Jingpo group began to dominate. After that, KIA Lisu leaders were systematically driven out or killed.

He concurs that today few Lisu are involved in the conflict other than as unwilling conscripts. He says the military strategy has always been to seek Lisu support to help them "win over" whoever it is they are fighting at the moment: the KIA, the Shan, the KNU (Karen National Union)—it doesn't matter who.

"The army has no loyalty to the Lisu, and [the] KIA is ruled by Jingpo Baptists; we [the Lisu] are always the pawns of one side or both." He adds that it's the same for all minorities. That's why he thinks the Crossbow Party's platform plank to infiltrate and democratize the army "sounds good, and of course it should be law. But unfortunately, it won't work." Discrimination against minorities is at the philosophical heart of army culture, according to J Yawu, who adds, "actually, their policy is to eliminate us."

I asked the senator what he thought of the new US engagement policy toward Myanmar: "The 'anti-anti,' pro-embargo position was not productive, the Chinese were the only ones who benefited from it. Obama's approach [is] good. I met Hillary [Clinton] when she visited Myanmar—I was very lucky and talked to her for twenty-four minutes! [An aide timed their con-versation.] I explained why the sanctions were not working, why the time for engagement has arrived. I guess a lot of people told her that," he beamed, albeit with a modest downward glance.

All this before dinner is unnerving. J Yawu's candor about politics is unlike the measured and cautious approach taken by Lisu I've encountered elsewhere. He doesn't seem afraid, yet I am afraid for him. I ask about the risk of criticizing powerful people and institutions, and he brushes off the paranoia I've learned in three reporting trips and from working next door in Thailand as a foreign correspondent in the 1990s.

"Oh, I am free, not censored [as a member of the opposition]—unlike my uncle with the USDP who cannot say a word without an okay from the government." He mentioned that he has been warned against using Bible quotes in public talks but doesn't always comply because, as he paraphrased the Bible, "The law is made for man, not men made for laws." He mentions that seventy-six Christian churches have been destroyed and not one Buddhist temple he knows of: "Though 40 percent of our country's people are ethnic minorities, overall 90 percent in Myanmar are [Theravada] Buddhists—because minorities assimilate and Buddhism is the state religion." (The balance is 4 percent each Christian and Muslim, with animists, Mahayana Buddhists, and Hindus splitting the final 2 percent.)

Over a delicious dinner of dishes combining Lisu and Jingpo elements, we heard about J Yawu and Jacinta's romance and recent rapprochement with the Roman Catholic Church. Their children speak Lisu, Jingpo, and Burmese, I'm told; I wonder how much English they understand. They are remarkably affectionate with each other and with the adults and while well-behaved, not cowed or particularly quiet.

> Well, we fell in love, and we are both Catholic. When my sweetheart became pregnant, I left the church and married her. I decided that if I can't be holy, at least I'll be honest—I didn't want to stay on as a sneaky priest, like some do. We couldn't have our marriage properly blessed because I was excommunicated, but she and I continued to attend church, though we couldn't take communion. We always sat in the front row to show that even though we sinned, we had not deserted the church. As our children began arriving, we brought them with us.
>
> For years I wrote letters to Pope Benedict, asking forgiveness and telling him I really think God's plan was for me to fall in love and help my country

through politics, not the church. Finally, just before Benedict abdicated in February 2013, he sent our bishop a message allowing my reinstatement! The day the bishop called me to give me this news was my happiest. I ran to find my sweetheart, and we went straight to the church and got married again.

Within a couple more days, that pope was gone.

The two smallest children have taken turns sitting in J Yawu's lap at dinner; their family circle appears to expand and contract organically until all the kids have reassembled back in the other end of the room, reading, giggling, and playing.

I ask J Yawu about the religious divides among Lisu and if he agreed with Ashley South, the Australian academic I'd met with in Rangoon who stated that "religious conflict is as great as political difference" in Kachin State.

"It's true. The various sects don't get along well, are full of schisms, and Protestants really look down on Catholics. On the other hand, the nonsectarian 'Unity Movement' is strengthening, and Lisu understand that to have a national voice, we must stick together politically."

"The thing about Catholics is that we can drink, and Protestant Lisu don't like that," he said, offering a tot of "traditional" medicinal cordial with a pickled bug and some interesting herbs in the bottom of the bottle. I mentioned that a young Assembly of God pastor had complained to me that "they [Catholics] think they can have it both ways." J Yawu laughed and agreed, telling me he'd distilled the cordial himself. Both J Yawu's father and grandfather were plant experts who taught him many plant-based cures that he relies on during his constituent walkabouts. He proceeded to expound on these remedies, including the helpful "honey is great for repelling leeches, and believe it or not, if you instantly apply earwax to a cobra bite, you won't die."

"The Catholic mission came late, and we are a tiny minority. But we're gaining popularity lately since Lisu like football and they see football players making the sign of the cross on TV. Pope Francis is also very popular. Most Lisu faith is not very complicated: just believe in God or you will go to hell."

This seems like a good moment to pop my question: "How did you manage to get elected? Being Catholic and your lack of family money must have been obstacles."

Flashing his most beatific smile of the evening, J Yawu responded, "Oh-h-h-h-h, my opponent!" as if that were sufficient to explain his victory.

The man was a Rawang, very rich and involved with a Rawang militia, a group supported by the military. People were disgusted by him because he led Rawang boys into a battle where they were used as cannon fodder/human shields by a joint force of [the] Karen National Union and Tatmadaw way down in the south. It had nothing to do with their cause, yet many were killed.

This caused people to hate the Tatmadaw even more, along with my Rawang opponent who they felt had led lambs to slaughter. The religious aspect was that my opponent was Assembly of God, and they don't like [the] Church of Christ [the two dominant evangelical sects in his Kachin State senate district]—so rather than vote for one of them, they voted for me, a Roman Catholic. I was known as a good guy because I'd done development work with NGOs in Kachin State . . . water systems, toilets, agricultural development. Since I was an EX-priest—no longer a priest—people didn't hold my religion against me so much. It was enough that I was religious, which Lisu think is always a good thing!

Demographics worked in my favor, too. My district used to be 40 percent Jingpo but had become less, maybe 30 percent, as the Lisu population grew to the number two spot, with the same or just a little less [population] than the Lowo. Lisu will always vote for a Lisu over a Rawang, especially since this Rawang had blood on his hands.

The final reason I won is that the Tatmadaw had not prepared enough phony ballots to turn the election for my opponent! They had only 10,000, but I received 29,000 votes. So even though they burned up another 2,000 NUP ballots, I still ended up with a margin of victory.

I have to ask again if it is not dangerous for him to speak so freely.

"Well, if there is a huge electoral victory by the USDP that is backed up by a military clampdown, I must rush to China," he says with a laugh. He added more thoughtfully, "We have friends and associates there. And we would have some warning if the government turns direction radically. They really don't want economic sanctions to return and stifle investment.

When I explained to the pope that this is what God wants me to do with my life, I believed it. I believe it still—because I cannot do more than this, I am in full swing!"

He leapt up to mime a line drive toward the back wall of his modest family digs, making the "whoosh" sound of a speeding projectile traveling a long distance.

4

China

Shu ma da!
(We can never die!)
 —*Lisu saying, also translated as "never say die!"*

Yunnan, August 2014

The strobe shoots twinkly points of light across the banquet hall; the music is amplified and enhanced with electric bird tweets, adding some country funk. Yu-yin Jiang, age twenty-six, sings with emotion about his village, backed by six young dancers getting down with their Lisu moves: hoeing the field, tossing the hay, sowing the seed. Their traditional costumes, updated in satin, shimmer and reflect the trippy lighting as they perform for about forty Han Chinese tourists focused on eating dinner.

The audience warms to the show as it refuels, however, and after about twenty minutes of Lisu song and dance, Yu-yin invites members to join in. As if waiting for their cue, about half leap up from their seats and onto the low stage.

Now everyone is having fun.

As in the group exercise in parks and town squares you see everywhere in China, here new members of the middle class get physical as they learn how to be tourists and absorb some Lisu culture. Un-shyly, to Lisu music and

*Lisu cultural show for Chinese tourists inside a jewelry mall in Tengchong, Yunnan.
Author photo.*

line-dance steps, they reenact agricultural rituals—digging earth, planting in
male-female pairs, slinging seed—probably not that far removed from their
own lives. Trays full of tiny shots of "liquor medicine" are passed out at the
end of the show and chugged before the crowd files out to board the bus for
the last two stops of the day.

The group from Baoshan clearly enjoyed its dinner break above one of
Tengchong's fancy new jade malls. Earlier, they'd purchased rings, bracelets,
pendants, name chops, and knickknacks from among fifty shops where arti-
sans handcraft wares in front of customers. Dozens of buses a day stop at
this mall, which gives no clue from the street that in addition to jade, cross-
cultural knowledge is traded inside.

From the second century BC, Tengchong, formerly called Tengyue, was a
regional market center on the southern branch of the Silk Road. It sits in a high
valley (1,640 meters, or 5,380 feet) in the Gaoligong foothills in far southwestern
China, 40 kilometers from the Myanmar border. Surrounded by volcanoes and
hot springs, it is adjacent to the most jade-rich region in the world.

Large-scale manufacturing and industry is absent here. The remote, pristine area was slated mainly for tourism more than twenty years ago as part
of China's master plan to build service and consumption sectors. The larger

goal was to develop a less export-dependent economy. The centrally controlled juggernaut of Chinese economic growth was cooling in 2015; as its currency and stock market lose value, whether the long-term plan will succeed in providing the world's second-largest economy with a "soft landing" is in question. Has China yet grown a middle class with strong enough purchasing power to sustain it?

Yu-yin Jiang, the Lisu cabaret leader, moved to Tengchong in 2005 at age seventeen from his village two hours north. "I wanted [to] earn more money and have a better life," he said. He arrived during the feverish building boom then transforming the town into a tourism center. Yu-yin looked around to figure out how he might get in on the action.

———————— ■-■ ————————

I first visited Tengchong in October 1997. It was an outpost from which to access remote Lisu hinterlands: no tourists, no airport, and a town of perhaps 15,000 people. My new thousand-page edition of the Lonely Planet travel guide to China spent a couple hundred words describing a walkable town of traditional wood architecture unvisited by many travelers.

The Dansha area, fifty miles from Tengchong and ten miles north of Guyong, was my main destination: an area of exquisite stream-crossed valleys, jewel-like Lisu villages, forested foothills, and low mountains. It was an eight- to ten-hour auto trip to reach Dansha from Tengchong on a good day, and the road was frequently washed out.

Anthropologist Otome Klein Hutheesing was my companion and translator on that trip; she frequently remarked that the Lisu we met here were "the same people" she'd lived with in Thailand for years—except perhaps "more friendly and open." We visited several wooden villages in this area at harvest time. Most Lisu were animist subsistence farmers; perhaps 20 percent had converted to Christianity. They wore the same colorful dress their forebears donned when they migrated to Shan and Kachin States in Burma and on into Thailand. They lived without electricity, running water, or much connection to the outside world. Although major opium cultivation had ended fifty years earlier, farmers told us they hadn't completely stopped growing it as a trade item until three years before. Otome's Lisu quickly adjusted to the local dialect, and in many conversations we learned that after a long period of suppression, they were again free to practice traditional religion. "During

Mao's time, this wasn't possible," Wo-ta, a small and finely made bear clan member, told us. He said he'd resisted joining the Christians, although they'd invited him over the years. Wo-ta lived in the grandest wood-beamed house in Dansha village, built around a large courtyard with a second-floor stuffed-full granary adjacent to his fields. He showed us his new tabia, built just five years earlier in the Chinese style. It had twelve cups and a Tibetan dorje bell on it that he'd dug up in his field. The village also had a spirit house, which he called a Nee-hee, just outside its boundary, where the Big Hill Guardian was worshipped. Wo-ta did not recognize the Thai spirit names Otome mentioned, however, including Yi-da-ma.

A Christian household in the same village, also built around a courtyard, had a Bible quote carved into its front door in Fraser's Lisu Script. The owner, Nusa, was a second-generation Christian whose living came from producing planks of wood from logs he bought from Chinese dealers. We saw no evidence of crosses or other Christian symbols in his house, but he told us his father had done away with the family tabia during the Cultural Revolution. Christians got together in each other's houses here, but an old traditional medicine woman, whom he called a Nyi-ma, was the one everyone went to when they got sick. In 1997, there were still no hospitals in the area.

Just ten years later, before "Hump Airport" (named in honor of the air route that contributed to the Allied victory against Japan) opened in Tengchong in 2009, its tourist office was claiming 2 *million* annual visits—most arriving on newly built roads from within Yunnan or adjacent provinces.

Tengchong is the site of massive real estate development and gleaming Oz-like infrastructure. A solar-panel–lit highway connects what is left of the old town to the airport and to blocks of empty apartments awaiting occupancy as second homes by China's rising classes. A marvel of a superhighway through sheer mountains between here and the nearest industrial center, Baoshan, has shortened the drive from ten hours to four. Thousands of urban trees have been planted, as in every Chinese city and town, in addition to massive afforestation projects of the last thirty years—32 million acres alone since 2008. These trees are intended to absorb carbon released by China's decades of coal-powered industrial and construction booms and to soften the effects on human beings trying to live amid all the commotion.

Getting back to Yu-yin's show: "I want to advertise Lisu culture and people to the rest of China. My show is all Lisu culture, no foreign culture, not Christian," he says when I ask how he came to be leading a troupe of Lisu youth entertaining Han Chinese at a jade mall. He, an animist, got the idea for the cabaret after working in Tengchong for a few years. In addition to himself, it consists of three young men and three young women, one of whom is his strikingly beautiful wife.

"We are ethnic people, many with no writing. We show our emotions to each other in dancing and singing," he says, adding that his father is also a musician, so it is his family business. Besides Chinese, he learned to write in Lisu (Fraser's Script) at his government school, but not very well. He also studied computers briefly after high school. For his current gig, he made new, Chinese-pop–style arrangements of Lisu music on a synthesizer, which a foreign friend helped him put on a DVD. The songs are in Lisu; he MCs the show in Chinese.

Yu-yin and his troupe are employees of the mall's Chinese owner. He says he is satisfied with the arrangement, which pays regularly and well. He and his wife send money home each month to his mother and father, who take care of their two-year-old son so both can work.

Have his parents ever come to see his show, I ask, imagining an old Lisu couple taking in their son's Vegas-style review. My question surprises him, then elicits a guffaw and look of incredulity.

"No, why would they? They do the dances themselves; they see them at home all the time!"

The Lisu in China are the ones who never left home. They've moved around a lot, however; home is huge, and life has undergone more profound changes here in the past twenty years than in any other national milieu. Minorities may still be looked down upon, but they are not systematically isolated as in Thailand and Myanmar because China's education and other policies weave them into social and urban fabrics. Many are involved in local administration. Lisu women in particular have gone on to higher education. The elite Yunnan Nationalities College offers courses in the Lisu language, although all Lisu under age fifty speak Chinese.

Lisu culture is the most varied in China, where the biggest population in the world has dispersed across mountain ranges and down river gorges over the centuries. Today and for the past several hundred years, most live in Yunnan—earlier, it was probably Sichuan around Lake Lugu (home of the matrilineal Mosuo, whose language is related to Lisu), and before that theories disagree (see Book I, Chapter 5). The migrating lifestyle has created a cultural mosaic of custom and costume united by language. In addition to traditional religion—itself a mix of animistic beliefs and borrowings from the Chinese—large numbers converted to Christianity or gave up religion entirely. Indeed, in China, rising to any significant position requires membership in the Communist Party, an avowedly atheist organization of 87 million. Practical and ambitious, many of the most successful Lisu aspire to join. I was assured by one Lisu driver who was an atheist that a lack of faith didn't take away from his Lisuness—on the contrary, it made him *more* Lisu.

Sixty-five years after the revolution, Lisu are more settled than at any other time in history. China is as opaque as it is huge, however, and access to reliable historical particulars wasn't possible for me. Parts of this void may be filled by others in the future. Impacts on the Lisu of the calamitous Great Leap Forward (1958–62) and the Cultural Revolution (1966–76), for example, are not knowable in an overall sense beyond the fact that these events caused convulsive change: many dropped traditional practices, took up Chinese ones, or migrated—including thousands into Burma. Ideology and scholarship are not separate in China; most of what has been written about Lisu and other minorities (certainly translated material) is either so fragmented as to lack broad usefulness or else has a strong political slant.

During the Cultural Revolution, Lisu and other minorities were charged with and found guilty of "Little Nation Chauvinism." Mao's ideological campaign to rid China of the "Four Olds"—including old culture—precipitated chaos, persecution, and famine for millions. Minority Tibetans and Muslim groups such as the Uighurs were particularly targeted, but suffering was widespread and no group or region escaped.

Many older Lisu men and women, however, were still wearing Mao caps with traditional dress in the mid-1990s and often gave me the "thumbs up" when I asked about him. Whether this reflected true feelings or was a reflexive response I don't know. Several told me that right after the revolution Mao gave them horses, land, and government grants—but these benefits soon disappeared. Mao also relaxed the quota on the number of children allowed to

Several Lisu in provincial market towns dress in traditional clothing, as does this woman traveling with a village group in a new car. Lisu in the Tengchong area have grown particularly prosperous, along with other citizens, over the past fifteen years. Author photo.

minorities in remote areas. Unlike urban Chinese, allowed one, and rural families, allowed two, the Lisu and other ethnic minorities often had more children. I interviewed several Lisu in the 1990s who had four or five.

Mao's death in 1976 marked the end of the Cultural Revolution, though it had been winding down the previous five years. Deng Xiaoping succeeded Mao and began building a more pragmatic and orderly society, still authoritarian but with capitalistic tendencies: the new focus was an economy based on manufacturing, exports, and the building of a consumer society.

The two-hour drive to Yu-yin's home village of Shao Hu Ba is through pretty valley floor-land banked by low mountains and hills, many still forested. The turnoff from the main road leading to each village or town is marked by a

massive carved pink stone monument, but the area is not as densely populated or cultivated as other non-precipitous areas we traveled through on the
way to Tengchong from Baoshan. The only industry here is cement; from
afar, factories suggest ancient castles and battlements—but when you get
close you see it is just another extraction operation. We don't veer from the
excellent, newly constructed road until close to our destination.

Thanks to China's cell phone coverage, meeting up with Yu-yin's father,
Yu-you Jiang, in a nearby market town is a breeze. We see other Lisu in traditional dress in the three-block-long market that runs through the center of
town, but he is the only one riding a motorcycle who waves and smiles at us.
He wears knee-length Lisu trousers, gators, and rattan leg bracelets topped
with a polo shirt and is soon leading our small Korean sedan to his village.
Half of the road on the last fifteen minutes to Shao Hu Ba is a paved lane
out of town that degenerates to gravel after a kilometer or so. When it further devolves into a hilly and mud-rutted car trail that takes 180 degree turns
around fields and within a couple feet of front doors in a Han hamlet, I feel
as though I've returned to the China of the 1990s.

We arrive just after midday. The village of a hundred families is empty
and quiet, a hodgepodge of cinderblock, cement, and wood houses—its
lanes steep and muddy. The paved road advanced to within a mile five years
ago; no one knows when it might fully connect the village to the marvel
of China's new highway system. Shao Hu Ba village reclines upon a south-
facing hillside; one house in a flat place has set up a tiny shop offering a few
essentials and brightly packaged snack foods. Yu-you says: "Before we had no
road . . . just climbing, walking, carrying. Things have improved."

A handsome restroom built of stone is the village's freshest-looking construction and only public infrastructure. I ask about a half-built church further up the hill, and Yu-you says that the church came to the village years
ago, he can't remember how many. Twenty families converted and started
to build, but they ran out of steam and never completed it—though they are
still Christians.

We walk up the slippery lane to Yu-you's family compound, made of wood
and built Chinese-style around a courtyard. This courtyard has several large
mirrors built into one interior wall, three feet tall and four feet wide.

"I am a singing and dancing specialist. I have been to Beijing to perform with
other musicians," he says. He got the idea for the mirrors in his courtyard

during his visit to the capital. When he expanded it three years ago he added them so "the young people I teach can see their good bodies dancing. I want to grow Lisu culture in the next generation." He sounds a lot like his son, who hasn't fallen far from the family's entrepreneurial tree. Yu-you ushers us through the courtyard and invites us to sit in the main room of his house. It is bare with a packed mud floor and smoky fire, a tabiya with nine cups, and a few old calendars with film stars decorating the walls. He fire-roasts popcorn and brings out two kinds of musical pipes to show us; we are soon joined by his wife carrying their grandson. Yu-yin stands up then and plays a tune accompanied by a slow-stepping dance that he calls the "rhythms of welcome." It is meant to communicate "sit in our house, visit our home, come by anytime," he says.

I ask him to tell me about this village and the biggest changes he's seen since the 1990s, and settle down to take notes. But his first statement—that Sho Hu Ba is 400 or 500 years old—takes me so aback that I immediately interrupt to ask how he knows it is so old. In 20 years of studying the Lisu, I've never heard of a Lisu village with such a long history.

Yu-you is unperturbed: "I know because of my tabiya; I can count back the generations who were in this place. My father told me our ancestors came from Luishi on the Nujiang before they immigrated here. My tabia has nine cups, one cup, one generation covering our family's time here. About fifty years each. I've been thinking that the next generation, my great-grandfather, who comes on the tabiya will replace the current oldest ancestor who has lived here."

This seems unlikely, but who am I to challenge him? Many tabiyas have nine cups, and this Lisu village looks like dozens of others: an impermanent way station without signs of long inhabitation. His claim reminds me how varied Chinese Lisu history is and how much reinvention the last century's convulsions must have inspired.

Yu-you grows two kinds of corn along with rice, buckwheat, and tea. The popcorn we are eating is from Tibet, he says, and is the same corn the ancestors ate. The corn fed to pigs is newer, from China.

"One big change is that everyone has enough to eat now; this was not true until ten or fifteen years ago," he says, adding that he still collects nuts, tea oil, rattan, and medicines in the forest. "We are not allowed to hunt animals anymore, but I still do a little—not like in the past when we were more hungry."

Yu-you, father of the cultural show star Yu-yin, plays a variety of traditional Lisu instruments and teaches youth in the Lisu village Sho Hu Ba music and dancing. Author photo.

"Now we have many kinds of food. We keep pigs and chickens and ducks for meat and eggs. No one used to grow rice, just buckwheat and corn—and my family didn't learn wet-rice farming until after the revolution. This was still quite new when I was growing up. Today I also grow beans, cabbage,

Yu-you counts back the generations with cups on his tabiya, calculating that Sho Hu Ba village must be 400 or 500 years old. Author photo.

chili, garlic, and pepper." He provides a sample of the latter that is drying outside the door in his courtyard: it looks like red peppercorns but is like nothing I've tasted before. It doesn't burn like chili, and it doesn't taste like pepper—instead, it sizzles with a strong, almost lemony flavor and numbs my tongue.

I ask if he collected the rattan to make the leg bracelets I've seen Lisu in Thailand and Burma also wear, and he nods yes: "When a boy sends rattan to a girl, it means I love you. When she sends gators back to him, it means I love you, too." He nods toward his wife and says she made his gators, which draws a chuckle from her that her little grandson immediately mimics.

Although born in 1967, a generation after the revolution, Yu-you says he received only thirty days of schooling and cannot read. However, father, like son, declares himself satisfied with his country, counting his blessings on his fingers: he lived in a bamboo and grass house until six years ago (this does not jive with what I think I know about the area's architecture); now he lives in a wood house. He has three children, two sons and a daughter, and nobody's died. Two are married (he was able to afford Yu-yin's hardworking bride, and his daughter fetched a respectable sum), and he will support his grandson if he want to go to college. And oh . . . he adds as an afterthought: he's had electricity for forty years—it came to the village when he was seven or eight.

Yu-you is full of surprises; none of the villages I visited in the Tengchong area in the 1990s had electricity, and none were built of bamboo. I hadn't visited this particular valley, though. Lisu lives in China are too varied to generalize, I keep learning—even as I find myself not quite believing everything I'm hearing. This is rare in my experience of interviewing Lisu. I question my Chinese interpreter several times about Yu-you's statements, wonder about her reliability, and miss having Otome to translate.

Most people in this village, about a hundred families, practice animism and ancestor worship like he does, Yu-you says. They have tabiyas in their homes; there is no communal worship place. When they get sick they consult a ne-pa (shaman), of whom there are three, who use divination sticks to determine how to contact the correct spirit to heal them. If they are not cured, they go to the hospital.

Christians also lack a common meeting place, since their church remains a foundation and a couple of deteriorating walls. They don't socialize with non-Christians much, according to Yu-you, except to attend each other's weddings. I ask if the Christians in this village drink alcohol. "No, normally they don't drink. But when they get together with us, they make an exception. And when they drink, they like to dance, too."

───────────■-■───────────

From the Tengchong area to the Nujiang is not far, twenty miles as the crow flies. But the softer geometry of foothills and pretty valleys turns suddenly vertical when you reach the Gaoligong mountains that form the west side of the Nujiang Valley. Traveling north along the river above Fugong, the valley narrows further into a gorge, and barren sheer mountains give way to escarpments just as steep but clothed in vegetation. The sense of being closed in and cut off increases, and one realizes how this geography has isolated its inhabitants throughout history. With no car bridges across the river until the 1980s and only a simple track running alongside it, even after the revolution the Lisu here have remained relatively undisturbed.

The spectacular gorge carved by the Nu along with two other rivers, the larger Mekong and the Shweli, all flowing north-south within 20–30 miles (and lesser ones running in various directions), creates a mountainous, transected region. For the last several hundred years, Lisu lived and developed their egalitarian culture in precipitous pockets of this unique geography—and it is from here that they migrated out into the world.

The beautiful valleys around Tengchong and Guyong and the stunning terrain of the Nu Valley feel like the homelands Lisu in Burma and Thailand long for in sad songs and poems. These are two places from which we know the Lisu have migrated.

The drive up the Nujiang gorge in the heart of today's Lisuland is an awake-dream. For more than half of the river's 600 kilometer scenic journey through Yunnan, the visual excitement is almost overwhelming. We kept stopping to take pictures that never adequately captured the scene. I felt a curious longing/anxiety both about documenting the experience and thinking about how to get back here—even while I *was* here. The lit-from-within greenness of 2,000 meter drops from ridge to river in August 2014's rainy season was more beautiful and surreal than I remembered, though the river raged with muddy water instead of resembling the swift blue-green knife I recalled from October 1997.

During that visit, I'd once seen fish in the kitchen of one of the modest restaurants we frequented. I ordered it since it wasn't offered most places. When the bill arrived, it was more than twice what I'd been paying everywhere else, and I asked why. The owner pointed to the plate, which by then contained only a few fish bones, and gestured toward the Nu, asking "have you seen that river?" as sufficient explanation. Thereafter I paid more attention; indeed, only once did I spot a fisherman attempting to harvest anything more than washed-up driftwood from its fierce, un-giving waters.

That was before the Chinese began systematically harnessing small bits of the Nu's enormous hydroelectric potential. Plans had been in the works since the 1980s, but only in the past twenty years have dozens of mini–electric plants sprouted on ridges above its banks. They provide cleaner and more local energy than the gigantic CO_2-belching coal-powered plants fueling most of China. I'd noticed a few small hydro projects in the 1990s, but by 2014, every 10 miles or so a generating facility had been built to power nearby villages. Today, virtually all villages are electrified and have cell phone service.

Construction on superhighway coming through the mountains to Liuku from the east will run right behind a giant Buddha. Such massive infrastructure projects have transformed China, making previously isolated provincial areas easily accessible. Author photo.

Following a single electric line a couple thousand meters up the vertical wall of the gorge to a tiny hamlet or even a single house at the top is evidence that "power to the people" is more than a political slogan.

A huge hydroelectric dam along the Nu, as well as several lesser ones, have been planned since the 1980s; like Three Gorges Dam, these would submerge thousands of villages and fields and cause severe environmental impacts. There have been resistance and delays in starting such projects, however. According to a personal communication from Piaporn Deetes of the NGO International Rivers (Berkeley, CA) on July 13, 2017, because of China's cooling economy, "the dams proposed on the Nu River have not [been] started, and there is no hydropower project on the Nu River proposed in the 13th Five-Year Plan for China's Economic and Social Development (2016–2020)."

The Chinese have constructed a few magnificent stone bridges and many light suspension crossings for pedestrians across the Nu in the past twenty years. Local people still use the old cables to save the time of walking to the new bridges, though. Cables had been improved by the late twentieth century; now there are usually two, one for each direction, engineered so that gravity and modern gliders make crossing a relative breeze. All one needs are nerves to match the new steel hardware that zips people across the raging Nu 150–200 feet (50–60 meters) above its surface.

In the twentieth century, the Chinese began calling this gorge "the Grand Canyon of the East" in reference to Arizona's well-known canyon in the United States. It is around here that most of China's 700,000 Lisu are concentrated in Nujiang Lisu Autonomous Prefecture (encompassing Lushui, Bijiang, Fugong, and Gongshan Counties), as well as in Weixi Lisu Autonomous County on the Mekong eighteen miles to the east. Nujiang was established as an autonomous district in 1954 and upgraded to a prefecture in 1957.

Liuku is a bustling little (by Chinese standards) city of 50,000. It is Nujiang's seat of government and main commercial center, located in Lushui County at the southern end of the prefecture. The valley widens out a bit here, and today Liuku straddles the Nujiang. The old city is on the west bank, along which a wonderful stone riverwalk meanders, and its new section is on the east bank. The modern part is much larger than the original town, and canyons of ten- and twenty-story high-rises dominate it. Soon it will be reached by an elevated superhighway advancing through the mountains from the east. Two main bridges cross the river in Liuku: one for pedestrians where people sell everything from magic charms, vegetables, and electronic goods to precious stones and crossbows, and one on which vehicular traffic moves very slowly. We stay at the Hotel Miami in the old city not far from the pedestrian bridge and must register at the police station before checking in. Hotels on this side of the river are geared to domestic travelers; their computers aren't yet in the national system that tracks foreigners moving about China.

On a Saturday morning we are tasting peppercorns in Liuku's old covered market, trying to track down the sizzling variety. My cell phone rings and it is Myanmar's Lisu senator J Yawu, sounding excited: "Come as soon as you can to my hotel lobby. The minister has agreed to meet!"

Fortuitously, my travel plans to China coincide with J Yawu's. He is in Liuku for an international conference, and we'd arranged to meet an hour from now to attend a Lisu church service and have lunch with the minister afterward.

Liuku is the capital of Nujiang Lisu Autonomous Prefecture, a town where Lisu make up the majority. A market by the main pedestrian bridge features crossbows, arrows, and the aconite poison hunters apply to arrow tips—despite hunting being illegal today. Author photo.

In the hotel's shiny marble lobby, I'm unnerved for a moment when I realize we're about to ditch church to meet with a different minister—Nujiang Lisu Autonomous Prefecture's foreign minister Molido. The evening before, J Yawu had told me chances of meeting him were slim because of his responsibilities as conference host.

Yet here I am, shaking the hand of a tall, fit man in his fifties with a silvering brush cut. As the liaison for Nujiang's administration, Beijing, and foreign countries for international projects, as well as for cultural and trade missions, he is a very influential Lisu. We begin our interview sitting in soft, oversized hotel lobby furniture, but my first question prompts a change of venue.

"It's a bit sensitive; this is more tea shop conversation," the sharp-eyed Lisu minister responds when I ask how power sharing between local government and central authorities works. "We have fifty-six nationalities in China and thirty autonomous prefectures; there are differences in geographical position, resources, and so on." He excuses himself for a few minutes, after which

Nujiang Autonomous Lisu Region's foreign minister Molido, left of the author, organized an impromptu lunch at a Liuku hotel, where Myanmar's Lisu senator J Yawu, left of the minister, kindly served as translator. Minister Molido did not learn the Chinese language until he was fourteen years old. Author photo.

we reconvene upstairs in a large private room with a seating area, where an impromptu banquet is readied for J Yawu's entourage, the minister and his aides, my husband, and me. Molido begins with a succinct overview:

> There are 530,000 people in Nujiang Prefecture's four counties. Two hundred and sixty thousand are Lisu, the largest group. More are becoming Christians all the time. The other big minorities are Dulong, Nu, and Leme. Only 11 percent of the people here [56,000] are Han Chinese. In Weixi Lisu Autonomous County to the east, in Deqe Prefecture, 80,000 of the 120,000 population are Lisu—the majority there are still animists. In all of Yunnan's sixteen prefectures, only three have no Lisu.
>
> China's total Lisu population is 700,000—and 600,000 of us live in Yunnan. Lisu are the third-largest group in the province; we follow the Chinese and the Lalo. Quite a few Tibetans also live here.

The Lisu are left behind in education, economic, and commercial development compared to other nationalities. In Nujiang we have thin soil, steep
slopes, and Lisu farmers don't multi-crop. We do our best with the land and
resources we have. In the past, Lisu migrated here and there around China,
living in temporary houses, always building and rebuilding, getting poorer
and poorer. Now we encourage people to build concrete and brick houses to
last for two generations.

Molido's relaxed authority in reciting facts and an agreed-upon narrative
brings home the reality that Lisu in China, unlike those in all other countries,
include *themselves* in the national voice. Perhaps this shouldn't be surprising;
there is only one party here. But it is still new to me to hear such an attitude
from a Lisu, although Yu-yin and his father, Yu-you, also expressed it. It contrasts with both J Yawu and Myanmar, where Lisu are new to political power
and mostly in opposition to the government (this interview took place before
the November 2015 elections), and Lisu in Thailand—where half aren't citizens,
they don't rise above village headman level, and they all hate the government.

The minister's view on the growth of Lisu political leadership tops my ad
hoc list of questions, so I ask about it in the context of my visit the month
before to Myanmar, where change since the late 1990s is dramatic and everyone is speculating about the general election that will take place in just over
a year.

There's no comparison. Our systems, our hierarchy, are different. Here we've
had peace a long time, while in Shan and Kachin States civil wars have been
almost continuous for sixty years.

Since 1949, in China the government has emphasized infrastructure and
cares about minorities. There are so many projects, especially roads, that
helped raise people up quickly as they connected our country together. We've
had political representation a long time. In Nujiang, Lisu are administrators,
professors, elected officials; Weixi is also known as a "City of Lisu" since most
of its leaders are Lisu. This happens because our best Lisu students go to university. We have universities in Kunming and Beijing where minority cultures
are a big part of the curriculum. China's minority policies are important to
its central policies because Lisu and other nationalities live in border regions
with security issues. And of course, we've had at least thirty years of continuous improvement, compared to Burma.

But frankly, the Lisu are still not very well-equipped and lag behind other minorities because of our land and, until recently, our remoteness. We are at the back of the herd in learning Chinese ways.

I myself spoke only Lisu, no Chinese, until I was fourteen. I have struggled with this language all my life. I did not insist that my own children learn Lisu. Their mother is Chinese, so it was my responsibility. I regret it now because my perspective has changed. I realize that one reason Lisu culture is not improving is that too often we learn other languages and forget our own. Yes, we need to imitate other cultures' wisdom but *not* to lose our own. When we embrace Christianity, for example, too often we throw out musical instruments and other aspects of culture.

Preserving culture is not easy, though, when your main jobs are education and economic development. For seven years in the 1980s I was a schoolteacher—we tried to teach in both Lisu and Chinese. It just didn't work, the kids were confused, and eventually we stopped in the early 1990s. [The Chinese government invented a Lisu writing system, used from 1957 and called New Lisu, that it abandoned in 1992 when it adopted Fraser's as the official Lisu script. Historically, only Christians used it, but they are a fast-growing segment of the Lisu population, and today its use is increasing secularly, in universities as well as by churches. Lisu all over the world can communicate in Fraser's, and it has been embedded in most computer operating systems via Unicode since 2009.]

I ask Molido if there are specific plans for Lisu cultural preservation and development in Nujiang. To get back to my original question about power sharing between local and central governments, who would be in charge of implementing such plans?

Plans are formulated at the top working through lots of committees and representatives—this is China. In Nujiang, we are charged with making them work within budget constraints, etc. The central government sends a lot more money into the prefecture than it gets from us; [it has] made serious investments here.

The idea for years was that because we are poor, we cannot focus on cultural values—just [on] surviving. Now, after years of economic development, we're getting a little well-to-do and beginning to promote customs and tourism more as we realize these things help us prosper. In the last four to five years, a big government project helps farmers with long-term planning, getting them to grow hard fruits and nuts. If a farmer is able to wait five years and care for twenty trees as they mature, eventually he will make 8,000 RMB ($1,250) per tree and come out of poverty.

Warming to the theme, Molido becomes animated, declaring, "We need the same kind of long-term planning for cultural preservation projects, like language, as we have for infrastructure and agriculture." I can see that he is a charismatic politician. He's certainly a busy man; just then he glances at his Rolex and jumps up, excusing himself to chair a session of the meeting in progress next door at the convention center.

J Yawu, who has been my interpreter, tells me after Molido leaves that he is in the running for the next prime minister of Nujiang. The Lisu minister from China has told the Lisu senator from Myanmar that when and if he rises, cultural preservation will be a central concern of his. Politicians come and go in the grander scheme—nonetheless, these particular ones are rocking this particular moment in the Lisu world as they map new territory for a small but persistent people.

Market day, Lishadi town, Fugong County

After the Cultural Revolution, farm collectives broke up, individual land rights gained ground, and commercial activities condemned for more than a generation were once again encouraged. For the Lisu (and the majority of Chinese who have always worked the land), a key rehabilitated custom is market days. These are held on a rotating basis in the largest towns within a rural vicinity.

People (mostly Lisu) from villages and hamlets around Lishadi pour into town on Tuesdays, many loaded with goods to sell. Women run most of the stalls and as family purse holders, they also do most of the shopping. Goods traded are DVDs, dried noodles, ready-made clothing, and electronic goods—along with produce, meat, savory and sweet snacks, herbal medicines, and a few handcrafts such as headdresses and crossbows. Socializing and showing off are de rigeur. Most Christian and animist women still wore either full ethnic dress or at least traditional skirts, aprons, or jewelry to market in 2014. Lishadi is the prettiest of Fugong's market towns for this reason and also because it is tucked into small emerald-green hills overlooking the Nujiang.

Market day in Lishadi on the Nujiang River is excellent for Lisu watching, as most women there don some elements of traditional clothing and accessories. Author photo.

Non-Christians (the minority here) are easy to spot at the crowded market's outdoor rice wine and spirit stalls. We also visit a hole-in-the-wall bar that looks like a cozy, alcohol-soaked family sitting room. Three or four men and a couple of women lounge on an old sofa and some mismatched chairs. A peek out its back door reveals that it leans out over the raging river a hundred feet below. Those who need to use its toilet "perch" are warned not to fall in. This is no joke; before midday, patrons are rapidly becoming too drunk

Author visits hole-in-the-wall drinking establishment in Lishadi, where even Lisu drunks expressed patriotism to China. Photo: Mark Goldschmidt.

to interview, and getting swept off by the Nu is not an unusual end around here. One soulful-looking young man determinedly putting back shots of local plum toddy told me he'd thought about becoming Christian, but he can't since he'd have to give up alcohol. I bring up the Catholic option, which he brushes aside emphatically: "Here in my area, Christians *do not* drink," reminding us yet again that for the Lisu, what you do (or don't do) is what counts. Another inebriate acted out a "big-house spirit" ceremony for me, distinguishing spirit and shaman roles by alternating between a high squeaky voice and a low rumbly one. He said he had no interest in Christianity and felt no pressure to convert. His happiness, he told me, comes from "our country: it is improving, we make business, we make farm." In China, even Lisu drunks are patriotic.

I meet Aki Li-tu, age eighty-five, at a market stall offering blue and white striped ladies' and men's ware, black vests, and other Lisu garb sewn with machine-produced prints and velvets. He tells me he is a dashipa, or medicine shaman, and he certainly looks the part with his fox-like visage and jaunty black hat. When I express interest in talking with him, his son offers to walk us to their village from the suspension bridge a few miles up the road

Lisu fashion is evolving. Author photo.

at Ngwa Chi-doo if we can meet him there in an hour or so. We share cell-phone numbers.

Our driver had returned to Fugong for business, so a while later we hop a local bus plying the gorge-hugging road to get to our meeting point. Ngwa Chi-doo is not far beyond the great oval hole in the Gaoligong mountaintop (160 feet wide by 120 feet tall, 50 by 30 meters) eroded by water and snow

The Stone Moon (Ya Ha Ba in Lisu), upper right, is a 50 meter by 30 meter great oval hole eroded near the top of a peak in the Gaoligong range just south of Ngwa Chi-doo village above the Nujiang River. When backlit by moonlight, it looks like a low moon itself. Author photo.

overlooking the Nu at 10,826 feet (3,300 meters). Called the Stone Moon (*Ya Ha Ba* in Lisu), this gap looks like a brilliant, low-hanging moon when lit from behind. According to Lisu legend it was cut through the mountain by the divine shepherd Adeng's magic arrow to save the earth from flooding. The floodwaters released by an angry Dragon King to kill the people harmlessly drained away through the gap, and Adeng and Ala, daughter of the king, survived and were united.

Aki Li-tu's son, Ah Ju, meets us by the scary, multi-patched pedestrian suspension bridge across the Nu, to begin our climb to Rhee Yato village. In the last ten years the Chinese have built several such bridges to replace metal zip lines they installed from the 1980s at popular crossings, which in turn had replaced rope "bridges" used by Lisu for hundreds years to haul themselves in wood harnesses over the gorge. The ropes are gone now—but to the unaccustomed, just crossing the bridge takes guts as it swings a lot and looks more fragile than it is.

It is a two-and-a-half-hour hike to reach the village atop the western (Gaoligong) side of the gorge; only short zigzags in the trail prevent it from being completely vertical. The path is seldom wider than 18 inches and is slippery with mud in places as a result of irrigation leaks and recent rain. Rest stops are a must. We cross a few other groups ascending and descending and meet up and join one that includes Dashipa Aki Li-tu and six or seven men, women, and teenagers carrying goods and a baby, returning from Lishadi's market. A couple of donkeys carrying bricks pass us, but this is chiefly a human highway. Our view of Stone Moon immediately to the south is astounding on this hot day with few clouds. We take in the scene at stops, relieved of the pain of the climb to which locals are inured. The eighty-five-year-old shaman lights his pipe at one such interlude.

Vast tracks of extreme hillside such as this have been reclaimed and terraced to maximize arable land. Some are not irrigated, containing tiny fields, but villagers in Rhee Yato's vertical landscape have built impressive systems of cement ditches and piped water to irrigate long, skinny fields wrapping around hillsides. Swidden agriculture has been abolished in the big river gorge, but I'm told it is still practiced in more remote valleys behind.

Aki Li-tu was born on this mountain in the 1930s. Sometime after the revolution, during what he calls "the commune time," he relocated from his original home near the village center, when the site was claimed by Christians to build a church, to his present mountainside perch of a house at its outer boundary. His wife died years ago, and he lives as a bachelor in a smoke-blackened hut of woven bamboo with a cool earthen floor. Its corners are filled with large field baskets, a few pots and pans, and piles of potatoes; his fire pit is heaped with ashes and fed by lengths of dried bamboo. He has an A+ view. The potatoes are a matter of pride; he grows them in one of his son's fields though he is retired now, living on a government pension. Usually, he takes his meals with his son and family, who live in a larger, tidier bamboo house nearby.

"In this area, we call healers dashipas, *not* ne-pas," Aki Li-tu corrects me as I begin our interview. In the Nu Gorge this is the common designation;

Aki Li-tu relaxes with a smoke on the hike up to his village, Rhee Yato. Author photo.

several Lisu, Christian and non-Christian, explain this to me, usually adding that ne-pas are in league with dark spirits. One obvious distinction between the two styles of Lisu healers is that ne-pas enter a trance state, when various spirits "ride" them and prescribe curatives and suggest offerings. Ne-pas don't remember what happens in ceremonies—the spirits speak through them, and their messages are witnessed by assistants or others who take note. By comparison, dashipas appear earthbound and pragmatic; they follow formulas depending on illness, clan, and other variables—and remain conscious. They can tell you exactly what they will do: which offering, which prayer the situation calls for. But like ne-pas, they consider themselves chosen by spirits because of their special talent and intuitive knowledge. Every healer I spoke with expressed his calling to be an economic burden rather than a blessing, but as one's fate, it is hard to avoid.

Whether the Lisu ne-pa tradition, documented in Thailand by E. Paul Durrenberger and others, began in China and was exported or was developed/

Aki Li-tu at his bamboo-burning hearth. Photo: Mark Goldschmidt.

borrowed along immigration trails isn't clear. It is plausible that ne-pas fell or were pushed out of favor in parts of China by communist ideology against superstition as one of the "olds" and that the dashipa tradition survived because its practice is less occult. Or, it could have something to do with Christianity. Evangelical missionaries who influence the Lisu also believe in spirits; but with the exceptions of God, Jesus Christ, and the Holy Spirit, all others are considered malevolent. In Tengchong-area conversations with Lisu, I wasn't corrected when I used the word *ne-pa* or told that they were in league with evil spirits. That isn't much evidence to go on, however, and I didn't meet any shamans there. In Nujiang, I had no trouble contacting several and interviewed four in quick succession.

Aki Li-tu was keen to share his tradition, perhaps because, beyond himself, only three of the village's fifty households still observe traditional ceremonies. Dashipa means "Old Friend Priest," he told me, a title that resonates with the mur-mu-pa role in Thailand. Mur-mu-pas, however, concentrate on civic

Aki Li-tu at home with author, piles of potatoes all around. Photo: Mark Goldschmidt.

ceremonies to keep villagers on good terms with local spirits and don't function as healers. He went over specific calls, such as *"Ah dee boo-do su dza nyee mee, Ah ti, nyi ye ka do yee dje ma,"* to summon help from one of the thirty-six spirits of rock, land, mountain, stream with whom he is in contact and explained steps of healing ceremonies in which mostly small animals are sacrificed. He has five assistants from his and other villages where he is called to service. His son tells me his father is a famous dashipa who receives requests for help from as far away as Fugong, but travel is getting harder for the eighty-five-year-old.

"I can no longer help him," Ah-Ju explains, looking sorry about it, "because seven years ago I became a Christian with my wife's family and had to stop assisting in animist ceremonies." Now Aki Li-tu asks for a travel fee instead of the traditional gift of meat, since no one else in his family can eat flesh tainted by spirits Christians are supposed to steer clear of.

"My great-grandfather was a dashipa, and I have been the chief dashipa for thirty years, after twenty years of being an assistant," Aki Li-tu says, adding that none of his current assistants is ready to step up. "I don't think there will be many more dashipas; unlike in the past, people can go to the doctor today when they become ill, and this is usually quite effective."

Such collegial appreciation of his fellow medical practitioners seems generous, considering they are likely to put his profession out of business.

Cho s'dur Liang lives in one of many villages south of Liuku, relocated there by the Chinese government over the past thirty years. He likes living in proximity to Christians "because they don't ask for my help." Author photo.

But I found this attitude shared by three other shamans I interviewed in the Nu Valley.

———————■ ■———————

Cho s'dur Liang, a dignified, lean man of seventy who lives in the newer suburban village of Tan-na-nu outside Liuku, expressed similar thoughts. Our conversation took place in his mud-brick courtyard on a hillside with a view to the east of the Nujiang, a couple of kilometers away. The pleasant outdoor living space is shaded by a couple of mature trees and planted with flowers—and is also used to store farm implements and piles of beer bottles for eventual recycling. The dashipa is a Gwapa clan member originally from an area north of the river, Lamakah, not far from Rhee Yato.

His village was one of fifty the government has relocated to a relatively less precipitous area west of the river, a few kilometers south of Liuku, over the past thirty years. Thousands of hillside acres were cleared for agriculture in an area formerly supporting one village. The main road through Tanna-nu still has close to a forty-degree grade and is a mixed community of 200 animist and 120 Christian households.

"I like living side by side with Christians because they don't ask for my help. They are good, and because the spirits are not for them, they lighten my load. I'm happy about that, since I work for free," Cho s'dur Liang says, referring to the financial hardship of being a healer on top of tending fields and other responsibilities.

Again, the dashipa is happy to demonstrate his work. He points to a tree in the courtyard, saying: "When someone is seriously ill, before the ceremony I make an icon of a spirit, like a horse, dragon, sword, or chopstick from this Samada tree. Then I make an image of the patient from mud. Shaking the bamboo sticks tells me which spirit to contact, and after sacrificing an animal, a goat or a chicken or even a pig, depending on what the spirit asks for, I offer rice, salt, alcohol, and water."

He says he conducts thanking ceremonies to the Old Friend Spirit, making offerings when the first rice or the first fruit appears. He goes to peoples' houses and provides blessings and benedictions, asking for health and prosperity and offering ancestor spirits blood, alcohol, pork, beef, or a mutton head the first day of the New Year. He tells me his clan, the Gwapa, does not use tabiyas and conducts most ceremonies outside. Gwapa means multiply, and his clan's story is central to a Lisu origin myth that, like most, involves a flood and a brother and sister who survive it and marry to repopulate the world. In his telling, a boy and a girl are born in each of nine successive sets of fraternal twins; they go out into the world to create the Chinese, Burmese, Indian, African, Lisu, and other races. The ninth set of twins included Gwa-mobie, the founder of his clan.

Cho s'dur Liang's father was also a dashipa; the son received his calling to carry on the tradition after his death. Growing up, he watched his father work but didn't pay that much attention and didn't require special training once the gift was bestowed. "I automatically think about spirits, they just come to my mind," he told me. "For example, I knew you were coming today so I stayed home to meet you."

He and his wife have three sons, no deaths. The first is an atheist, the others animists. They married "in communist time" when bride price was not allowed, but he paid 2,000 and 5,000 yuan, respectively, for his first two sons' brides. He didn't have to pay for his youngest's wife because her father, having no sons of his own, adopted him. "But currently, bride price is higher, about 120,000 yuan," the dashipa said, "because the Chinese habit of aborting female fetuses has led to a shortage affecting the market."

I asked my standard question: what are the biggest changes affecting you and your country over the last twenty years?

"I don't know if my sons will follow me the way I followed my father. There are fewer animists in the next generation; maybe it's good because fewer animals will be sacrificed. I'm just happy if people recover, I don't care if it's because of me or another doctor. Overall, things are better now: electricity and roads everywhere, more people go to the doctor and they don't have to pay fees. The treatments are as good as mine. Being a dashipa is a heavy load to carry as I get old."

———————————■·■———————————

Seventy-three-year-old Suer-ye-tsa is a dashipa and Woh clan member who lives just up the hill from Cho s'dur Liang in another courtyard house but one more barren, without trees or plantings. He and his wife, Sha-kan-na, married in 1961. His father paid 380 yuan, one goat, one cow, one pig, and a huge crock of alcohol (he makes a circle with his arms, fingers barely touching, to show its size) for her bride price. Family planning wasn't yet compulsory; they had nine children, and only one died. Medical services were available in their original village 30 kilometers beyond Lishadi on the west side of the Nujiang. They relocated to Tan-na-nu twenty years ago. Now retired, husband and wife receive a monthly government pension of 65 yuan each (just over $10).

"In our clan, the dashipa is called Ne-gu-pa," he explains, adding the now familiar disclaimer that he is *not* a ne-pa and that ne-pas are witch doctors who deal with evil spirits. Like the others, Suer-ye-tsa is keen to describe his interactions with the spirit world and seems especially proud of his ability to talk them into leaving his clansmen alone.

Sporting a cowboy hat and using a winnowing basket as a prop, he acts out a healing ceremony, explaining each aspect. It takes place on a hill above the village, with four assistants usually helping him. First he calls the heaven spirit, Mu-Ah-pa, considered a grandfather, and then the earth spirit, Mu-Wee-ah, or grandmother. He goes through several steps: branches of four types of

Suer-ye-tsa, age seventy-three, demonstrates a Woh clan healing ceremony. Author photo.

trees are placed in holes, with white paper cutouts tied to each. Twelve cups filled with a mixture of rice, salt, alcohol, bread, and popcorn are placed in front of them in a tray. The animal intended for sacrifice is tied next to the offering, a hearth of three rocks is made, and a fire is started.

He calls Mu-Ah-pa: "Take this animal, three years old." He goes from kneeling to standing as he holds up the offerings and throws the contents of one cup into the air.

Then, holding up the remaining eleven cups, he calls out the sick person's name as the animal is killed by assistants. Its hair is then burned off and it is cut in pieces and cooked, so spirits can be offered cooked meat. The dashipa continues to call Mu-Ah-pa and Mu-Wee-ah and to ask for their blessing on the sick person while this is going on.

When all is prepared, the tone of the ceremony changes somewhat:

"We make this offering. You take this meat and *exchange* it for our friend. You leave him or her so she will be healthy again. Spirit, leave this person, and when he or she is well, he or she will do many good things."

With each entreaty, another offering cup is tossed, until all are empty.

"You don't want to eat the bone and hair of [sick person's name]. You give him or her 100 years, 1,000 years. You don't desire to eat us, the dashipa and assistants, or the other people in the village. This offering is ENOUGH! Look to the north, look to the south, eat animal flesh, don't eat human flesh—not here."

When the ceremony is done, the branches are thrown away below the village, not at the offering site, and the remaining meat is taken home. Everyone eats together and drinks alcohol—but no music, dancing, or singing is allowed.

Suer-ye-tsa, like the other dashipas I've met, concedes that only a few young people are interested in keeping up traditions, and even they are not able to become dashipas or ne-gu-pas. "I can't tell you why, but I have observed fewer and fewer. I can't predict the future," he says with a shrug.

As for the past: "Until around fifteen years ago, everyone was poor and it was a very hard time. Much better now, today is good."

———————■-■———————

Both Chos-o-pho, a shaman of the La clan, and his wife, Yu-gee-pa, are seventy-two years old, from Pee-Ja village. It was sited on a mountain behind the main Nujiang gorge near Gongshan, and they tell me it doesn't exist anymore. He is soulful and refined; she, lively and outspoken. They moved to this intensively cultivated and now deforested (except the ridges) area south of Liuku in 2001, accepting the government's offer to resettle in one of six drab new rowhouses built on a shelf carved from the mountain. It came with a few acres and is tucked into a hilly neighborhood of small farms about 5 kilometers west of the river. A new paved road to the village replaced the old one last year, built by villagers who were well paid by the government for their labor and even received overtime. The shaman and his wife made monthly payments to the government over ten years, totaling a few thousand RMB, for the new family homestead—which they now

*Chos-o-pho, a shaman of the La clan, and his wife, Yu-gee-pa, practice different religions,
since she followed their children in converting to Christianity. Author photo.*

own. Constructed of cement bricks, it is a solid dwelling with dark red steel
doors and windows.

Chos-o-pho is slowly recovering from a fall down a hill one moonless night
two months earlier: "I rolled and rolled, I couldn't stop, and my injury was
quite serious," he explains. He knows from an X-ray that three ribs were
broken and says his internal organs were badly bruised. He is getting better,
through rest and the use of herb poultices. When I comment on how steep
the land here is, he says "Pee-Ja was much more steep, like this." He holds his
arm out in front of him, bending it at the elbow to make a perfect 90-degree
angle, to illustrate.

The couple has four living children, two sons and two daughters. Another
nine died in the mountains as infants or young children. They had no electricity or roads, water had to be carried, and only traditional medicine was available. Unlike others I have met, these two speak only Lisu and never learned
Chinese. There were no schools in their area when they grew up; however,
their children received education and all speak Chinese.

Chos-o-pho appears still to be in pain but carries himself with dignity.

"My tradition is called Cha-ga," he tells me, "and I am a ne-gu-pa. Today, most of the people I help have already gone to the doctor; they still feel sick, so they turn to spiritual healing. I am good, in fact famous, in this area, and many people will testify to my curing skills."

Like most Lisu shamans, he knows automatically what spirits to make offerings to. He began assisting a ne-gu-pa when he was twenty and now has four assistants of his own, ranging in age from their mid-twenties to around fifty. But he doesn't see any of them as particularly gifted or likely to take over after he is gone. "Our tradition is probably almost over," he says, adding modestly, "but I can't foresee the future."

Yu-gee-pa seems to agree, rolling her eyes when the subject of her husband's assistants comes up. "They don't know much," she says with a cluck, although she herself converted to Christianity and goes to the doctor when seriously ill. First her children and grandchildren converted, and then she followed them.

"We respect each other," she says of her husband's avocation. "I go away when he is conducting ceremonies so the spirits are not disturbed by me."

The four dashipas I spoke with, taken together and by their own reckoning, lead to the conclusion that their tradition will soon be gone. I looked for a young dashipa in vain and was told by everyone I asked that there aren't any. The combined forces of Christianity and modern medicine have made the profession obsolete. Even remote villages such as the mountaintop Rhee Yato, where the dashipa Aki Li-tu resides, are integrated into China's services and infrastructure. My cheap cell phone connects from there on the first try to the driver back in Fugong. I call to say I will not make it to the main road at 4:00 p.m. as planned.

Instead, we walk around the dashipa's village. It has the familiar deserted feel of Lisu villages in the daytime. A fine stilted bamboo house belongs to the village pastor, who is not at home but which his neighbor nonetheless invites me to take a look at. Several lesser bamboo houses are strung out along a shelf of land below it, and a variety of others, some wood with cement foundations, are tucked on pads of land carved out of the hillside. Most didn't look in much better repair than Aki Li-tu's potato-strewn abode.

There is, however, one large new two-story cement house wearing a fresh coat of pale turquoise. Pristine and grand, it looks as if it were dropped from the sky to this hilltop.

A woman with a huge smile appears on its front porch, greeting us like old friends and waving us to enter. When she holds up her radiant infant, I recognize that she was in the group we'd hiked up the trail with earlier. Baby strapped on her back and burdened with bundles like everyone else, on the trail she had hardly projected the image *lady of the manor*.

At forty-six years old, in China and perhaps most places, Fu Yu Zhi is an unlikely new mother. She and her daughter make a beaming couple who welcome us to enter and take a seat.

"I had two sons, but one died when he was eighteen," Fu Yu Zhi explains as she dandles her glowing baby. "My husband and I wrote to the government asking permission to have another child. They said okay, and now my baby girl is a year old. I am very happy."

I ask how she became rich and why she chose to build such a house here.

I, my parents, and my grandparents were all born in this village. I love it here, it is my native area. No need to buy this or that in the store: we have fruit, we have vegetables and meat, everything we need we grow or raise ourselves, and it [is] always fresh.

We began to be prosperous after becoming Christian fifteen years ago. No drinking and not as much fellowship. Fellowship, feasting the village, etc., is very expensive. The church encouraged us to save money because we were poor. When I started raising chickens and pigs for market, we began to save.

As for the house, after saving for many years, we built it with government support. They provide half the cost to anyone who builds a concrete house. Every brick was carried up the mountain on a donkey's back; it took more than a year to collect materials before we could build.

Fu Yu Zhi shares this fairytale success story seated in her light and airy new living room, which the family appears not to have fully moved into. As in Aki Li-tu's hut, big baskets, piles of clothing, and bags of rice and shopping casually line its walls and infringe on the space. Lisu houses, even fancy new ones, apparently lack closets. While proud of her accomplishments, she isn't house-proud in a Western bourgeois sense, and her husband is out working his fields as usual. I share some sesame-encrusted cookies purchased in the

Fu Yu Zhi and her family occupy the newest, largest, and fanciest house in the remote
mountaintop village of Rhee Yato, where she was born. She attributes her prosperity
to conversion to Christianity fifteen years ago. Giving up drinking and raising pigs for
market (instead of village feasting) provided her family with an economic edge, she says.
Author photo.

Lishadi market, and she serves us fruit and a delicious concoction she identifies as "juice" that is lightly but clearly fermented. Made from the same plum-
like fruit non-Christian Lisu use to produce a strong liquor, she becomes
vague when I ask how she makes it.

I wonder how many young people today choose to stay in villages like
Rhee Yato. Or, how many leave as they get older because of the physical
fitness the location requires? I note that hers is the only new house I saw in
the village.

"Yes, it is true that many young people want to run away. But some learn it is too expensive in town. Older people understand this, and most of my neighbors stay here. One of my sons left and became a driver for a couple years. Then he got into an accident and lost his driving license. Now he is back home with us, working our fields with his father. Village kids all go to school in Fugong City [about two hours by bus, after the hike down the mountain]. They live there during the week and come home on weekends for years, so they grow up knowing both places."

She gestures out the window at "this place" with its bird's-eye view of tiny thatched village across the gorge in the magnificent Biluo range, only a few kilometers away. "In the end, they must decide for themselves what life they want, to go or to stay" she says with one of the happiest Lisu shrugs I've seen so far.

Conclusions, and Notes on Where Lisu Might Go from Here

Until recently, being as good as everyone else in one's own small society—the goal of many Lisu—was judged by most of them as preferable to trying to assimilate into a national culture from the bottom. Who wants to be shunned and discriminated against? But as the option of remaining isolated and independent disappears from the earth, Lisu (and other groups) face tough, limited, and often limiting choices.

I have observed the Lisu in three national settings over 30 years of spectacular globalization, from the mid-1980s to 2015. It has been extraordinary to witness the incremental pivot from their traditional "live-far-from-the-ruler" playbook toward engagement with the state-dominated worlds they inhabit. Most still retain strong Lisu identity, though there have been key losses. Loss of full Lisu language ability in the younger generation is probably the greatest of these, occurring among the most successful urbanized Lisu. Whether Fraser's writing system will catch on and grow with increased Internet use is an open question. It is impossible to know whether this people, numbering only 1.5 million, will exist as a distinct culture 100 or even 50 years from now. I do know that their procrastination in assimilating presents a valuable and probably short window of opportunity to examine cultural adaptation.

Timing is of the essence. Unlike those of us long integrated into nation-states, the Lisu did not adapt to being subjects of the state until *after* globalization had entered full swing. Through them, any number of issues and ideas surrounding culture, nationalism, and globalization become more legible. Having three environments in which to examine and compare such issues provides unique controls.

What specific aspects of culture, both outward markers and at deeper psychological levels, are most affected by the modern ordering of the world—in China, Myanmar, and Thailand? Which are not? The strength and reach of state power has grown steadily over the past few hundred years but particularly since the mid-twentieth century. The impacts, especially on minority and underdog populations, may be ignored at the world's peril as ethnic, sectarian, and other sub-national conflicts have become increasingly lethal in the past sixty years. Do Lisu have anything unique to teach about nurturing useful aspects of ethnic identity to peacefully navigate—and not be destroyed by—integration into nation-states?

While the analogy is not exact, studying the Lisu is a bit like following triplets who were separated not at birth but soon after they began talking, to examine how they and their culture—as individuals and a group—adapt and function in different globalizing national circumstances.

Their hard lives, egalitarian style, and historical use of migration to survive inevitably result in a range of individual success. What stands in high relief, however, is a clear pattern of agency and individual empowerment—the Lisu *still* want to be first among equals. Today, this means playing catch-up against the odds in a world that has moved past them. An in-built quest for myi-do, combined with their distinct and bemused resignation, seems to provide a wellspring of motivation as well as resiliency in surviving disappointment.

These qualities alone make the Lisu a valuable case study in adaptation and a model for a study in applied anthropology.

My father-in-law, the cultural anthropologist Walter Goldschmidt, had a habit of being provocative. Something he said in another context, almost a throwaway line, always stayed with me: "Well, you know, cultures are far more varied than people."

This idea is likely connected to the time he came of age within anthropology, the 1930s. Because there are only so many personality types, it is the crucibles of culture, environment, and history that form and reward some traits and repress others, creating such different cultural results as Frenchmen, Scots highlanders, Masai tribesmen, and Japanese Samurai. Ruth Benedict, one of Franz Boas's star students, presented theories examining the essential relationships among culture, personality, art, and language in *Patterns of Culture* in 1934. It was one of the most influential anthropological works of that period, although, of course, challengers have emerged and psychological studies have complexified the field beyond recognition in ensuing years.

As I rewrote and updated this book—first due for publication in 1999—in 2015, I kept a running list of "big thoughts" as well as details of particular interest I worried would slow the narrative. "Maybe this will fit somewhere in the *conclusion*," I'd think to myself, jotting down an idea in a document that grew to several pages. Reviewers for the publisher of my original manuscript pointed out that it lacked this essential element—a conclusion—and recommended I add one.

I am not an anthropologist; the Lisu have compelled and fascinated me over time, and I hope my research and observations interest readers and add value to the existing literature, especially in China and Myanmar. However, my work is not academic, scientific, or particularly theory driven. As a writer in the "show-don't-tell" school of journalism, I hesitate to tell readers what to think about what they just read. Walter's comment, though, applied to the Lisu, kept bubbling up as I contemplated doing just that.

If cultures are so varied, there must be unique and specific things to learn from the Lisu—whose culture rewards hardworking, competitive, risk-taking, charming/funny individuals who can lead without dominating. Lisu lessons are likely to be time-sensitive given the latish hour at which they fully engaged in the globalization process that is impacting all of our cultures. Humans face problems and issues both universal and time-specific. Some groups come up with better ideas or solutions than others or at least with good habits worth sharing and disseminating. This was an idea earlier anthropologists used to help answer the question, why study other cultures—particularly those judged "more primitive" than the studier's?

Why be concerned with the Lisu now?

People under forty can be excused for not knowing that anthropology used to be more broadly influential than it is today. Interest in the field was far-ranging, from power elites to pop culture—and it peaked in the 1960s and 1970s before the Internet and globalization expanded, exploded, and fragmented the information "that everybody knows." Anthropology's rise followed its inclusion of women, Jews, and other minorities in preceding decades, as Western societies began looking to the social sciences to help solve big problems. Those able to popularize anthropological insights sold millions of books, and some had near rock-star notoriety—Franz Boas, Margaret Mead, Ruth Benedict, Zora Neale Hurston, Louis and Mary Leakey, Jane Goodall, Lévi-Strauss, Desmond Morris, Colin Turnbull, Diane Fossey, Carlos Castenada, and Donald Johanson—the list of the influential grew long and branchy. As a teen and young adult from an immigrant, book-reading, but not particularly intellectual family in California, I read the work and attended lectures of all of the above. I offer this personal example to illustrate that anthropology was indeed mainstream in this period. Public intellectuals in primatology, sociology, urban studies, and psychology all fed the rising star of the study of humankind. Richard Dawkins's view of evolution expressed in his 1976 best-seller *The Selfish Gene* seemed to begin tipping the scales back toward nature and the quantitative measures of hard science—and away from the perceived subjectivity of ethnography, which weights observation and qualitative judgments—as the more reliable way to study human behavior.

Anthropology's diminishing influence in the public mind has paralleled the rise of globalization. I wouldn't attempt to connect the two, but I have pondered the timing, wondering if the shrinking number of "primitive" people left to study in the field created an opening for more lab-oriented, gene-centered, biological studies of humans. Father-in-law Goldschmidt lamented that as a discipline, anthropology lost its seat at the table in discussing approaches and solutions to big issues—to the world's harm, he believed. He attributed the loss to several factors, one being that it became a victim of its own popularization. Oversimplified ideas such as nature versus nurture, national character, or the fiction that groups are ever *really* isolated from the influence of states and global economics all lost currency as complexity and interrelatedness were accepted as new norms in a globalizing world. Also, anthropological studies no longer have the power to shock as when Margaret Mead first wrote about Samoa. The pith and excitement of insights gleaned

One of the 5,000 Lisu who followed the Morse family to Hidden Valley in 1965, this old man recounts the hardships of the journey and first years there. A young Lisu woman, raised in the relative comfort of a lowland Muhladi village outside Putao town, listens. Author photo.

from early anthropological studies fired imaginations more when local and regional variations appeared greater, before the Internet exposed us to so many images, and when we believed what we learned from people different from ourselves had intrinsic value.

Many of the greatest challenges in the world today, however, remind us that the study of genes or biology is unlikely to yield practical tools to counter terrorism. Nations often fail to deal effectively with ethnic, tribal, and sectarian violence and migration crises or help minorities assimilate successfully. These failures might even create an opening to turn back toward more cultural approaches of engagement. Since nature versus nurture created a false dichotomy and problematic oversimplification, the time could be ripe for a new meme: the *integrated human circuit*—hardwiring (nature) programmed by software (culture).

This brings me back to the Lisu and the value of studying their experience. Loss and opportunity go together as they join the modern world and move into urban settings or at least less isolated ones. Their culture is being put to new tests that require different skills from those that kept them alive in the past. However, Lisu talents of adaptability, mobility, and attitude have always undergirded their survival; such agility will no doubt serve them in the future.

Many see loss of language as the tragic death knell of a small minority's ethnic identity. Such loss has been greatest among younger Lisu who moved to cities—often the most educated—and their children. Other Lisu migrants to cities are cast-outs, prostitutes, and addicts. Solid statistics don't exist, but leaders I spoke with estimate that 20 percent to 30 percent of Lisu have left their villages, and a larger percentage have a solid foot in both worlds today.

Must second-generation language always be a defining cultural loss? Does nostalgia get in the way of clear thinking about change, inevitable in all human experience? I discussed this at length over several days with David Morse. He is the oldest son of Eugene and Helen Morse, now the patriarch of a missionary clan that has worked among the Lisu since the 1930s. He belongs to the third generation and is a Lisu native speaker who has lived in Chiang Mai, Thailand, for the past forty years. Now in his sixties, about five feet eight inches tall and a little stocky, Morse was born in Burma where he developed his linguistic talents and inventiveness far from any city. He learned English when he was five but did not become fluent until he was twelve.

As a teen in 1965, he fled on foot with his extended family from Putao Valley in northern Burma, traversing mountains and settling in an uninhabited, un-demarcated, "cursed" territory called Hidden Valley on India's Assam border. Unbidden, 5,000 Lisu joined them. General Ne Win's military government had ordered missionaries, anthropologists, and other foreigners to leave Burma. Kachin State and much of the country roiled with violence and insurgency, which, along with a desire to stick with the Morses, triggered some Lisu's migratory instincts. For the first years, the group survived on scant resources, hunting skills, and wits to build a remote Lisu Christian society of twenty villages in no-man's land. The long arm of the law reached and deported the Morses in 1972 when the area was adjudicated to be part of

Burma. Many Lisu stayed on, building the pioneer settlements into a prosperous area.

From reading Eugene Morse's book *Exodus to a Hidden Valley*, I knew that as a sixteen-year-old, David, with poor eyesight that went untreated in those years and unable to hunt with his peers, conceived of and led a vital project with his younger brothers and Lisu friends. They salvaged parts from aircraft that had crashed over Burma's "Hump" in World War II and hand-fabricated other parts—first building a generator and then a hydroelectric system using a nearby river and jungle products such as rattan and pig fat. It produced 20 volts of electricity, which the Lisu expanded and used years after the Morses left. David also modified more than one typewriter to use the Lisu Fraser's Script; when the settlers opened a school after two years in the wilderness, students shared printed, stenciled textbooks in their own language. He taught science and math, and children also studied Burmese, Kachin, and English. The younger Morse children, who returned to junior and senior high schools in Terre Haute, Indiana, after this six-year adventure, as well as children of Lisu families who drifted back to Putao, were not behind academically when they returned to civilization.

Much more recently, Morse designed new Lisu fonts and developed the Advanced Lisu Script (ALS), suited to the Internet age and instant messaging. ALS eliminates Fraser's upside-down and backward letters. As perhaps the best-known Lisu writing expert, in 2009 he successfully pleaded the case to adopt Fraser's Comprehensive Script for international keyboard software standards to the UNICODE Consortium. It has since been accepted by participating countries, including China.

Conceding the implications of language loss and that younger Lisu increasingly use the national languages in which they are educated, David Morse alternates between first and third person in expressing faith in this culture's viability in the future: "Being Lisu goes even deeper, beyond where we live, how we live, what kinds of clothes we wear. Lisu conquer adversity, that's what they do, that's what we experienced in Hidden Valley. Incredible perseverance. I don't know if we would have survived, certainly not as well as we did, without their skills. God certainly had a hand in it, but my parents and grandparents were always in 'the Lord helps those who help themselves' camp, and we always stress self-reliance in Lisu churches. This is completely in line with Lisu culture."

Morse mentioned one unexpected outcome he's observed regarding the decline of swidden farming and increasing land pressure:

Two or three families can no longer just break off and move away, the ingrained Lisu habit, when there is a problem—there's no more new land to move to in villages or cities. I know folks who have strengthened and grown Lisu identity after they left the mountains because they have to stick together in cities and figure out new ways to solve disputes. As they become more educated, they learn to get along in larger, less clannish groups. They've learned how to organize, that's a new skill for most. There is a push for cultural committees in all countries where Lisu live today—older Lisu and leaders are especially worried about preserving culture. They're doing something about it, though sometimes too late.

Thai Lisu put together the most truly international conference so far, convened in Chiang Mai in 2015 and attended by Thai, Chinese, Burmese, Indian, and Laotian Lisu.

Over the past decades, David put a dozen tape recorders into the hands of people coming through Chiang Mai on their way to distant Lisu enclaves—but most never returned with the songs and stories he asked them to record. He's become more upbeat, however, about current efforts to preserve Lisu material because the Internet has made an international Lisu space possible. Now that a common writing system has gained acceptance and YouTube hosts a "Lisu Zone," you can hear twenty sub-dialects and view all sorts of singing, talking, and dancing online. Lisu are rapidly becoming computer literate, and many are active in reaching across borders to communicate in their own language. They have taken to social media such as Facebook in a huge way. Courting songs, many sung over cell phones for ten or twenty minutes, have taken off and caused scandals as the electronic age enables anonymous callers to woo telephonically without intermediaries or other social controls and constraints.

The prospect of new virtual Lisu communities bridging the gap and safeguarding some pith of Lisuness amid all the change and loss is his hope: "But there is so much vocabulary, for different kinds of plants and forest craft and food, that is already lost to this generation in Thailand. The oral tradition, storytelling, singing . . . they have wisdom embedded, but it takes a lot of time to transmit, and no one has time in Thailand—where there is so much

Lisu (identifiable from their shoulder bags) line up on a chilly morning in Fugong on the Salween River Gorge, waiting for the bank to open. Photo: Mark Goldschmidt.

new information to learn. Burma is easier because it remained isolated longer and there is political representation, and China, well, it's hard to know what's going on there."

I mentioned that I observed the most organized Lisu cultural preservation movement by far in Myanmar, where every area has an active committee and the government is working with cultural ministers to publish a national library of minority histories in Burmese, English, and each ethnic group's writing system.

The necessity for Lisu to embrace literacy in their own language to keep aspects of their culture alive long term is hard to dodge. It could be their core challenge, and it is shot through with uncertainty. Developing new Lisu literature and documenting oral tradition by writing down stories and songs top the priority lists of cultural committees. Most existing written literature has Christian content exclusively—but there is consensus that modern and secular content is essential for their written language, and possibly even their spoken one, to survive beyond the next couple of generations. Christians in Myanmar seemed the most united on this theme, and they lead in Lisu literacy. A number of small Lisu-language magazines, mostly published in Yangon, have appeared recently.

Lisu have been slower to embrace literacy and education than other minority groups, particularly in Thailand. Morse says, "It took them longer to value it, but, as soon as they do, Lisu do well in school. That came out in Hidden Valley; Lisu kids returning to Putao were ahead of peers attending state schools. They are competitive, and their oral tradition helps because they have incredible memories. They actually like to take tests."

Yet embracing school, not to mention literacy in their own language, has been hard. It is probably most difficult in Thailand for Lisu to get a good education, but, conversely, this country offers the best opportunities for those able to break through barriers. Christianity has not taken hold in the Buddhist Kingdom as it has in Myanmar and China, and Christian Lisu are generally more likely to become educated. Non-Christian Lisu profiled in the Thai section of this work do not represent the majority—some, like Mimi Saeju and Del Phaywong Guat, paid a steep price in long childhood separations from family for the privilege of attending school. Others, like Mayura Sinlee and Cho-me Orn-anong, prove Morse's point by breezing through college, including correspondence courses, in the Thai language. The fact that the fathers of both women were Thai village headmen could indicate that in this hierarchical society, Lisu are picking up habits of elite privilege not seen when there was no defined leadership class. But since there will always be variation, it is impossible to rule out the quest for individual myi-do as the driving force behind their successes. It is ironic that literacy prospects in the Lisu language are best in Myanmar—the least developed Lisu national space.

Children living in Lisu areas there have recently begun to learn to read and write in their own language in government-approved after-school programs run by cultural committees. But of the three countries, China has put by far the most resources toward educating minority populations, though now the Lisu language is generally not taught in school until the college level. Academically gifted Lisu in China are the most likely of all to gain higher education.

On the other end of the scale, Lisu on the lowest rungs of society include prostitutes, AIDS sufferers, addicts, and drug mules. They are far more prevalent in all three countries—today particularly Thailand—than in the 1990s.

According to Morse, the speed of change itself has sucked many into the drug trade, which centers on methamphetamine, not opium. "Oh, I needed a smartphone to do business, I wanted a flat-screen TV, I was going to run drugs till I got one and then quit" are stories he has heard visiting Lisu in Thai prisons. He asks rhetorically: "Imagine if, instead of going from party-line to individual phone to cell phone, as we did, if your first telephone is also a computer and video camera?" Their entrepreneurial spirit also draws Lisu to the drug trade: "It is their nature to want to be boss, employer—not employee," says Morse, noting a long-observed trait. The Lisu willingness to risk has landed many in trouble, including being shot, wounded, or killed in skirmishes with drug traders or police and the army, themselves often corrupt.

The Lisu way is still to write one's own fate through individual and persistent effort. Prospects for success vary from country to country and depend on factors outside individuals' control more than when they roamed statelessly. Many are attuned to and energized by new opportunities. In 2016 all Lisu environments were in rapid flux, which adds to the difficulty—and importance—of learning from their experience. I spoke with several Lisu who migrated the farthest and now live in the United States in Virginia, Minnesota, and Colorado. All are Christian "fake refugees" from Myanmar. One young man whose family came to America when he was eight interned at Google in California last summer, where he installed Lisu keyboard software in its Internet browser, Chrome. He's now in Singapore for a semester abroad and finishing his BS in computer science. He likes life in Colorado, but all of the older Lisu told me they will return home, at least to visit, as soon as they have the "protection" of US citizenship.

Lisu no longer have the option of living far from the ruler. Both present and future will test their culture's resiliency, ingenuity, and strength—but, as always, this challenge unfolds as myriad individual contests. Does the Lisu never-say-die (*Shu Ma Da*) ethos predict group survival? As the Lisu often say, generally with a shrug, "*Al-ee du LA, al-le SWA.*"

Whatever comes, count on it.

Notes

PREFACE

For Claude Lévi-Strauss's observation about mankind and monoculture, see
Claude Lévi-Strauss, *Tristes Tropiques*, translated by John Weightman and Doreen
Weightman (New York: Penguin Books, 2012 [1955]), 38.

INTRODUCTION

For descriptions of the Lisu, see Che Shen, Xiaoya Lu, and Pin Liao, *Life among
the Minority Nationalities of Northwest Yunnan*, China's Nationalities Series
(Beijing: Foreign Languages Press, 1989), 121; Prasert Chaipigusit, "Anarchists
of the Highlands? A Critical Review of a Stereotype Applied to the Lisu," in
Anarchist Hill Tribes Today: Problems in Change, ed. John McKinnon and Bernard
Vienne (Bangkok: White Lotus–Orstom, 1989), 173–90; Paul W. Lewis and Elaine
Lewis, *Peoples of the Golden Triangle: Six Tribes in Thailand* (London: Thames and
Hudson, 1984), 241; Eugene Morse, *Exodus to a Hidden Valley* (New York: Readers

Digest Press, 1974), 59, 65; Otome Klein Hutheesing, *Emerging Sexual Inequality among the Lisu of Northern Thailand: The Waning of Dog and Elephant Repute* (Leiden: E. J. Brill, 1990), 19.

Book I: MEET THE LISU

Part 1: Lisu World

1. WHO ARE THE LISU?

On description of the Nujiang gorge, see Yang Guangmin, *Women Not to Be Blocked by Canyon: The Lisus*, Women's Culture Series: Nationalities in Yunnan (Kunming, China: Yunnan Educational Publishing House, 1995), 4, and illustrations.

On description of Lisu territory in Burma, see Morse, *Exodus to a Hidden Valley*, 21–22.

On early explorers' and geographers' description of the Lisu, see C. M. Enriquez, *Races of Burma*, 2nd ed., Handbooks for the Indian Army (Delhi: Manager of Publications, 1933), 65–66; Mireille Mazard, "The Art of (Not) Looking Back: Reconsidering Lisu Migrations and 'Zomia,'" in *Globalizing Migration History: The Eurasian Experience (16th–21st Centuries)*, ed. Jan Lucassen and Leo Lucassen (Leiden: Brill, 2014), 215–46.

On the meanings of myi-do, see Klein Hutheesing, *Emerging Sexual Inequality*, 97–100.

On Lisu style of humor, ibid., 19.

For an interpretation of anarchism that resonates with Lisu culture, see James C. Scott, *Seeing Like a State: How Certain Schemes to Improve the Human Condition Have Failed* (New Haven, CT: Yale University Press, 1998); James C. Scott, *Two Cheers for Anarchism: Six Easy Pieces on Autonomy, Dignity, and Meaningful Work and Play* (Princeton, NJ: Princeton University Press, 2012); James C. Scott, *The Art of Not Being Governed: An Anarchist History of Upland Southeast Asia* (New Haven, CT: Yale University Press, 2009).

On Lisu migration, habitation patterns, and social organization, see Morse, *Exodus to a Hidden Valley*; Alain Yvon Dessaint, "Economic Organization of the Lisu of the Thai Highlanders" (PhD dissertation, University of Hawaii, Honolulu, 1972), 16–49.

On Morse family history living among Lisu, see Morse, *Exodus to a Hidden Valley*, 32–41.

On the contrasting styles of gumsa (hierarchical) and gumlao (egalitarian) political systems in Burma and their application to the Lisu, see Edmund Ronald Leach, *Political Systems of Highland Burma: A Study of Kachin Social Structure* (London: G. Bell, 1954), 197–212; E. Paul Durrenberger, "Lisu Ritual, Economics, and Ideology," in *Ritual, Power, and Economy: Upland-Lowland Contrasts in Mainland Southeast Asia*, ed. Susan Diana Russell (Dekalb: Northern Illinois University, 1989), 103–20.

On the Lisu preference for reaching consensus on group decisions, see Morse, *Exodus to a Hidden Valley*, 49–53, 199–201.

2. Mythic Origins

Lisu origin myth about Wu-sa (sky god) making a man and a woman out of beeswax recounted in Klein Hutheesing, *Emerging Sexual Inequality*, 24–25.

On Lisu myth involving nine sets of twins, Cho s'dur Liang, interview with author, Tan-na-nu village outside Liuku, Yunnan, China, 2014.

On the rejection of writing systems by the Lisu and other peoples of Southeast Asia, see James C. Scott, *The Art of Not Being Governed: An Anarchist History of Upland Southeast Asia* (New Haven, CT: Yale University Press, 2009), 220–34.

On the Lisu use of forgetting as a coping mechanism for homelessness, see Klein Hutheesing, *Emerging Sexual Inequality*, 35–36.

On the convenience of not having a history, see Scott, *Art of Not Being Governed*, 234–37.

3. History and Origin Theories

On Zomia as a "non-state space," see Willem van Schendel, "Geographies of Knowing, Geographies of Ignorance: Jumping Scale in Southeast Asia," *Environment and Planning D: Society and Space* 20, no. 6 (2002): 647–68; Jean Michaud, *Historical Dictionary of the Peoples of the Southeast Asian Massif* (Lanham, MD: Scarecrow, 2006); Jean Michaud, "Editorial—Zomia and Beyond," *Journal of Global History* 5, no. 2 (2010): 187–214; Scott, *Art of Not Being Governed*, 1–39.

For early mention of the Lisu presence in the Yunnan-Kweichow-Sichuan border area in Southeast China, see Fan Ch'o, *Man Shu (Book of the Southern Barbarians)* (Ithaca, NY: Cornell University Department of Far Eastern Studies, 1961 [circa 685]).

On Robert Morse's theory about Lisu origins in Chiang, see Robert H. Morse, *The Lisu of Northern Thailand* (Auburn, NY: Asia Library Services, 1975); Joseph Rock, *The Ancient Na-khi Kingdom of Southwest China* (Cambridge, MA: Harvard University Press, 1947), 124.

Reinhart Hohler's theory that the Lisu's ancestral home is in Yunnan is based on author interviews, Thailand and Yunnan, 1996–97.

4. MODERN TIMES

For indication of out-migration of Lisu from China to Burma's Kachin and Shan States, see James George Scott and J. P. Hardiman, *Gazetteer of Upper Burma and the Shan States*, 5 vols. (Rangoon: Superintendent of Government Printing, Burma, 1900).

5. MIGRATION

For general and particular background on Lisu migration, see Dessaint, "Economic Organization of the Lisu," 26–49.

Interview with Sin-lee clan member from Dton Loong village, Thailand, by Otome Klein Hutheesing [n.d.], as told to author.

On the portability of housing among the Lisu in Thailand, see E. Paul Durrenberger, "The Economy of a Lisu Village," *American Ethnologist* 3, no. 4 (1976): 633–44.

For estimates of the Lisu population in the early twentieth century, see James George Scott, *Burma and Beyond* (London: Grayson and Grayson, 1932), 288; Enriquez, *Races of Burma*, xiii.

For Enriquez's account of recruiting Lisu for the army and their promotion while serving, see Enriquez, *Races of Burma*, 1, 101.

Block quotation on one Christian Lisu's military service from Eligah Illia, interview with author, translated by Bobby Morse, Myanmar, 1997.

For the story about how a headman's unfairness influenced out-migration from one Lisu village, see Dessaint, "Economic Organization," 36–37.

Opium/Heroin History sidebar

For background on heroin production in Southeast Asia, see Alfred W. McCoy, *The Politics of Heroin in Southeast Asia* (New York: Harper and Row, 1972). Quotation on government decision about opium production on p. 89.

For more contemporary information on Southeast Asia's drug trade, see Tom
Kramer, Martin Jelsma, and Tom Blickman, *Withdrawal Symptoms in the Golden
Triangle: A Drugs Market in Disarray* (Amsterdam: Transnational Institute, 2009);
Pierre-Arnaud Chouvy, ed., "Drug Trafficking in and out of the Golden Trian-
gle," in *An Atlas of Trafficking in Southeast Asia: The Illegal Trade in Arms, Drugs,
People, Counterfeit Goods, and Natural Resources in Mainland Southeast Asia* (Lon-
don: I. B. Taurus, 2013), 29–52.

6. Identity and Cultural Flux

Background on Han Chinese woman becoming Lisu from Cha-tsu-mai, interview
with author and Otome Klein Hutheesing, Yunnan, China, 1997.

Quotation about Christian Lisu preserving Lisu traditional culture from David
Ngwa-za Fish, interview with author, outside Mogok, Myanmar, 1997.

On Lisu couples living matrilineally in Thailand, see E. Paul Durrenberger, "Lisu
Political Form, Ideology, and Economic Action," in *Highlanders of Thailand*, ed.
John McKinnon and Wanat Bhruksasri (Kuala Lumpur: Oxford University Press,
1983), 218.

7. View from the Village

A Temporary Encampment

For general background on Lisu housing, see E. Paul Durrenberger, "The Ethnog-
raphy of Lisu Curing" (PhD dissertation, University of Illinois, Champaign-
Urbana, 1971), 18–19; Lewis and Lewis, *Peoples of the Golden Triangle*, 256; Morse,
Exodus to a Hidden Valley, 80–81.

On the location of Lisu villages, see Scott, *Burma and Beyond*, 289.

Story about permission to dig up a ruined Chinese pagoda in northern Thailand,
Durrenberger interview and correspondence with author, United States, 1997,
2016.

On Lisu skepticism about spiritual rituals, see E. Paul Durrenberger, "Belief and
the Logic of Lisu Spirits," *Bijdragen tot de tall- Land-en Volkenkunde / Journal of the
Humanities and Social Sciences of Southeast Asia* 136 (1980): 26.

On the Lisu tendency to site villages at high elevations, see Enriquez, *Races of Burma*,
65.

On Lisu attitudes toward cleaning, see Klein Hutheesing, *Emerging Sexual Inequality*, 70.

Social Organization and Symbolic Significance

On the suggestion that Lisu congregate in villages primarily for protection, see E. Paul Durrenberger, *A Socio-Medical Study of the Lisu of Northern Thailand*, Final Report (Silver Spring, MD: Walter Reed Army Institute of Research, 1970), 14.

For descriptions of Lisu allegiance groups organized around sisters, see ibid., 14; Dessaint, "Economic Organization," 44.

For Lisu songs that sentimentalize villages, see Klein Hutheesing, *Emerging Sexual Inequality*, 85.

Dispute Solving

Description of "Lisu Trial" in Yunnan from Robert Morse (more detailed source reference is unavailable).

Headman's description of solving disputes from Alay Pa, interview with author, Dton Loong, Thailand, 1997.

On the prevalence of negotiation in Lisu society, see E. Paul Durrenberger, "Law and Authority in a Lisu Village: Two Cases," *Journal of Anthropological Research* 32, no. 4 (1976): 301–25.

Part 2: Being a Lisu

8. CHILDHOOD: LEARNING BY DOING

On a Lisu mother's reaction to her child sucking her thumb, see Klein Hutheesing, *Emerging Sexual Inequality*, 46.

For description of Lisu women pitying her for not having a child of her own, ibid., 14.

On Lisu children's experience of play, ibid., 137.

On Lisu women's attitudes toward babysitting, ibid., 137–38.

On Lisu children graduating from one "gang" to the next, see E. Paul Durrenberger, *A Socio-Medical Study of the Lisu of Northern Thailand*, Report 6: Lisu Rites of Passage (Silver Spring, MD: Walter Reed Army Institute of Research, 1970).

Girls: To Work Earlier and Play Closer to Home

Recollections of life as a young girl in a Lisu village from Margaret Morse, interview with author, Chiang Mai, Thailand, 1997.

Boys: Running Free and Learning to Survive

Recollections of life as a young boy in a Lisu village from Tommy Morse, interview with author, Chiang Mai, Thailand, 1997.

9. MEN, WOMEN, COURTSHIP, AND MARRIAGE
New Year Celebrations: Setting the Stage for Romance

On competition among Lisu girls to have the best New Year's outfit, see Lewis and Lewis, *Peoples of the Golden Triangle*, 241.

For a description of unmarried girls stealing a boy on New Year's, interview with author, Yunnan, China, 1997.

Gender Roles, Courtship, and Sexuality

For a description of the chopsticks metaphor among the Lahu, see Shanshan Du, *"Chopsticks Only Work in Pairs": Gender Unity and Gender Inequality among the Lahu of Southwest China* (New York: Columbia University Press, 2002), 30.

For a description of the Lisu folktale revealing man's intimate connection to dogs, see E. Paul Durrenberger, "Of Lisu Dogs and Lisu Spirits," *Folklore* 88 (1977): 61–63.

On the regulation of sexual speech within Lisu culture, see Klein Hutheesing, *Emerging Sexual Inequality*, 72, 94–95, 102–4, 106–7.

On elephant and dog analogies among the Lisu, ibid., 100.

On Lisu women's discussion of sex and genitals, ibid., 102, 147–48.

On life for Lisu women beginning after marriage, Otome Klein Hutheesing, interview with author, Thailand, 1996.

On Lisu compliance with community-condoned marriages, see E. Paul Durrenberger, *A Socio-Medical Study of the Lisu of Northern Thailand*, Report 11: Negotiating a Marriage (Silver Spring, MD: Walter Reed Army Institute of Research, 1970).

On the Lisu "dressing ceremony" and premarital sex, see Guangmin, *Women Not to Be Blocked*, 14–15.

On quasi-elopements among the Lisu, see Klein Hutheesing, *Emerging Sexual Inequality*, 110.

Negotiating Bride Wealth

For general background on courtship, marriage, and bride prices among the Lisu, see Dessaint, "Economic Organization," 140–53; Lewis and Lewis, *Peoples of the Golden Triangle*, 268–69; Guangmin, *Women Not to Be Blocked*, 16–19.

On Lisu marriage negotiations, see E. Paul Durrenberger, *A Socio-Medical Study of the Lisu of Northern Thailand*, Report 11: Negotiating a Marriage, and Report 12: The Tiger Enters the Case: A Sequel to the Marriage Negotiations (Silver Spring, MD: Walter Reed Army Institute of Research, 1970); Klein Hutheesing, *Emerging Sexual Inequality*, 110–18.

On bride takers and bride givers, see Leach, *Political Systems*, 255–57.

For the description of a marriageable Lisu girl as a "wet-rice field," see Klein Hutheesing, *Emerging Sexual Inequality*, 78.

10. THE HOUSEHOLD: THE PLACE FOR FAMILY AND WORK

On the lack of tolerance for laziness among the Lisu, see E. Paul Durrenberger, *Lisu Religion*, Center for Southeast Asian Studies Monograph Series (Dekalb: Northern Illinois University, 1989), 21.

Dualism in Division of Labor

On the division of work into male and female domains, see Klein Hutheesing, *Emerging Sexual Inequality*, 65–66.

Food, Feasts, and Liquor

Dessaint, "Economic Organization," 131–39.

Clothes

On Lisu clothing, see Guangmin, *Women Not to Be Blocked*, 20–23; Lewis and Lewis, *Peoples of the Golden Triangle*, 244–52; Klein Hutheesing, *Emerging Sexual Inequality*, 139–40.

The Home/Jungle/Field Connection

On the relationship between the jungle and gender roles, see Klein Hutheesing, *Emerging Sexual Inequality*, 61, 63, 65, 75–76.

Chant said while burning a swidden quoted from Dessaint, "Economic Organization," 86.

11. Cosmic Views

Spiritual and Physical Worlds Converge

For general background on Lisu religion and the use of shrines, see Durrenberger, *Lisu Religion*; Lewis and Lewis, *Peoples of the Golden Triangle*, 256, 260–62.

Description of offending the Apa-mo from Abu, interview with author, Doi Chang, Thailand, 1997.

On the practicality of Lisu religion, see Durrenberger, *Lisu Religion*, 1.

On the existence of a higher god called Wu-sa-pa-mo, see Klein Hutheesing, *Emerging Sexual Inequality*, 37, 46, 49.

On the four main groups of spirits, see Durrenberger, "Ethnography of Lisu Curing," 156, 176–99.

Calendar of the Thai Lisu Year sidebar

On the timing of Lisu celebrations, see Durrenberger, "Ethnography of Lisu Curing," 154–55.

Lisu Curing and Dealing with Spirits on a Daily Basis

On the Lisu shaman's interaction with spirits, see E. Paul Durrenberger, "Lisu Curing: A Case History," *Bulletin of the History of Medicine* 50 (1976): 357–67; E. Paul Durrenberger, "A Lisu Shamanistic Séance," *Journal of the Siam Society* 64 (1976): 151–60; E. Paul Durrenberger, "Lisu Shamans and Some General Questions," *Journal of the Steward Anthropological Society* 7 (1975): 1–20; E. Paul Durrenberger, "Misfortune and Therapy among the Lisu of Northern Thailand," *Anthropological Quarterly* 52, no. 4 (1979): 204–10.

On Lisu women as nurturers of spirits, see Klein Hutheesing, *Emerging Sexual Inequality*, 39.

On the experience of soul loss, see Durrenberger, "Ethnography of Lisu Curing," 101–2; Durrenberger, *Lisu Religion*, 25–27; E. Paul Durrenberger, "A Soul's Journey: A Lisu Song from Northern Thailand," *Asian Folklore Studies* 34, no. 1 (1975): 35–50; E. Paul Durrenberger, "Lisu Etiological Categories," *Bijdragen tot de tall- Land-en Volkenkunde / Journal of the Humanities and Social Sciences of Southeast Asia* 113 (1977): 90–99; E. Paul Durrenberger, *A Socio-Medical Study of the Lisu of Northern Thailand*, Report 13: Soul Calling (Silver Spring, MD: Walter Reed Army Institute of Research, 1970).

On Lisu shamans, see Durrenberger, *Lisu Religion*, 13–16.

On Lisu medicine women and healthcare, see ibid., 17; Klein Hutheesing, *Emerging Sexual Inequality*, 141–44.

Background on Lisu sons and proverbs from David Ngwa-za Fish, interview with author, outside Mogok, Myanmar, 1997.

On death and burial practices among the Lisu, see E. Paul Durrenberger, "An Interpretation of a Lisu Tale," *Folklore* 89, no. 1 (1978): 101; Lewis and Lewis, *Peoples of the Golden Triangle*, 270; Klein Hutheesing, *Emerging Sexual Inequality*, 41.

Impact of Christianity . . . Just One More Influence?

Background on the Morse family's involvement with the Lisu from Tommy Morse, interview with author, 2014; Morse, *Exodus to a Hidden Valley*.

On the Lisu use of polarities, see Durrenberger, *Lisu Religion*, 19–20, 26–27.

On Lisu commonalities with Christians, see Morse, *Exodus to a Hidden Valley*, 59–60, 187–89.

On continuities between Christian converts and others among the Akha, see Deborah E. Tooker, "Identity Systems of Highland Burma: 'Belief,' Akha Zan, and a Critique of Interiorized Notions of Ethno-Religious Identity," *Man* 27, no. 4 (1992): 799–819.

Observations about Christian missionaries adapting Lisu spiritual beliefs from Bobby Morse, interview with author, 1997.

Quotation about Lisu pragmatism from Helen Morse, interview with author, Chiang Mai, Thailand, 1998.

Quotation about Christian Lisu from Abino Leeja, former Lisu headman, interview with author, Doi Chang, Thailand, 1997.

12. ECONOMY

On Lisu agriculture, see E. Paul Durrenberger and Kathleen Gillogly, "Greed in a 'Tribal' Economy? Acquisitiveness and Reciprocity in Lisu Society," *Economic Anthropology* 1 (2014): 88–103; E. Paul Durrenberger, "Rice Production in a Lisu Village," *Journal of Southeast Asian Studies* 10, no. 1 (1979): 139–45; Dessaint, "Economic Organization," 50–104; Guangmin, *Women Not to Be Blocked*, 1–3.

On reciprocity in Lisu economy, see E. Paul Durrenberger, "The Economy of Self-Sufficiency," in *Highlanders of Thailand*, ed. John McKinnon and Wanat Bhruksasri (Kuala Lumpur: Oxford University Press, 1983), 87–97.

Economic Activities in the Forest

General references on hunting and gathering: Dessaint, "Economic Organization," 81–83; Richard B. Harris and Ma Shilai, "Initiating a Hunting Ethic in Lisu
Villages, Western Yunnan, China," *Mountain Research and Development* 17, no. 2
(1997): 171–73; Morse, *Exodus to a Hidden Valley*, 95–100; author interviews.

On coffin planks, see Francis Kingdon-Ward, *Burma's Icy Mountains* (London: Jonathan Cape, 1949), 241.

Sweat: The Lisu Capital

On the centrality of Lisu labor and decisions about planting, see Dessaint, "Economic Organization," 104–28.

Lisu Women: Economic Partners

On Lisu women's control of money, see Klein Hutheesing, *Emerging Sexual
Inequality*, 227.

The Lure of Land

Quotation about Lisu desire for land from Morse, *Exodus to a Hidden Valley*, 64–65.

On drinking practices among the Lisu, see Klein Hutheesing, *Emerging Sexual
Inequality*, 141.

On the distribution of resources among the community, see Durrenberger, "Belief
and the Logic of Lisu Spirits," 26.

On Lisu liquor production, see Dessaint, "Economic Organization," 83–84.

On agricultural offerings to the spirits, ibid, 181, 183.

On the Lisu practices of hiring labor, relying on sons-in law, and maintaining strong
allegiance groups, ibid., 43–48, 106–20.

On the relative returns on subsistence and cash crops, see ibid., 76–77, 120–28;
Durrenberger, "Rice Production," 139–45; Durrenberger, "Economy of a Lisu
Village," 633–44.

On the influence of road construction and the shift to different cash crops in recent
years, see Durrenberger and Gillogly, "Greed in a 'Tribal' Economy," 88–103.

On the general absence of capital and credit among the Lisu, see Dessaint, "Economic Organization," 179.

Book II: THE LISU BY COUNTRY—SKETCHES OF THAILAND, MYANMAR, AND CHINA

1. COMPARING LISU NATIONAL SCENES: FULL OF OPPORTUNITIES TO BE WRONG

For recent assessments of Thai civil liberties and rule of law, see Freedom House, "Thailand," accessed April 3, 2015, https://freedomhouse.org/report/freedom-world/2015/thailand; World Justice Project, "Thailand," WJP Rule of Law Index 2015, accessed July 29, 2015, http://data.worldjusticeproject.org/pdf/rule-of-law-index-THA.pdf; Shadow Report on Eliminating Racial Discrimination: Thailand, Shadow Reports at United Nations, CERD Committee Meeting, Geneva, Switzerland, August 9–10, 2012.

2. THAILAND

On the origins and early settlement of Lisu in Thailand, see Jane Richardson Hanks and Lucien Mason Hanks, *Tribes of the North Thailand Frontier*, Monograph 51 (New Haven, CT: Yale University Southeast Asia Studies, 2001), 78–82.

For additional information on the coffee company, see Doi Chaang Coffee Company, "About Us: Our Story," accessed April 3, 2015, https://doichaangcoffee.com/learn.

On the emergence of Lisu headmen as liaisons to the Thai government, see Klein Hutheesing, *Emerging Sexual Inequality*, 83; Dessaint, "Economic Organization," 25; Durrenberger, "Ethnography of Lisu Curing," 190; Mayura Sinlee Seagrave, interview with author, Chiang Mai, Thailand, 2014.

On the Lisu Lodge resort, see Asian Oasis, "Lisu Lodge: Hill Tribe Adventure Experience," accessed July 29, 2015, http://www.asian-oasis.com/product/lisu-lodge-hilltribe-adventure-thailand/; Del Phaywong Guat, interview with author, Chiang Mai, Thailand, 2014.

On Lisu distrust of si-so relations, see Dessaint, "Economic Organization," 165–67.

On the Lahu protest of land confiscations, see "Thai Military Stops Lahu Minority from Filing Complaint on Land Rights to Junta," *Prachatai*, October 13, 2014, accessed November 2014, http://prachatai.org/english326/node/4401; Wiwat Tamee, interview with author, Chiang Mai, Thailand, 2014.

On problems of Lisu seeing Thai citizenship, see Amanda Flaim, *Summary Report for the UNESCO Highland Peoples' Survey* (Bangkok: UNESCO Office for Asia and the Pacific, 2011); Amanda Flaim, "Problems of Evidence, Evidence of Problems: Expanding Citizenship and Reproducing Statelessness among Highlanders of Northern Thailand," in *Citizenship in Question: Evidentiary Birthright and Stateless-ness*, ed. Benjamin N. Lawrance and Jacqueline Stevens, 147–64 (Durham, NC: Duke University Press, 2016); Sakda Seanmi, interview with author, Chiang Mai, Thailand, 2014.

On the aftermath of the 2014 coup in Thailand, see Amy Sawitta Lefevre and Panarat Thepgumpanat, "A Year after Thai Coup, Stability Trumps Growth for Business," *Irrawaddy*, May 22, 2015, accessed June 18, 2015, http://www.irrawaddy.com/asia /a-year-after-thai-coup-stability-trumps-growth-for-business.html; United Nations Office of the High Commissioner for Human Rights, "UN Human Rights Chief Alarmed by Thai Government's Adoption of Potentially Unlimited and 'Draconian' Powers," accessed April 2, 2015, http://www.ohchr.org/EN /NewsEvents/Pages/DisplayNews.aspx?NewsID=15793&LangID=E; Ali-ma Loy-yee-pa, interview with author, Dton Loon, Thailand, 2014; Mimi Saeju, interview with author, Chiang Mai, Thailand, 2014.

3. Burma/Myanmar

On missionary work of the Morse and Morrison families, see Morse, *Exodus to a Hidden Valley*; Gertrude Morse and Helen M. Morse, *The Dogs May Bark: But the Caravan Moves On* (Joplin, MO: College Press, 1998); Chin Khua Khai, "The Assemblies of God and Pentecostalism in Myanmar," in *Asian and Pentecostal: The Charismatic Face of Christianity in Asia*, 2nd ed., ed. Allan Anderson and Edmond Tang (Oxford, UK: Regnum Books International, 2011), 212–16; Helen Morse, interview with author, Chiang Mai, Thailand, 2014. On Baptist mission-ary work by the Tegenfeldts, see Herman G. Tegenfeldt, *A Century of Growth: The Kachin Baptist Church of Burma* (South Pasadena, CA: William Carey Library, 1974).

On early Lisu populations in Burma, see James Outram Fraser, *Handbook of the Lisu (Yawyin) Language* (Rangoon: Government Printing, 1922), i–xi; Enriquez, *Races of Burma*.

On contemporary military conflict in Myanmar, see Nyein Nyein, "Military Pres-ence Grows in Hpakant amid Further Clashes," *Irrawaddy*, accessed June 25, 2015, http://www.irrawaddy.com/burma/military-presence-grows-in-hpakant-amid -further-clashes.html; Kachin Women's Association Thailand (KWAT), "The 4th

Anniversary of the Renewal of War in Kachin Areas," statement released June 9, 2015, accessed July 29, 2015, http://kachinwomen.com/kachinwomen /publications/statements/137-the-4th-anniversary-of-the-renewal-of-war-in -kachin-areas; Nyein Nyein, "Elections Are the End of the Beginning," *Irrawaddy*, July 9, 2015, accessed July 29, 2015, http://www.irrawaddy.com /interview/elections-are-the-end-of-the-beginning.html.

On Zomia, see van Schendel, "Geographies of Knowing"; Michaud, "Editorial— Zomia and Beyond"; Scott, *Art of Not Being Governed*.

On the persecution and forced migration of the Rohingya minority in Myanmar, see Nobel Zaw, "Population Control Bill Could 'Stop the Bengalis': Wirathu," *Irrawaddy*, May 18, 2015, accessed June 18, 2015, http://www.irrawaddy.com /burma/population-control-bill-could-stop-the-bengalis-wirathu.html; Susan Cunningham, "Myanmar's Rohingya Boat People Are Safe for Now—But Root Issues Unsolved," *Forbes*, June 3, 2015, accessed June 18, 2015, https://www.forbes .com/sites/susancunningham/2015/06/03/myanmars-rohingya-boat-people-are -safe-for-now-but-root-issues-unsolved/; Lawi Weng, "Burma Says 'Boat People' Crisis Not Caused by Rohingya Strife," *Irrawaddy*, May 18, 2015, accessed June 18, 2015, http://www.irrawaddy.com/burma/burma-says-boat-people-crisis-not -caused-by-rohingya-strife.html; Todd Pitman and Aye Aye Win, "No Major Breakthrough at Meeting on Asian Boat People Crisis," *AP: The Big Story*, http:// bigstory.ap.org/urn:publicid:ap.org:e09a61ef295d49fe9053eeba13d4de29; Mark Davis and Australian Broadcasting Corporation, *Journey into Hell*, news show *Four Corners*, June 22, 2015, film, 44 minutes, http://www.abc.net.au/4corners /stories/2015/06/22/4257490.htm.

On the status of women in sex-segregated societies, see Wednesday Martin, "Poor Little Rich Women" (op. ed.), *New York Times*, May 16, 2015, accessed July 31, 2017.

4. CHINA

Descriptions of life in Yunnan in the Tengchong area and the Nujiang Valley are from author's personal observations and interviews in 1997 with Wo-ta (translated by Otome Klein Hutheesing) and in 2014 with Yu-yin Jiang, Yu-you Jiang, J Yawu, Minister Molido (translated by J Yawu), unnamed man in bar, Aki Li-tu, Ah-Ju, Cho s'dur Liang, Suer-ye-tsa, Chos-o-pho, and Fu Yu Zhi.

On hydroelectric and dam projects in the Nujiang Valley, "Interactive: Mapping China's Dam Rush." Accessed March 21, 2014. https://www.wilsoncenter.org /publication/interactive-mapping-chinas-dam-rush.

Contextual information from Associated Press, "China Says 'Golden Triangle' Source of Most Dangerous Drugs," *Irrawaddy*, June 24, 2015, http://www .irrawaddy.com/asia/china-says-golden-triangle-source-of-most-dangerous-drugs .html; Leonard Bolton, *China Call* (Springfield, MO: Gospel Publishing House, 1984).

On "fake refugees" (Lisu from Myanmar who seek political asylum through the UN Refugee program in Malaysia), it is impossible to verify or update numbers in this group or to trendspot in regard to political reform. In an email dated July 19, 2017, External Relations Officer Yante Ismail of the United Nations High Commission for Refugees (www.unhcr.org.my) explained that his agency does not break down statistics according to what he characterized as "sub-ethnic groups." At press time in 2017, 132,500 of UNHCR's 149,200 registered refugees were from Myanmar. The largest ethnic group are the Rohingyas, with 59,000, and the smallest, the Kachins, with 3,500. This illustrates the problem of obtaining accurate data on minorities in Myanmar, discussed in this chapter and also in Book I, Chapter 1. Who are the Lisu? Lisu are counted along with several other minorities as "Kachin," although they have a different language and culture. Knowing how many Lisu are among the 3,500 Kachin applicants for refugee status is a guessing game. Probably they comprise a small portion because Lisu are far outnumbered by the Jinghpaw in Kachin State, who live more in conflict areas and are more likely to be refugees since they make up the majority of the Kachin Independence Army (KIA)—among the few remaining AEGs that have not signed a peace treaty with the central government as of today.

Conclusions, and Notes on Where Lisu Might Go from Here

For an early, influential work on the relationships among culture, personality, art, and language, see Ruth Benedict, *Patterns of Culture* (Boston: Houghton Mifflin, 1934).

For a work on evolution that shifted interest away from ethnographic methods, see Richard Dawkins, *The Selfish Gene* (New York: Oxford University Press, 1976).

For contemporary information on Southeast Asia's drug trade, including its connection to HIV and other blood-borne diseases, see Kramer, Jelsma, and Blickman, *Withdrawal Symptoms in the Golden Triangle*.

Thoughts on the current state of the Lisu informed by author interviews with Walter Goldschmidt, David Morse, and four Lisu living in the United States; background on David Morse's life from Morse; and Lisu Bible-based preference to be employer, not employee, from Morse, *Exodus to a Hidden Valley*, 156–71, 15–16.

Bibliography

INTERVIEWS

All interviews were with author. They took place through interpreters unless indicated in the text that subject spoke English. Some interpreters are named.

Abino Leeja, former Lisu headman, Doi Chang, Thailand, 1997.

Abu, Doi Chang, Thailand, 1997.

Aki Dawoo, Putao Valley and Myitkyina, Myanmar, 2014 (two interviews).

Aki Li-tu, dashipa, Ree Ya To village, Nujiang, 2014.

Alay Pa, Dton Loong, Thailand, 1997.

Ale Baba, Doi Laan, Thailand, 2014.

Ale-ma Ee-su, Doi Laan, Thailand, 2014.

Ali-ma Loy-yee-pa, Dton Loong, Thailand, 2014.

Andrew, village near Myitkyina, Burma, 1997.

Ashley South, Rangoon, 2014.

A-wu, Doi Laan, Thailand, 2014.

Bobby Morse, Thailand and Myanmar, 1997 (multiple interviews).

Cha-tsu-mai, with author and Otome Klein Hutheesing, Yunnan, China, 1997.

Cho-me Orn-anong, Doi Chang and Chiang Mai, Thailand, 2014.

Cho s'dur Liang, Tan-na-nu village outside Liukhu, Yunnan, China, 2014.

Chos-o-pho, Pee-Ja village, outside Liukhu, Yunnan, China, 2014.

David Morse, Chiang Mai, Thailand, 2014 (multiple interviews).

David Ngwa-za Fish, outside Mogok, Myanmar, 1997.

Del Phaywong Guat, Chiang Mai, Thailand, 2014.

Eligah Illia, translated by Bobby Morse, Myanmar, 1997.

Eugene Morse, Chiang Mai, Thailand, 1997–98 (multiple interviews).

Fu-he-ma, outside Putao, Myanmar, 2014.

Helen Morse, Chiang Mai, Thailand, 1997–98 (multiple interviews).

J Pa-da, Citi-lo 1 village, Putao Valley, Myanmar, 2014.

J Yawu, Yangon, Myanmar, and Liukhu, Yunnan, China, 2014 (multiple interviews).

Julius, village near Myitkyina, Myanmar, 1997.

Margaret Morse, Chiang Mai, Thailand, 1997.

Mayura Sinlee Seagrave, Chiang Mai, Thailand, 2014.

Mimi Saeju, Chiang Mai and Doi Lan, Thailand, 2014 (multiple interviews).

Ngwa Pi-too, Da-goo Sheetza village, Putao, Myanmar, 2014.

Sakda Saenmi, Chiang Mai, Thailand, 2014.

Suer-ye-tsa, Tan-na-nu village outside Liukhu, Yunnan, China, 2014.

Timothy (Ko-boo-day), Putao town, Myanmar, 2014.

Tommy Morse, Chiang Mai, Thailand, 1997, 2014 (multiple interviews).

Tom Parks, Bangkok, Thailand, 2014.

Unnamed man, Nyisaladi, Putao Valley, Myanmar, 2014.

Unnamed man waiting for bus, Mae Hong Son, Thailand, 1998.

Unnamed pastor, Bahmadi village, Putao Valley, Myanmar, 2014.

Unnamed residents, Citi-lo 1 village, Putao Valley, Myanmar, 2014.

Unnamed residents, Da-goo Sheetza village, Putao Valley, Myanmar, 2014.

Unnamed residents, Nyi Salidi village, Putao Valley, Myanmar, 2014.

Victoria Vorreiter, Chiang Mai, Thailand, 2014.

Wiwat Tamee, Chiang Mai, Thailand, 2014.

PERIODICALS

AP: The Big Story

Bangkok Post

Forbes

Irrawaddy [Rangoon, Burma, and Chiang Mai, Thailand]

Khaosod English

Mekong Review

The Nation [Thailand]

New York Times

New York Times Review of Books

New Yorker

Prachatai

The Star [Penang, Malaysia]

Straits Times [Singapore]

WEBSITES AND SOURCES

Asian Oasis. "Lisu Lodge: Hill Tribe Adventure Experience." Accessed July 29, 2015. http://www.asian-oasis.com/.

Doi Chaang Coffee Company. "About Us: Our Story." Accessed April 3, 2015. https://doichaangcoffee.com.

Front Line Defenders. http://www.frontlinedefenders.org/taxonomy/term/13143.

Freedom House. "Thailand." Accessed April 3, 2015. https://freedomhouse.org.

Kachin Women's Association Thailand (KWAT). "The 4th Anniversary of the Renewal of War in Kachin Areas." Statement released June 9, 2015. Accessed July 29, 2015. http://kachinwomen.com/.

United Nations Office of the High Commissioner for Human Rights. "UN Human Rights Chief Alarmed by Thai Government's Adoption of Potentially Unlimited and 'Draconian' Powers." Accessed April 2, 2015. http://www.ohcr.org/EN/NewsEvents/Pages/DisplayNews.aspx?NewsID=15793&LangID=E.

World Justice Project. "Thailand." WJP Rule of Law Index 2015. Accessed July 29, 2015. http://worldjusticeproject.org/rule-of-law-index.

FILMS

Davis, Mark, and Australian Broadcasting Corporation. *Journey into Hell*. News show *Four Corners*. June 22, 2015. 44 minutes. http://www.abc.net.au/4corners /stories/2015/06/22/4257490.htm.

BOOKS, ARTICLES, CONFERENCE PAPERS, AND THESES

Anderson, Benedict. *Imagined Communities: Reflections on the Origin and Spread of Nationalism*. Revised ed. London: Verso, 2006.

Ayabe, Masao. "Diversity in Uniformity: Self-Classification among the Lisu of Thailand." Paper presented at the 6th International Conference on Thai Studies, Chiang Mai, Thailand, October 14–17, 1996.

Baker, Chris. "The 2014 Thai Coup and Some Roots of Authoritarianism." *Journal of Contemporary Asia* 46, no. 3 (July 2, 2016): 388–404. https://doi.org/10.1080/00 472336.2016.1150500.

Benedict, Ruth. *Patterns of Culture*. Boston: Houghton Mifflin, 1934.

Bolton, Leonard. *China Call*. Springfield, MO: Gospel Publishing House, 1984.

Boyes, Jon. *Tiger-Men and Tofu Dolls: Tribal Spirits in Northern Thailand*. Chiang Mai, Thailand: Silkworm Books, 1997.

Bradley, David. "Onomastic, Orthographic, Dialectal, and Dialectical Borders: The Lisu and the Lahu." *Asia Pacific Viewpoint* 38, no. 2 (1997): 107–17. https://doi.org /10.1111/1467-8373.00033.

Chaipigusit, Prasert. "Anarchists of the Highlands? A Critical Review of a Stereotype Applied to the Lisu." In *Anarchist Hill Tribes Today: Problems in Change*, ed. John McKinnon and Bernard Vienne, 173–90. Bangkok: White Lotus–Orstom, 1989.

Ch'o, Fan. *Man Shu (Book of the Southern Barbarians)*. Ithaca, NY: Cornell University Department of Far Eastern Studies, 1961 [circa 685].

Chouvy, Pierre-Arnaud, ed. *An Atlas of Trafficking in Southeast Asia: The Illegal Trade in Arms, Drugs, People, Counterfeit Goods, and Natural Resources in Mainland Southeast Asia*. London: I. B. Taurus, 2013.

Conrad, Yves. "Lisu Identity in Northern Thailand: A Problematique for Anthropology." In *Anarchist Hill Tribes Today: Problems in Change*, ed. John McKinnon and Bernard Vienne, 191–221. Bangkok: White Lotus–Orstom, 1989.

Crawford, Christa Foster. "Cultural, Economic, and Legal Factors Underlying Trafficking in Thailand and Their Impact on Women and Girls from Burma." *Thailand Journal of Law and Policy* 12 (2009). http://www.thailawforum.com /articles/Trafficking-in-Thailand%20.html.

Crooker, Richard Allen. "Opium Production in North Thailand: A Geographical Perspective." PhD dissertation, University of California, Riverside, 1986.

Dawkins, Richard. *The Selfish Gene*. New York: Oxford University Press, 1976.

Dessaint, Alain Yvon. "Economic Organization of the Lisu of the Thai Highlanders." PhD dissertation, University of Hawaii, Honolulu, 1972.

Dessaint, Alain Yvon. "Lisu World View." In *The Highland Heritage: Collected Essays
on Upland North Thailand*, ed. Anthony R. Walker, 315–38. Singapore: Suvarnabhumi Books, 1992.

Diran, Richard K. *The Vanishing Tribes of Burma*. London: Weidenfeld and Nicolson,
1997.

Du, Shanshan. *"Chopsticks Only Work in Pairs"*: *Gender Unity and Gender Inequality
among the Lahu of Southwest China*. New York: Columbia University Press, 2002.

Durrenberger, E. Paul. "Belief and the Logic of Lisu Spirits." *Bijdragen tot de tall-
Land-en Volkenkunde / Journal of the Humanities and Social Sciences of Southeast
Asia* 136 (1980): 21–40.

Durrenberger, E. Paul. "Blessing in Lisu Culture and Practice." In *Merit and
Blessing in Mainland Southeast Asia in Comparative Perspective*, ed. Cornelia Ann
Kammerer and Nicola Tannenbaum, 116–33. New Haven, CT: Yale University
Southeast Asia Studies, 1996.

Durrenberger, E. Paul. "The Economy of a Lisu Village." *American Ethnologist* 3, no.
4 (1976): 633–44. https://doi.org/10.1525/ae.1976.3.4.02a00050.

Durrenberger, E. Paul. "The Economy of Self-Sufficiency." In *Highlanders of Thailand*, ed. John McKinnon and Wanat Bhruksasri, 87–97. Kuala Lumpur: Oxford
University Press, 1983.

Durrenberger, E. Paul. "The Ethnography of Lisu Curing." PhD dissertation, University of Illinois, Champaign-Urbana, 1971.

Durrenberger, E. Paul. "An Interpretation of a Lisu Tale." *Folklore* 89, no. 1 (1978):
94–103. https://doi.org/10.1080/0015587X.1978.9716093.

Durrenberger, E. Paul. "Law and Authority in a Lisu Village: Two Cases." *Journal of
Anthropological Research* 32, no. 4 (1976): 301–25. https://doi.org/10.1086/jar.32
.4.3630019.

Durrenberger, E. Paul. "Lisu Curing: A Case History." *Bulletin of the History of Medicine* 50 (1976): 356–71.

Durrenberger, E. Paul. "Lisu Etiological Categories." *Bijdragen tot de tall- Land-en
Volkenkunde / Journal of the Humanities and Social Sciences of Southeast Asia* 113
(1977): 90–99.

Durrenberger, E. Paul. *Lisu: Opium Producers of the Golden Triangle*. 197?.

Durrenberger, E. Paul. "Lisu: Political Form, Ideology, and Economic Action." In
Highlanders of Thailand, ed. John McKinnon and Wanat Bhruksasri, 216–26.
Kuala Lumpur: Oxford University Press, 1983.

Durrenberger, E. Paul. *Lisu Religion*. Center for Southeast Asian Studies Monograph Series. Dekalb: Northern Illinois University, 1989.

Durrenberger, E. Paul. "Lisu Ritual, Economics, and Ideology." In *Ritual, Power,
and Economy: Upland-Lowland Contrasts in Mainland Southeast Asia*, ed. Susan
Diana Russell, 103–20. Dekalb: Northern Illinois University, 1989.

Durrenberger, E. Paul. "A Lisu Shamanistic Séance." *Journal of the Siam Society* 64 (1976): 151–60.

Durrenberger, E. Paul. "Lisu Shamans and Some General Questions." *Journal of the Steward Anthropological Society* 7 (1975): 1–20.

Durrenberger, E. Paul. "Misfortune and Therapy among the Lisu of Northern Thailand." *Anthropological Quarterly* 52, no. 4 (1979): 204–10. https://doi.org/10.2307/3317854.

Durrenberger, E. Paul. "Of Lisu Dogs and Lisu Spirits." *Folklore* 88 (1977): 61–63.

Durrenberger, E. Paul. "The Regional Context of the Economy of a Lisu Village in Northern Thailand." *Southeast Asia* 3 (1974): 569–75.

Durrenberger, E. Paul. "Rice Production in a Lisu Village." *Journal of Southeast Asian Studies* 10, no. 1 (1979): 139–45. https://doi.org/10.1017/S0022463400011887.

Durrenberger, E. Paul. *A Socio-Medical Study of the Lisu of Northern Thailand*, Reports 4, 6–13, final. Silver Springs, MD: Walter Reed Army Institute of Research, 1970.

Durrenberger, E. Paul. "A Soul's Journey: A Lisu Song from Northern Thailand." *Asian Folklore Studies* 34, no. 1 (1975): 35–50. https://doi.org/10.2307/1177739.

Durrenberger, E. Paul. "The Southeast Asian Context of Theravada Buddhism." *Anthropology* 5 (1981): 45–62.

Durrenberger, E. Paul. "Understanding a Misunderstanding: Thai-Lisu Relations in Northern Thailand." *Anthropological Quarterly* 48, no. 2 (1975): 106–20. https://doi.org/10.2307/3316614.

Durrenberger, E. Paul. "Witchcraft, Sorcery, Fortune, and Misfortune among Lisu Highlanders of Northern Thailand." In *Understanding Witchcraft and Sorcery in Southeast Asia*, ed. C. W. Watson and Roy Ellen, 47–66. Honolulu: University of Hawaii Press, 1993.

Durrenberger, E. Paul, and Kathleen Gillogly. "Greed in a 'Tribal' Economy? Acquisitiveness and Reciprocity in Lisu Society." *Economic Anthropology* 1 (2014): 88–103.

Durrenberger, E. Paul, and Nicola Tannenbaum. "Household Economy, Political Economy, and Ideology: Peasants and the State in Southeast Asia." *American Anthropologist* 94, no. 1 (1992): 74–89. https://doi.org/10.1525/aa.1992.94.1.02a00050.

Enriquez, C. M. *Races of Burma*, 2nd ed. Handbooks for the Indian Army. Delhi: Manager of Publications, 1933.

Flaim, Amanda. "Problems of Evidence, Evidence of Problems: Expanding Citizenship and Reproducing Statelessness among Highlanders of Northern Thailand." In *Citizenship in Question: Evidentiary Birthright and Statelessness*, ed. Benjamin N. Lawrence and Jacqueline Stevens, 147–64. Durham, NC: Duke University Press, 2016. https://doi.org/10.1215/9780822373483-009.

Flaim, Amanda. *UNESCO Highland Peoples' Surveys I and II*. Bangkok: UNESCO Office for Asia and the Pacific, 2010.

Fraser, James Outram. *Handbook of the Lisu (Yawyin) Language*. Rangoon: Government Printing, 1922.

Gillogly, Kathleen A. "Transformations of Lisu Social Structure under Opium Control and Watershed Conservation in Northern Thailand." PhD dissertation, University of Michigan, Ann Arbor, 2006.

Goodman, Jim. *The Akha: Guardians of the Forest.* Peoples and Cultures of Southeast Asia Series. Chiang Mai, Thailand: Teak House, 1997.

Goodman, Jim. *Grand Canyon of the East.* Kunming, China: Yunnan Publishing Corporation Group, Yunnan Peoples Publishing House, 2010.

Goodman, Jim. *Meet the Akhas.* Bangkok: White Lotus, 1996.

Guangmin, Yang. *Women Not to Be Blocked by Canyon.* Women's Culture Series: Nationalities in Yunnan. Kunming, China: Yunnan Education Publishing House, 1995.

Hanks, Jane Richardson, and Lucien Mason Hanks. *Tribes of the North Thailand Frontier.* Monograph 51. New Haven, CT: Yale University Southeast Asia Studies, 2001.

Harris, Joseph. "Uneven Inclusion: Consequences of Universal Healthcare in Thailand." *Citizenship Studies* 17, no. 1 (2013): 111–27. https://doi.org/10.1080/13621025.2013.764220.

Harris, Richard B., and Ma Shilai. "Initiating a Hunting Ethic in Lisu Villages, Western Yunnan, China." *Mountain Research and Development* 17, no. 2 (1997): 171–76. https://doi.org/10.2307/3673832.

Jatuworaphruek, Thawit. "Ritual of Power and the Transformation of Lisu Ethnicity." Paper presented at the 6th International Conference on Thai Studies, Chaing Mai, Thailand, October 14–17, 1996.

Jatuworaphruek, Thawit. "Salalu Ritual of Reproductive Ethnicity of the Poor Lisu in Chang Mai." Paper presented at the workshop "Ethnic Communities in Changing Environments," Center for Ethnic Studies and Development, Chiang Mai University, Thailand, February 22–26, 1997.

Khai, Chin Khua. "The Assemblies of God and Pentecostalism in Myanmar." In *Asian and Pentecostal: The Charismatic Face of Christianity in Asia,* 2nd ed., ed. Allan Anderson and Edmond Tang, 211–26. Oxford: Regnum Books International, 2011.

Kingdon-Ward, Francis. *Burma's Icy Mountains.* London: Jonathan Cape, 1949.

Klein Hutheesing, Otome. "Distortions of Social Reality, Disorientation of Culture: The Lisu Case." Paper presented at International Symposium on the Environment and Regeneration of Culture: Perspectives of Gender, Family, Ethnicity, and State, Universti Sains Malaysia, Minden, Penang, December 14–17, 1992.

Klein Hutheesing, Otome. *Emerging Sexual Inequality among the Lisu of Northern Thailand: The Waning of Dog and Elephant Repute.* Leiden: E. J. Brill, 1990.

Klein Hutheesing, Otome. "Facework of a Female Elder in a Lisu Field, Thailand." In *Gendered Fields: Women, Men, and Ethnography,* ed. Diane Bell, Patricia Caplan, and Wazir-Jahan Begum Karim, 93–102. London: Routledge, 1993.

Klein Hutheesing, Otome. *Gender at the Margins of Southeast Asia: "Male" and "Female" in Developing Southeast Asia,* ed. Wazir-Jahan Begum Karim, 75–97. Oxford: Berg, 1995.

Klein Hutheesing, Otome. "How Does a 'Tai' Spirit Come to Be on a Lisu Home Altar? A Note on the Merger of Lowland and Highland Cosmologies." In *Proceedings of the 4th International Conference on Thai Studies*, 133–42. Kunming, China: Institute of Southeast Asia Studies, 1990.

Klein Hutheesing, Otome. "Linking the Lisu to the HIV/AIDS Epidemic: Observations of a Cultural-Political Kind." Paper presented at the 1st Workshop on Sociocultural Dimensions of HIV/AIDS Control and Care in Thailand, Chiang Mai, January 1994.

Klein Hutheesing, Otome. "Male Jargon, Female Talk: Verbal Exchanges on Academe and the Mundane." *Kajian Malaysia: Journal of Malaysian Studies* 12 (1994): 185–209.

Klein Hutheesing, Otome. "A Mountain Culture Faces AIDS: The Lisu of Northern Thailand." In *Contemporary Cultural Anthropology*, 5th ed., ed. Michael Howard, 366–68. New York: HarperCollins, 1996.

Kramer, Tom, Martin Jelsma, and Tom Blickman. *Withdrawal Symptoms in the Golden Triangle: A Drugs Market in Disarray*. Amsterdam: Transnational Institute, 2009.

Leach, Edmund Ronald. *Political Systems of Highland Burma: A Study of Kachin Social Structure*. London: G. Bell, 1954.

Lévi-Strauss, Claude. *Tristes Tropiques*. Translated by John Weightman and Doreen Weightman. New York: Penguin Books, 2012 [1955].

Lewis, Paul W., and Elaine Lewis. *Peoples of the Golden Triangle: Six Tribes in Thailand*. London: Thames and Hudson, 1984.

Lintner, Bertil. *Burma in Revolt: Opium and Insurgency since 1948*. Bangkok: Westview and White Lotus, 1994.

Lintner, Bertil. *Land of Jade, a Journey from India through Northern Burma to China*. Bangkok: White Orchid, 1996.

Maitra, Asim. *Profile of a Little-Known Tribe: An Ethnographic Study of Lisus of Arunachal Pradesh*. New Delhi: Mittla, 1993.

Mazard, Mireille. "The Art of (Not) Looking Back: Reconsidering Lisu Migrations and 'Zomia.'" In *Globalizing Migration History: The Eurasian Experience (16th–21st Centuries)*, ed. Jan Lucassen and Leo Lucassen, 215–46. Leiden: Brill, 2014. https://doi.org/10.1163/9789004271364_009.

McCoy, Alfred W. *The Politics of Heroin in Southeast Asia*. New York: Harper and Row, 1972.

McKinnon, John, and Wanat Bhruksasri, eds. *Highlanders of Thailand*. Kuala Lumpur: Oxford University Press, 1983.

Michaud, Jean. "Editorial—Zomia and Beyond." *Journal of Global History* 5, no. 2 (2010): 187–214. https://doi.org/10.1017/S1740022810000057.

Michaud, Jean. *Historical Dictionary of the Peoples of the Southeast Asian Massif*. Lanham, MD: Scarecrow, 2006.

Mirante, Edith. "Between China and Myanmar: Southeast Asia: Refugees in Crisis." *The Diplomat*. Digital magazine of *Asia Pacific*, March 7, 2016.

Mitton, G. E. *Scott of the Shan Hills*. London: John Murray, 1936.

Morse, Eugene. *Exodus to a Hidden Valley*. New York: Readers Digest Press, 1974.

Morse, Gertrude, and Helen M. Morse. *The Dogs May Bark but the Caravan Moves On*. Joplin, MO: College Press, 1998.

Morse, Robert H. *The Lisu of Northern Thailand*. Auburn, NY: Asia Library Services, 1975.

Packer, George. "The Courage of Migrants." *New Yorker*, May 27, 2015.

Phongpaichit, Pasuk, and Ssungsidh Piriyarangsan. *Corruption and Democracy in Thailand*. Chiang Mai, Thailand: Silkworm Books, 1994.

Rashid, Mohd Razha, and Pauline H. Walker. "The Lisu People: An Introduction." In *Farmers in the Hills: Ethnographic Notes on the Upland Peoples of North Thailand*, ed. Anthony R. Walker, 157–64. Singapore: Suvarnabhumi Books, 1986.

Ren, Mei'e, Yang Renzhang, and Haoshen Bao. *An Outline of China's Physical Geography*. Beijing: Foreign Language Press, 1985.

Rock, Joseph. *The Ancient Na-khi Kingdom of Southwest China*. Cambridge, MA: Harvard University Press, 1947. https://doi.org/10.4159/harvard.9780674289192.

Scott, James C. *The Art of Not Being Governed: An Anarchist History of Upland Southeast Asia*. New Haven, CT: Yale University Press, 2009.

Scott, James C. *Seeing Like a State: How Certain Schemes to Improve the Human Condition Have Failed*. New Haven, CT: Yale University Press, 1998.

Scott, James C. *Two Cheers for Anarchism: Six Easy Pieces on Autonomy, Dignity, and Meaningful Work and Play*. Princeton, NJ: Princeton University Press, 2012.

Scott, James George. *Burma and Beyond*. London: Grayson and Grayson, 1932.

Scott, James George, and J. P. Hardiman. *Gazetteer of Upper Burma and the Shan States*. 5 vols. Rangoon: Superintendent of Government Printing, Burma, 1900.

Shadow Report on Eliminating Racial Discrimination: Thailand. Shadow Reports at United Nations, CERD Committee Meeting, Geneva, Switzerland, August 9–10, 2012.

Shen, Che, Xiaoya Lu, and Liao Pin. "The Lisu People—a Merry Nationality." In *Life among the Minority Nationalities of Northwest Yunnan*. China's Nationalities Series. Beijing: Foreign Languages Press, 1989.

Simms, Claudia, and Thomas Tarleton. "The Lisu of the Golden Triangle." In *The World and I*, Culture Crossroads Inset, "The Rituals of Rice Planting" and "Reliance on Opium" (October 1987): 463–66.

Steinberg, David I. *Burma/Myanmar: What Everyone Needs to Know*, 2nd ed. Oxford: Oxford University Press, 2013.

Strangio, Sebastian. "Death or Freedom." *Mekong Review* 2 (February–April 2016): n.p.

Tegenfeldt, Herman G. *A Century of Growth: The Kachin Baptist Church of Burma*. South Pasadena, CA: William Carey Library, 1974.

Tooker, Deborah E. "Identity Systems of Highland Burma: 'Belief,' Akha Zan, and a Critique of Interiorized Notions of Ethno-Religious Identity." *Man* 27, no. 4 (1992): 799–819. https://doi.org/10.2307/2804175.

Tooker, Deborah E. *Space and the Production of Cultural Difference among the Akha Prior to Globalization: Channeling the Flow of Life.* Amsterdam: Amsterdam University Press, 2012.

van Schendel, Willem. "Geographies of Knowing, Geographies of Ignorance: Jumping Scale in Southeast Asia." *Environment and Planning: D, Society and Space* 20, no. 6 (2002): 647–68. https://doi.org/10.1068/d16s.

von Geusau Alting, Leo. "Dialectics of Akhazarn: The Interiorizations of a Perennial Minority Group." In *Highlanders of Thailand,* ed. John McKinnon and Wanat Bhruksasri, 241–77. Kuala Lumpur: Oxford University Press, 1983.

Vorreiter, Victoria. *Songs of Memory, Traditional Music of the Golden Triangle.* Thailand: Resonance, 2009.

Wang, Zung. "Lisu Tribe: Its Socio-Cultural Life." Thesis submitted to the University of Myitkyina in partial fulfillment of the requirement for the degree Master of Research in the Department of History, Kachin State, Myanmar, 2012.

Wyatt, David K. *Thailand: A Short History.* New Haven, CT: Yale University Press, 1982.

Yin, Ma. *China's Minority Nationalities.* Beijing: Foreign Language Press, 1989.

Young, Gordon. *Hilltribes of Northern Thailand: A Socio-ethnological Report.* Bangkok: Siam Society, 1962.

Index